GENDERED SUBJECTS

The Editors

Margo Culley teaches Women's Studies and American Literature within the English Department at the University of Massachusetts, Amherst. She has recently been the Co-Director of the Black Studies/Women's Studies Faculty Development Project and has taught graduate courses in feminist pedagogy.

Catherine Portuges, Director of the Women's Studies Program at the University of Massachusetts, Amherst, is also a member of the Department of Comparative Literature. Her work on psychoanalytic approaches to the interpretation of film and literature includes essays on Colette, de Beauvoir, Duras, Varda and Freud's *Dora*.

Both editors have held Mellon Foundation Fellowships at the Wellesley Center for Research on Women. They lecture and consult frequently on topics related to curriculum development and feminist pedagogy.

GENDERED SUBJECTS

THE DYNAMICS OF FEMINIST TEACHING

Edited by Margo Culley and Catherine Portuges

Routledge & Kegan Paul
Boston, London, Melbourne and Henley

378.125
G325

First published in 1985
by Routledge & Kegan Paul plc

9 Park Street, Boston, Mass. 02108, USA

14 Leicester Square, London WC2H 7PH, England

464 St Kilda Road, Melbourne,
Victoria 3004, Australia and

Broadway House, Newtown Road,
Henley on Thames, Oxon RG9 1EN, England

Set in Journal 10/12pt. by
Columns, Reading, Great Britain
and printed in Great Britain
by T.J. Press (Padstow) Ltd,
Padstow, Cornwall

Library of Congress Cataloging in Publication Data

Gendered subjects.

Bibliography: p.
Includes index.
1. Women—Education (Higher)—United States—
Addresses, essays, lectures.   2. Afro-American women—
Education (Higher)—United States—Addresses, essays,
lectures.   3. Women college teachers—United States—
Addresses, essays, lectures.   4. Women's studies—
United States—Addresses, essays, lectures.   I. Culley,
Margo.   II. Portuges, Catherine.
LC1756.G46   1985   378'.125'088042   84-18079

British Library CIP Data available

ISBN 0-7100-9907-X

Contents

Introduction

The phrase 'feminist pedagogy' couples the contemporary and the traditional, joining current political movements with a concern for the transmission of knowledge more ancient than the Greek word for teaching. Now, two decades after the first Women's Studies courses appeared on campuses, their place in American higher education happily needs little demonstration. As the number of programs in the US approaches 500, few campuses remain untouched by the intellectual ferment. Some programs offer graduate degrees, and the number of research centers with membership in the National Council for Research on Women continues to grow. Concurrently, efforts to bring material on women into the 'mainstream' curriculum gain momentum. These developments are not limited to the US: feminist research and teaching are thriving around the world. It is a challenging moment to be engaged in feminist research and teaching for, as Florence Howe has noted, 'It is now difficult to keep up with more than a segment of women's studies scholarship – even within a single discipline' (*Women's Studies Quarterly*, vol. 2, no. 2, summer 1983, p. 2).

The early and mid-1970s produced a richness of material *descriptive* of the challenge and exhilaration of teaching and learning about women. At recent professional meetings, increasing numbers of sessions on aspects of feminist pedagogy indicate growing interest in developing and elaborating *theory* about the dynamics of the feminist classroom. But few theoretical studies have so far reached print. With the accumulation of the experience and evidence of the last two decades, we now have the opportunity to think even more deeply and systematically

1

about our teaching. We know that to bring women fully into the curriculum means nothing less than to reorganize all knowledge, and that changing *what* we teach, means changing *how* we teach. Educators involved in this late-twentieth-century revolution in teaching and learning must continue to explore and to articulate — through reflection and dialogue — the content of this new conjunction 'feminist pedagogy.' Perhaps the better phrase is 'feminist pedagogies,' for the essays in this volume are neither homogeneous nor doctrinaire. They reflect a range of classroom experience; from a small elite New England liberal arts college with a long tradition of male education, to a large state university in California; from a Seven Sisters women's college to an urban community college. Despite the differences in their experience, however, educators whose teaching practices have been transformed by the feminist revolution in learning do share some common perspectives which allow an approach to definitions.

Feminist pedagogy postulates the existence of two separate but interlocking sets of concerns, each with its own dynamic. First, its practitioners define themselves as feminists and implement that self-definition through work that challenges the economic, socio-political, cultural and psychological imperatives based on gender. Those engaged in feminist pedagogy work to correct the academy's traditional myopia — a myopia that verges on blindness — by applying feminist principles to the classroom situation. Such application, far from reductive or doctrinaire, contains the potential for reconstructing and revitalizing the ways in which knowledge is acquired, sanctioned and perpetuated.

Aware of the ways in which the pedagogical situation may reproduce discriminatory, even destructive, attitudes and expectations about women, feminist teachers in their praxis enact a conscious (and also unconscious) array of behaviors and attitudes that bear in important ways on the issue of gender. Focus on both the apparent and hidden structures of the classroom yields, among other things, continuing discussion of the question of authority in the feminist classroom. Feminist teachers also explicitly confront the popularly understood schisms between the public and the private, between reason and the emotions. Feminist pedagogy legitimates personal experience as an appropriate arena of intellectual inquiry, and insists on a wedding of affect and intellect. Most feminist educators understand that knowledge is not neutral, that teacher and student alike bring 'texts' of their own to the classroom which shape the transactions within it.

How, then, one might ask, does feminist pedagogy differ from plain good teaching? To be sure, the practice of feminist educators has not developed in isolation from the more widespread developments in teaching theory and practice of the 1960s and 1970s. During these years, student interrogations of traditional classroom formats, as well as the desire of some faculty members to be more responsive to political and cultural upheavals, produced changes within ivied walls. Classrooms long considered the domain of primarily white students between the ages of eighteen and twenty-one were changed in important ways by policies of 'open enrollment' and the arrival of 'reentry' or 'nontraditional students' from diverse racial, ethnic, and class backgrounds, including numbers of older women students. Along with shifts in student concerns and student populations came the need to rethink the organization and delivery of 'knowledge,' as traditionally vested in the composition of the academic canon across the disciplines.

This gradual — and at times dramatic — reconsideration and reconstruction highlighted the need for new ways of teaching. Learner-centered and learner-active education became the focus of various experiments with humanistic, experiential, and psychological approaches to pedagogy in the USA and Europe. Working in Brazil, Paulo Freire's genius was to combine learner-centered education with explicit goals for social change. Freire's *Pedagogy of the Oppressed* (New York: Seabury Press, 1970) is the text most often referred to by the writers in this volume whose theory and practice of feminist pedagogy has been influenced by contemporary educational theory. But little of the progressive educational theory of the last several decades — Freire included — addressed questions of gender. Research has been done on sex equity and on sex-role stereotyping, particularly at the elementary school level. Nevertheless, little has been done to bring theories of teaching and learning together with a heightened consciousness of gender.

Because our teaching is so important, and so personal, talking openly about it is challenging, frightening and stimulating — an activity at once embraced and avoided. Few topics generate such intensity of discussion and debate at feminist conferences and on campuses around the country among those involved in teaching about women. At least such was our experience in presenting a paper with colleagues in 1979 at the New York University Institute for the Humanities Conference, commemorating the thirty-year anniversary of the publication of

Simone de Beauvoir's *The Second Sex*. The large attendance at that seminar, and the intensity and urgency of discourse surrounding it, convinced us that the time had come (after ten years of 'hands on' experience) for a serious assessment and overview of feminist pedagogy. Debate continued at a Women's Studies Forum on feminist pedagogy at the Modern Language Association Convention in Houston, in 1980, where we conceived the idea for this volume. As practitioners in a field newly institutionalized in higher education, we felt the need to move beyond oral presentations, small group discussions and private reflection in our attempts to theorize about the nature of our experience as feminist teachers. This collection of essays is the result.

Contributors to this volume raise provocative, even compelling, questions. Approaching feminist pedagogy from different perspectives of political orientation, gender and race, and across a variety of educational settings, they reflect upon the particularly charged space that the feminist classroom often becomes. Both the students' and teachers' 'agendas' are subject to scrutiny here, for teaching is not viewed as a strictly cognitive delivery of information, but rather as a complex intellectual and emotional engagement.

In this collection we have combined a number of 'classic' statements on feminist pedagogy from the early and mid-1970s with recent original essays, making what we believe to be significant and exciting contributions to the field. We have not arranged the essays chronologically, but in groups emphasizing the thematics of feminist pedagogy. Part one, 'Frameworks and Definitions,' offers broad theoretical perspectives on the realities of the classroom. 'The Politics of Nurturance' (Margo Culley, Arlyn Diamond, Lee Edwards, Sara Lennox and Catherine Portuges) explores the psychodynamics of feminist teaching. One consequence of Adrienne Rich's radical challenge to 'take women students seriously' is developed in Janice Raymond's description of an epistemology of 'passionate knowledge.' Another essay in this group, by Frances Maher, makes the connections between new feminist scholarship and interactive learning. The section concludes with an analysis by Gloria Bonder of Women's Studies in Argentina, where pedagogic strategies take account of 'the subject and intersubjective, the cognitive and emotional processes of an oppressed group facing established knowledge about women and the social reality.'

As the new scholarship on women has changed the content and structure of knowledge in every field, pedagogy has begun to mirror those changes in exciting ways. Part two, 'Transforming the Disciplines,' explores the implication of feminist pedagogy for particular disciplines. The teaching of history, as Robert Bezucha argues, traditionally based on an assumed split between the public and the private spheres, is transformed when both course content and classroom discourse about it challenge the terms of that division. The teaching of law, an enshrined pedagogy of rote and intimidation, becomes entirely new when Janet Rifkin encourages critical consciousness in the exploration of new modes of conflict-resolution. Helene Keyssar's 'Staging the Feminist Classroom' describes one experiment in theater in which the feminist process is as much the subject of study as the play under production. These essays, while obviously not able to represent all fields where feminist scholarship has transformed pedagogy, suggest ways the new learning may be embodied in the teaching process of other disciplines.

Traditionally, learning passed from master to novice, and unquestioned authority was vested in those older and therefore wiser. Part three, 'Teacher as Other,' looks at this role division. What are the consequences — ask Erlene Stetson and Judith McDaniels — when the teacher inhabits a marginal position in the culture? What authority does the black woman or the 'out' lesbian bring to the classroom when her position in the institution is likely to be precarious? Diedrick Snoek explores contradictions of a different nature for the male feminist at a traditional college: he may wish to divest himself of the automatic authority granted by his gender, but what if his students prove resistant to, and suspicious of, his intellectual and political perspectives?

In the feminist classroom, life-experience and theory interact as legitimately complementary, but sometimes competing, authorities. Two 'classic' essays — 'Breaking Silences: Life in the Feminist Classroom' (Nancy Hoffman) and 'Black-Eyed Blues Connections' (Michele Russell) — explore in detail a theme recurrent in this volume: the transforming power of the personal as the subject and method of feminist education. Other contributors insist on the importance of theory, confronting the myth that theory is alien to women, while admitting its seductive power. Joan Cocks writes about teaching feminist theory, Catherine Portuges about combining film and psychoanalytic theory, and Nancy K. Miller urges her graduate students in French to put 'the codes (and modes) of metacritical discourse' to the service of a feminist analysis.

Once experience becomes an appropriate subject of intellectual inquiry, the classroom is forever changed. And one consequence of that change is that traditional structures of authority in the classroom come under scrutiny. Susan Freidman takes issue with the popular idea of the non-hierarchical feminist classroom in an effort to reclaim and redefine the possibility of authority for women. Personal experience brings with it all forms of affect to the classroom, and one challenge to the feminist teacher (unlikely to be trained in such strategies) is to use affective energy in creative and productive ways. Margo Culley explores the particularly problematic uses of anger in the feminist classroom.

To achieve what Johnnella Butler calls 'Everywoman's Studies,' feminist teaching strategies as well as intellectual visions must be based in a multicultural reality. Contributors to part seven 'Communication Across Differences,' explore how race (Mary Helen Washington, Johnnella Butler and Elizabeth Spelman), gender and class (John Schilb) and political orientation (Barbara Hillyer Davis) inform feminist inquiry.

While these essays raise important issues in the hope of producing further dialogue, many other topics remain unexplored. More attention must be paid to the intersection between cognitive development and feminist teaching and might extend to the teachers' as well as the students' development. At different stages in our work, we experience different needs for control, and we fluctuate in our availability to students – indeed, in our engagement in teaching itself. How far can our changing sense of our work-selves be accounted for by changes in age, professional accomplishment and the climate in which we operate? More work must be done on feminist teaching in multicultural and multilingual contexts, including international feminist education. We look for more work on feminist pedagogy and the sciences, an arena where the connections promise to be particularly exciting. Moreover, settings outside formal schooling must be central to our thinking about feminist pedagogy, and our theorizing must also take us back to the elementary and secondary classroom. Finally, those involved in the effort to 'mainstream' material about women in the curriculum must explore the pedagogical implications of their work for the traditional classroom.

Every anthology is, in some sense, a collective enterprise. Even so, the editors of this collection are especially fortunate in their contributors, who have demonstrated the kind of cooperative spirit that has come to characterize the feminist academic endeavor. This book could not have happened without our companions in learning and teaching: the students, faculty and staff of the Women's Studies Program at the University of Massachusetts, Amherst. It is through more than a decade of almost daily interaction with these valued friends and colleagues that we have learned what we know about feminist pedagogy.

Margo Culley
Catherine Portuges
Amherst, Massachusetts
1984

PART ONE

Frameworks and definitions

1

The politics of nurturance[1]

Margo Culley, Arlyn Diamond, Lee Edwards, Sara Lennox, Catherine Portuges

After more than a decade of feminist teaching, of working with large numbers of students in Women's Studies courses and in feminist courses in 'mainstream' departments, we have come to accept one truth about our classrooms: they are indeed highly charged arenas of inquiry. To explain the intensity and urgency of the dialogue, the sometimes chaotic explosiveness of the transactions within these classrooms, we have to look beyond the material we are teaching, beyond even our pedagogical processes which challenge the organization of knowledge and the operation of institutions. Our very presence within the academy as 'woman thinking,' or the female authority, alters the fundamental construction of gender in our culture. Being who we are, doing what we do, enmeshes us (and our students) in contradictions, contradictions potentially generative of change in our educational system, perhaps even in the deepest structures of our gender arrangements.

With her characteristic lucidity, Simone de Beauvoir, in reflecting upon her own heritage, offers us a framework for understanding the contradictions inherent in our work:[2]

> I grew accustomed to the idea that my intellectual life — embodied
> by my father — and my spiritual life — expressed by my mother —
> were two radically different fields of experience which had abso-
> lutely nothing in common. This imbalance, which made my life
> a kind of endless debate, is the main reason I became an intel-
> lectual.

11

The feminist intellectual in the classroom is indeed in a position of permanent imbalance and endless debate. As women teachers, and especially as women teachers in our Women's Studies classrooms, we are both our fathers' daughters and our daughters' mothers. That is, many of us entered our professions expecting, perhaps naively, that the mantle of clarity, dignity and grace would be our inheritance as we rose inevitably through an institutional hierarchy based on merit. Yet, as de Beauvoir points out in *The Second Sex*, the correspondence between the idea of female virtue and the image of the mother tends to work against our capacity to achieve, or even aspire to, such professional 'success.'[3] As mothers, we are expected to nurture; as professionals, we are required to compete. The context in which our nurturing is to take place is the patriarchal context in which we teach. To the extent that our goal within and outside the classroom is the overthrow of the institutionalized patriarchy which currently structures our knowledge and our relationships, the contradictions we as teachers simultaneously represent are heightened. It may be that full consciousness of the dimensions of these contradictions will not suffice to dissolve them, but our awareness of our circumstances may finally enable us to preserve the positive maternal qualities of nurturance and caring in our efforts to transform the classroom.

The contemporary American university or college produces people trained to be useful members of an advanced capitalist society. The graduates are expected to be knowledgeable in areas the society has already determined have value: they are processed to accept, as natural modes of comprehending the world, production goals, competition, hierarchical structures and the need to separate the personal from the public self. Trustees or legislatures ask the institution to 'graduate' a certain number of bodies each year, at a certain limited cost. The institution, in turn, sets minimal faculty-student ratios, research and service goals. The faculty determines that so many credits distributed in a certain way represents a 'good' education. As a result of all these decisions — and the formation of self they imply — students and teachers are always attempting to advance themselves: to produce something tangible — a book, a paper, a grade — which will make them an associate professor, a graduate student, or a senior. We live in a world of numbers, office hours and competition for limited resources.

These contexts of our educational system hold consequences for us, as women and as feminists. As women, our own position is precarious, and the power we are supposed to exercise is given grudgingly, if at all. For our students, for ourselves, and for our superiors, we are not clearly 'us' or 'them.' The facts of class, of race, of ethnicity, of sexual preference — as well as gender — may cut across the neat division of teacher/student. Because of the politics we hold in common with our students as feminists, we think we are mutually and similarly committed to changing our institutions. However, our different 'investments' in our positions make our ideas of what should be changed inevitably divergent.

In our culture, the role of nurturer and intellectual have been separated not just by gender, but by function; to try to recombine them is to create confusion. Our psychoanalytic models are primarily useful when talking about feelings as distinct from abstract ideas or information. Neither one's mother nor one's therapist has to grade one's dreams or one's toilet training, or to make sure that one understands the difference between Wollstonecraft's philosophy and Engels's, or the labor conditions in Lowell in the nineteenth century, or Virginia Woolf's style. It is hard to know, in the finite world of the classroom, how to fulfill both functions. Some of us are more drawn to one role — mother or professor — than the other. Nevertheless, we would not be teachers now if we had not, at one point in our lives, had a powerful commitment to the idea of being intellectuals. As a result of our successes in the system, we are more deeply and passionately ambivalent about the intellectual life than our students can be. The mutual enterprise of the classroom, the kind of openness, freedom, and flexibility it demands, is thus made more difficult by the realities of what we have become in order to achieve our educational goals — and even by those goals themselves. Finally, unlike our students, we have long-term responsibilities to our programs: students will graduate; (some) professors remain. If we want to have Women's Studies, we have to make sure that we will be around in sufficient numbers to be effective.

Thus, the context in which we teach tends to limit and corrupt our ability to deal with the issues we are discussing here — especially if we think of ourselves as isolated nurturant or therapeutic figures. We need to be clear about those aspects of our role as teachers which are currently unavoidable, so we can identify them and their consequences for our students and ourselves, and separate them from the kinds of 'developmental' issues also operative.

Theorists since de Beauvoir have illuminated still further paradoxes embedded in our positions, complexities beyond — or beneath — the material conditions of our work. Dorothy Dinnerstein in *The Mermaid and the Minotaur* and Nancy Chodorow in *The Reproduction of Mothering* underscore the relevance of psychological dynamics to our current dilemmas.[4] Both writers point out the particular oedipal asymmetries involved in the basic structures of relationship between the two parents and their child. These asymmetries result in ambivalence and conflict, focused particularly in the crucial issues of power, control and authority. The resulting antagonisms manifest themselves in adult life in the split between visions of 'clean,' intellectual, remote beings, who are typically seen as male; and 'dirty,' emotional, accessible beings, who are typically seen as female. Our childhood gods metamorphose into demons; we despise the mother we can possess, while we yearn for the father who eludes us.

Dinnerstein and Chodorow argue that the fact that women have primary responsibility for infant care in this culture has profound consequences for adult life. And we would suggest, by extension, that the psychodynamics which they elaborate can help us understand the charged arenas of our classrooms. To recapitulate Dinnerstein's thesis in its simplest form: it is the woman in her female body who is, to the infant, all joy, all power, as well as the first source of disappointment and the first object of rage. The woman is the person from whom the boy child and the girl child must separate in their movement toward autonomous personhood. This process is usually understood as involving some anger at the mother and a transfer of positive feelings toward the father (who has remained a somewhat distant and uncontaminated figure).

Of course, the classroom recapitulates the family in approximate ways only, but we have found it most helpful to understand that students and teachers alike bring 'texts' to these classrooms, texts inscribed far beyond their boundaries. Our students see us as something more, or certainly something other, than simply their teachers. We are, inescapably, also their mothers — necessary for comfort but reinforcing a feared and fearful dependency if such comfort is too easily accepted. But we are also, in part, their fathers — word-givers, truth-sayers — to the extent we incorporate what Dinnerstein calls the father's 'clean' authority in our female bodies. The poet Anne Halley would call us 'bearded mothers' as we betray our body's traditional significance — for good or ill — with every word we utter. As our maternal power is feared, our paternal authority is mistrusted.

But the visions our students have of us tell only half the story.

For we, the teachers, are implicated in the classroom dynamics as fully as our students. Like them, we have our own 'texts,' our own unarticulated needs and expectations, our often unconscious desires with regard to our students' lives, attitudes, opinions, emotions, and relationships to us. Teachers see students as unruly daughters who must be both reformed and protected; students see teachers as old-fashioned mothers — powerful enough to command children, but necessarily rejected by all who would call themselves adults.

It is here that we invoke, with some trepidation (aware that the classroom setting is not a therapeutic situation) the psychoanalytic terminology of transference and countertransference. This language has given us access to the emotionally loaded nature of our feminist classrooms. We had always known that we were in the business of introducing powerful course *content* to our students. Nevertheless, it was only when we investigated our own 'texts,' and those of our students, that we could fully understand why unexpected 'happenings' in the feminist classroom continued to 'interrupt' course agendas. These included outbreaks of temper, tears, denunciation and divisiveness, notions that courses must offer total salvation or else fail, strong feelings of vulnerability, awareness that students/teachers love or hate students/teachers, that students/teachers see or reject themselves/their sisters/mothers/fathers in the course content or interactions in the classroom.

Classical psychoanalytic theory holds that in the transference experience the patient repeats central human relationships of the past in order to obtain previously thwarted satisfactions or to overcome guilt or anxiety. Transference, then, is a reliving of the past, an editing of the present in terms of the paradigms of the past; taken in its most encompassing sense, it is a vital force in all significant encounters with others, and in the psychoanalytic context evokes major human relations not formerly accessible to consciousness. Many theorists consider the transference relationship to be the cornerstone of the therapeutic endeavor, acknowledging that it is also the most demanding and difficult part of analytic technique. Schematically defined, the concept of transference refers to the whole range of affects in which our experience of another is colored by patterns of self- and object-representations pervading our subjective world. In subjecting the patient's spontaneously unfolding attitudes and affective reactions to intensive, cooperative scrutiny, the therapeutic alliance becomes a microcosm of the patient's inner object-world and thus facilitates exploration of conscious and unconscious expectations and meanings. When it succeeds, the transference offers the patient the possibility of reconstructing the inner object-world and of entering into a new, less distorted mode of interacting with others. If the transference is one of the most valuable sources of material for analysis, one of its most salient motivations, it also poses the greatest obstacle to success. One's desires for nurturance remain largely ungratified by the analyst, who has been trained not to gratify the patient's longings to act out unfulfilled needs for love or aggression. This stage of emotional celibacy compels the analysand to seek other, more appropriate targets upon whom to displace both libidinal and aggressive impulses, all of which are expected to appear in analytic sessions under the close supervision of the analyst.

As feminist teachers, we have been struck by the applicability of this admittedly fragmentary overview of transference theory to the special interplay of affect visible in the feminist classroom. Obviously, we are not analysts and the classroom is not the couch. Yet our mutual presence as female teachers and students creates a highly charged, fantasy-laden recapitulation of the mother/daughter nexus, that lifelong relationship imbued with a complex and contradictory dynamic of individuation and fusion, reminiscent of the infant's needs for separation and differentiation from the mother. Our students, whose ages range from seventeen to sixty, tend most frequently to come to us in their twenties, a period of crucial developmental identity. Alternating between a lingering, somewhat regressive dependency on their mothers and a potential for equality with — or even superiority over — them may create deep ambivalence toward their teachers. In *Memoirs of a Dutiful Daughter*, de Beauvoir speaks of the pervasive power of her own mother by suggesting that any reproach made by her, even the slightest frown, was a threat to the daughter's existential security. 'Without her approval,' she says, 'I no longer felt I had any right to live.'[5] Such a remark resonates equally in the pedagogical imperative that confronts the teacher-mother and her student-daughter. Powerlessness, rage and guilt conflate with longing, love and dependency just when our students are confronted by a woman professor, purveying at the same time the maternal breast and authoritative word of the texts embodying our deepest concerns as women.

Of course, this model of transference also implies its reciprocal notion of countertransference. Splitting off parts of ourselves, we lodge them in our students in ways that stipulate that for every two bodies in the room there will be at least four beings. We must learn, as teachers, to understand the nature of our own fantasies and their sources, as well as what precipitates their appearance in this context we had been trained to think of as free from affect, aloof from irrationality. Students appear before us as our daughters and our selves, as better than we were (and, therefore, threatening our self-esteem), as worse than we are (and, therefore, calling forth our fantasies of omnipotence and power in our wish to 'improve' them). They are our stepchildren, sometimes ungrateful for the help we, naively, think we offer disinterestedly, as infant seducers inordinately needy of attention we feel we must withhold if they (and we) are to survive. They are our rivals and our mirrors, the hope and fear of our unknown futures, the redeemers and betrayers of our rejected, cherished pasts.

The feminist classroom is thus transformed into a privileged space, the *locus desperatus* of reenacting, and perhaps examining for the first time, both threatening and joyous psychic events at a telling moment in the students' developmental life. We can begin to learn how to gather this material into new wholes, but only if we drop the masks of our own non-involvement. Our detached wish merely to help our students to become better learners, more competent female adults, is only part of the story, for it omits the intensity of our own emotional involvement. We must not confuse our projected wishes and fears with the students' real identities: if we do, we only contribute to the uncontrolled 'acting out' that at times is let loose in the feminist classroom. Instead, we can admit our complicity in the ambivalence and even negativity, as well as the highly charged positive feelings, our students inspire in us; we can disarm the images and undefensively, freely, allow new patterns to emerge.

From the transference analogy we can, perhaps, learn that as teachers we bear the burden of cultural images associated with the female intellectual: brainy woman, mythic teacher, sexless virago, phallic mother. Just as the analyst can provide a context that permits the patient to know longing and anger without necessarily responding behaviourally to such transferential affects, so too can we facilitate our students' development and intellectual progress by remembering the projections they may bestow upon us in no less measure than we idealize or demean them. True, we are denied the luxury of actively soliciting each individual's feelings in the group teaching we do; yet if we recognize and accept our students' attachments or disappointments without making them 'pay' for these transferences, we may be able to empower each other to become mutually whole and autonomous. The classroom can indeed be an eroticized milieu, alternately enhancing and suppressing the psychic energy needed for growth, and releasing primitive, narcissistic material from all participants. If we can work both within ourselves and collectively to understand what we contribute to the mother/daughter transference configuration, we can utilize both that bond and the analyst's mode of caring, informed detachment.

Not the least consequence of this analysis is the conclusion that the turmoil of the feminist classroom may not be entirely our fault. Knowing in advance that our students' love for and rage against us may erupt into our teaching, and that our own psychic material will also be engaged, we can understand with some clarity why so much more is taking place in these classrooms than what has been announced on the course syllabus.

In one real sense, the feminist classroom may become the place where the cultural split between mother and father may be healed. The feminist intellectual appropriates the *word* for herself and its power to name the manifestations of patriarchy. It may be that as women academics we have become the fathers, entered into the realm of history which men have always controlled. Yet, in a more profound sense feminism repudiates the law and order of the father and transforms history by bringing to it what we know about being mothers and being mothered. If, as Dorothy Dinnerstein indicates, the rage at mothers daring to be fathers derives from a terror that women will abandon the side of life responsible for keeping the world partly safe and sane, feminism can assert that its project is not to abandon the feminine standpoint, but to insert its best qualities into history.

Not just the content, but the form of knowledge is at stake here. It has been argued[6] that

> the Western scientific way of knowing, purportedly sexually neutral, is actually genderized; its acquisition of knowledge emerges as an active masculine process by a subject distanced from its passive, feminized object. Such fixed separation of subject and object correlates with rigid boundaries, intra-psychic ones between self and other, ideological ones between Culture and Nature.

In the feminist classroom, women who have been mothered by women resist the drawing of these rigid boundaries and admit to the fusion of affect and intellect. Or, as Muriel Dimen writes: 'Eyes accustomed to the shifting light of everyday social halftones, emotional fire-works, and private darkness can see best what lies between sub-ject and object, and chart the path between what is and what might be.'[7]

The feminist classroom is the place to use what we know as women to appropriate and transform, totally, a domain which has been men's. Let us acknowledge and welcome what everyone has always known — that more goes on in the classroom than the transmission of information. Let us welcome the intrusion/infusion of emotionality — love, rage, anxiety, eroticism — into intellect as a step toward healing the fragmentation capitalism and patriarchy have demanded from us. Our admitted histories and contexts, when subjected to examination, can alter the form and content of how we learn and teach. Affirming that we and our students are concrete subjects of the learning process, our model becomes dialectical rather than positivistic. For us as teachers, revealing ourselves as human beings is especially frightening and perilous, for it means we divest our-selves of what little institutional protection and power we possess, making us doubly vulnerable. But we count on the fact that the femi-nist classroom contains women who learned how to mother as well as be mothered. And for all its irrational dimensions, the demand for nurturance and support is finally a rational one, and we must dare to embody and empower the vision of a supportive and nurturant community of women. From this experiential here and now, we can begin to elaborate a new feminist epistemology, and to foster and encourage the subjects of that feminist transformation — our Women's Studies students.

In doing so, we would be honoring Simone de Beauvoir's prac-tice as a professor, deeply engaged with her students yet committed to a critical observation of this very phenomenon. We can now benefit perhaps more than ever before from her efforts to encom-pass and articulate her experience as a woman, an intellectual, a teacher, without avoiding painful, sometimes irreconcilable contra-dictions. Her transformative vision dedicated to demystification acknowledges ambivalence, paradox, even despair, as she moves back and forth between the contradictory aspects of herself, teaching us the appropriate dynamism of the psychic divisions between the double quests for autonomy and intimacy so familiar to women.

Notes

1 This paper was originally prepared as a talk in five parts given at the conference The Second Sex: Thirty Years Later, sponsored by the Humanities Institute at New York University in September 1979. Written under the influence of new scholarship on mothers and daughers, the essay was conceived, written, and presented as a collaborative effort. The extent of the collaboration is evident in the fact that the authors can no longer tell who wrote which part, though each is convinced she alone thought of the title.

2 Simone de Beauvoir, *Memoirs of a Dutiful Daughter*, New York: Harper & Row, 1959, p. 41.

3 Simone de Beauvoir, *The Second Sex*, ed. and trans. by H. M. Parshley, New York: Alfred A. Knopf, 1952.

4 Dorothy Dinnerstein, *The Mermaid and the Minotaur*, New York: Harper & Row, 1976; and Nancy Chodorow, *The Reproduction of Mothering: Psychoanalysis and the Sociology of Gender*, Berkeley: University of California Press, 1978.

5 De Beauvoir, *Memoirs of a Dutiful Daughter*, p. 39.

6 Evelyn Fox Keller, 'Gender and Science,' *Psychoanalysis and Contemporary Thought*, vol. 1, no. 3 (1978), pp. 409-33.

7 Muriel Dimen, 'Theory from the Inside Out, Or Process is Our Most Important Product,' from The Second Sex Conference Papers, New York University, 1979.

2

Taking women students seriously[1]

Adrienne Rich

I see my function here today as one of trying to create a context, delineate a background, against which we might talk about women as students and students as women. I would like to speak for a while about this background, and then I hope that we can have, not so much a question period, as a raising of concerns, a sharing of questions for which we as yet may have no answers, an opening of conversations which will go on and on.

When I went to teach at Douglass, a women's college, it was with a particular background which I would like briefly to describe to you. I had graduated from an all-girls' school in the 1940s, where the head and the majority of the faculty were independent, unmarried women. One or two held doctorates, but had been forced by the Depression (and by the fact that they were women) to take secondary school teaching jobs. These women cared a great deal about the life of the mind, and they gave a great deal of time and energy — beyond any limit of teaching hours — to those of us who showed special intellectual interest or ability. We were taken to libraries, art museums, lectures at neighbouring colleges, set to work on extra research projects, given extra French or Latin reading. Although we sometimes felt 'pushed' by them, we held those women in a kind of respect which even then we dimly perceived was not generally accorded to women in the world at large. They were vital individuals, defined not by their relationships but by their personalities; and although under the pressure of the culture we were all certain we wanted to get married, their lives did not appear empty or dreary to us. In a kind of cognitive dissonance, we knew they were 'old maids' and therefore supposed to be bitter and lonely; yet we saw them vigorously involved with life. But despite their existence as alternate models of women, the *content* of the education they gave us in no way prepared us to survive as women in a world organized by and for men.

From that school, I went on to Radcliffe, congratulating myself that now I would have great men as my teachers. From 1947 to 1951, when I graduated, I never saw a single woman on a lecture platform, or in front of a class, except when a woman graduate student gave a paper on a special topic. The 'great men' talked of other 'great men,' of the nature of Man, the history of Mankind, the future of Man; and never again was I to experience, from a teacher, the kind of prodding, the insistence that my best could be even better, that I had known in high school. Women students were simply not taken very seriously. Harvard's message to women was an elite mystification: we were, of course, part of Mankind; we were special, achieving women, or we would not have been there; but of course our real goal was to marry — if possible, a Harvard graduate.

In the late 1960s, I began teaching at the City College of New York — a crowded, public, urban, multiracial institution as far removed from Harvard as possible. I went there to teach writing in the SEEK program, which predated open admissions and which was then a kind of model for programs designed to open up higher education to poor, black, and Third World students. Although during the next few years we were to see the original concept of SEEK diluted, then violently attacked and betrayed, it was for a short time an extraordinary and intense teaching and learning environment. The characteristics of this environment were a deep commitment on the part of teachers to the minds of their students; a constant, active effort to create or discover the conditions for learning, and to educate ourselves to meet the needs of the new college population; a philosophical attitude based on open discussion of racism, oppression, and the politics of literature and language; and a belief that learning in the classroom could not be isolated from the student's experience as a member of an urban minority group in white America. Here are some of the kinds of questions we, as teachers of writing, found ourselves asking:

1 What has been the student's experience of education in the inadequate, often abusively racist public school system, which rewards passivity and treats a questioning attitude or indepen-

dent mind as a behavior problem? What has been her or his experience in a society that consistently undermines the self-hood of the poor and the non-white? How can such a student gain that sense of self which is necessary for active participation in education? What does all this mean for us as teachers?

2　How do we go about teaching a canon of literature which has consistently excluded or depreciated non-white experience?

3　How can we connect the process of learning to write well with the student's own reality, and not simply teach her/him how to write acceptable lies in standard English?

When I went to teach at Douglass College in 1976, and in teaching women's writing workshops elsewhere, I came to perceive stunning parallels to the questions I had first encountered in teaching the so-called disadvantaged students at City. But in this instance, and against the specific background of the women's movement, the questions framed themselves like this:

1　What has been the student's experience of education in schools which reward female passivity, indoctrinate girls and boys in stereotypic sex roles, and do not take the female mind seriously? How does a woman gain a sense of her *self* in a system — in this case, patriarchal capitalism — which devalues work done by women, denies the importance and uniqueness of female experience, and is physically violent toward women? What does this mean for a woman teacher?

2　How do we, as women, teach women students a canon of literature which has consistently excluded or depreciated female experience, and which often expresses hostility to women and validates violence against us?

3　How can we teach women to move beyond the desire for male approval and getting 'good grades' and seek and write their own truths that the culture has distorted or made taboo? (For women, of course, language itself is exclusive: I want to say more about this further on.)

In teaching women, we have two choices: to lend our weight to the forces that indoctrinate women to passivity, self-depreciation, and a sense of powerlessness, in which case the issue of 'taking women students seriously' is a moot one; or to consider what we have to work against, as well as with, in ourselves, in our students, in the content of the curriculum, in the structure of the institution, in the society at large. And this means, first of all, taking ourselves seriously: recognizing that central responsibility of a woman to herself, without which we remain always the Other, the defined, the object, the victim: believing that there is a unique quality of validation, affirmation, challenge, support, that one woman can offer another; believing in the value and significance of women's experience, traditions, perceptions; thinking of ourselves seriously, not as one of the boys, not as neuters, or androgynes, but as *women*.

Suppose we were to ask ourselves, simply: what does a woman need to know? Does she not, as a self-conscious, self-defining human being, need a knowledge of her own history, her much politicized biology, an awareness of the creative work of women of the past, the skills and crafts and techniques and powers exercised by women in different times and cultures, a knowledge of women's rebellions and organized movements against our oppression and how they have been routed or diminished? Without such knowledge women live and have lived without context, vulnerable to the projections of male fantasy, male prescriptions for us, estranged from our own experience because our education has not reflected or echoed it. I would suggest that not biology, but ignorance of our selves, has been the key to our powerlessness.

But the university curriculum, the high-school curriculum, do not provide this kind of knowledge for women, the knowledge of Womankind, whose experience has been so profoundly different from that of Mankind. Only in the precariously budgeted, much-condescended-to area of Women's Studies is such knowledge available to women students. Only there can they learn about the lives and work of women other than the few select women who are included in the 'mainstream' texts, usually misrepresented even when they do appear. Some students, at some institutions, manage to take a majority of courses in Women's Studies, but the message from on high is that this is self-indulgence, soft-core education: the 'real' learning is the study of Mankind.

If there is any misleading concept, it is that of 'co-education': that because women and men are sitting in the same classrooms, hearing the same lectures, reading the same books, performing the same laboratory experiments, they are receiving an equal education. They are not, first because the content of education itself validates men even as it invalidates women. Its very message is that men have been the shapers and thinkers of the world, and that this is only natural. The bias of higher education, including the so-called sciences, is white and male, racist and sexist; and this bias is expressed in both subtle and blatant ways. I have mentioned already the exclusiveness of grammar itself: 'The student should test himself on the above questions'; 'The poet is representative. He stands among partial men for the complete man.' Despite a few half-hearted departures from custom, what the linguist Wendy Martyna has named 'He-Man' grammar prevails throughout the culture. The efforts of feminists to reveal the profound ontological implications of sexist grammar are routinely ridiculed by academicians and journalists, including the professedly liberal *Times* columnist, Tom Wicker, and the professed humanist, Jacques Barzun. Sexist grammar burns into the brains of little girls and young women a message that the male is the norm, the standard, the central figure beside which we are the deviants, the marginal, the dependent variables. It lays the foundation for androcentric thinking, and leaves men safe in their solipsistic tunnel-vision.

Women and men do not receive an equal education because outside the classroom women are perceived not as sovereign beings but as prey. The growing incidence of rape on and off the campus may or may not be fed by the proliferations of pornographic magazines and X-rated films available to young males in fraternities and student unions; but it is certainly occurring in a context of widespread images of sexual violence against women, on billboards and in so-called high art. More subtle, more daily than rape is the verbal abuse experienced by the woman student on many campuses — Rutgers for example — where, traversing a street lined with fraternity houses, she must run the gauntlet of male commentary and verbal assault. The undermining of self, of a woman's sense of her right to occupy space and walk freely in the world, is deeply relevant to education. The capacity to think independently, to take intellectual risks, to assert ourselves mentally, is inseparable from our physical way of being in the world, our feelings of personal integrity. If it is dangerous for me to walk home late of an evening from the library, *because I am a woman and can be raped*, how self-possessed, how exuberant can I feel as I sit working in that library? How much of my working energy is drained by the subliminal knowledge that, as a woman, I test my physical right to exist each time I go out alone? Of this knowledge, Susan Griffin has written:[2]

more than rape itself, the fear of rape permeates our lives. And what does one do from day to day, with *this* experience, which says, without words and directly to the heart, *your existence, your experience, may end at any moment*. Your experience may end, and the best defense against this is not to be, to deny being in the body, as a self, to . . . avert your gaze, make yourself, as a presence in the world, less felt.

Finally, rape of the mind. Women students are more and more often now reporting sexual overtures by male professors — one part of our overall growing consciousness of sexual harassment in the workplace. At Yale, a legal suit has been brought against the university by a group of women demanding an explicit policy against sexual advances toward female students by male professors. Most young women experience a profound mixture of humiliation and intellectual self-doubt over seductive gestures by men who have the power to award grades, open doors to grants and graduate school, or extend special knowledge and training. Even if turned aside, such gestures constitute mental rape, destructive to a woman's ego. They are acts of domination, as despicable as the molestation of the daughter by the father.

But long before entering college the woman student has experienced her alien identity in a world which misnames her, turns her to its own uses, denying her the resources she needs to become self-affirming, self-defined. The nuclear family teaches her that relationships are more important than selfhood or work; that 'whether the phone rings for you, and how often,' having the right clothes, doing the dishes, take precedence over study or solitude; that too much intelligence or intensity may make her unmarriageable; that marriage and children — service to others — are, finally, the points on which her life will be judged a success or a failure. In high school, the polarization between feminine attractiveness and independent intelligence comes to an absolute. Meanwhile, the culture resounds with messages. During Solar Energy Week in New York I saw young women wearing 'ecology' T-shirts with the legend 'Clean, cheap and available' — a reminder of the 1960s anti-war button which read, 'Chicks say yes to men who say no.' Department store windows feature female mannequins in chains, pinned to the wall with legs spread, smiling in positions of torture. Feminists are depicted in the media as 'shrill,' 'strident,' 'puritanical,' or 'humorless,' and the lesbian choice — the choice of the woman-identified woman — as pathological or sinister. The young woman sitting in the philosophy classroom, the political science lecture, is already gripped by tensions between her nascent sense of self-worth, and the battering force of messages like these.

Look at a classroom: look at the many kinds of women's faces, postures, expressions. Listen to the women's voices. Listen to the silences, the unasked questions, the blanks. Listen to the small, soft voices, often courageously trying to speak up, voices of women taught early that tones of confidence, challenge, anger, or assertiveness, are strident and unfeminine. Listen to the voices of the women and the voices of the men; observe the space men allow themselves, physically and verbally, the male assumption that people will listen, even when the majority of the group is female. Look at the faces of the silent, and of those who speak. Listen to a woman groping for language in which to express what is on her mind, sensing that the terms of academic discourse are not her language, trying to cut down her thought to the dimensions of a discourse not intended for her (*for it is not fitting that a woman speak in public*); or reading her paper aloud at breakneck speed, throwing her words away, deprecating her own work by a reflex prejudgment· *I do not deserve to take up time and space.*

As women teachers, we can either deny the importance of this context in which women students think, write, read, study, project their own futures; or try to work with it. We can either teach passively, accepting these conditions, or actively, helping our students identify and resist them.

One important thing we can do is *discuss* the context. And this need not happen only in a Woman's Studies course; it can happen anywhere. We can refuse to accept passive, obedient learning and insist upon critical thinking. We can become harder on our women students, giving them the kinds of 'cultural prodding' that men receive, but on different terms and in a different style. Most young women need to have their intellectual lives, their work, legitimized against the claims of family, relationships, the old message that a woman is always available for service to others. We need to keep our standards very high, not to accept a woman's preconceived sense of her limitations; we need to be hard to please, while supportive of risk-taking, because self-respect often comes only when exacting standards have been met. At a time when adult literacy is generally low, we need to demand more, not less, of women, both for the sake of their futures as thinking beings, and because historically women have always had to be better than men to do half as well. A romantic sloppiness, an inspired lack of rigor, a self-indulgent incoherence, are symptoms of female self-depreciation. We should help our women students to look very critically at such symptoms, and to understand where they are rooted.

Nor does this mean we should be training women students to 'think like men.' Men in general think badly: in disjuncture from their personal lives, claiming objectivity where the most irrational passions seethe, losing, as Virginia Woolf observed, their senses in the pursuit of professionalism. It is not easy to think like a woman in a man's world, in the world of the professions; yet the capacity to do that is a strength which we can try to help our students develop. To think like a woman in a man's world means thinking critically, refusing to accept the givens, making connections between facts and ideas which men have left unconnected. It means remembering that every mind resides in a body; remaining accountable to the female bodies in which we live; constantly retesting given hypotheses against lived experience. It means a constant critique of language, for as Wittgenstein (no feminist) observed, 'The limits of my language are the limits of my world.' And it means that most difficult thing of all: listening and watching in art and literature, in the social sciences, in all the descriptions we are given of the world, for the silences, the absences, the nameless, the unspoken, the encoded — for there we will find the true knowledge of women. And in breaking those silences, naming our selves, uncovering the hidden, making ourselves present, we begin to define a reality which resonates to *us*, which affirms *our* being, which allows the woman teacher and the woman student alike to take ourselves, and each other, seriously: meaning, to begin taking charge of our lives.

Notes

1 Originally given as a talk at the New Jersey College and University Coalition on Women's Education, 9 May 1978. First published in the USA, *On Lies, Secrets, and Silence: Selected Prose 1966-1978* by Adrienne Rich, New York: W. W. Norton, 1979, pp. 237-45. Reprinted by permission of W. W. Norton & Company, Inc. Copyright ©1979 by W. W. Norton & Company Inc. and with permission of Virago Press Ltd, London (UK publishers).
2 Susan Griffin, *Rape: The Power of Consciousness*, New York: Harper & Row, 1979, p. 61.

3

Classroom pedagogy and the new scholarship on women

Frances Maher

Introduction

What are the implications for classroom pedagogy as it relates to the new scholarship on women and the new consciousness of women's issues? This article is an analysis of the factors contributing to the need for particular pedagogies, or ways of teaching, when dealing with women as students and with women's experiences as subject-matter. The word 'pedagogy' is often defined to include curricular choices. Here, however, the focus will be on processes of teaching and learning, and classroom interactions as they relate to what and how people learn.

The assumptions behind this search for appropriate teaching styles for and about women are threefold. One is that, as Adrienne Rich says, 'women's minds and experiences are intrinsically valuable and indispensable to any civilization worth the name' (1979, p.235). The second is that the public examination of women's lives, those of half the race, has been virtually buried until recently. Thus we need to construct a language, a worldview (or views), a research methodology, and a pedagogy to discover, examine and describe a set of experiences which, up until now, did not officially exist.

Thirdly, appropriate teaching styles to recover the female experience can also be applied to the education of all people. Although women have been particularly silent and silenced, 'official' truths and traditional teaching methods have distorted other truths and experiences, as well — such as those of minority and working-class women and men. The traditional mode of university teaching, that of the lecture, presumes

29

that an expert will present to the students an objective, rationally derived and empirically proven set of information. This mode, no matter how complete, can only reflect one version (usually the one dominant in the culture). It does not necessarily hold personal meaning for all students — they may simply memorize it on the teacher's terms, for a grade or career goal. (Thus we have the common distinction of learning 'for yourself' or for 'the test.) Moreover, this traditional version of education as the wisdom of generations is especially pernicious for women (and other oppressed groups) because its content has often ignored or demeaned them. They are memorizing truths to which their own historical, cultural, and personal experience gives the lie.

A pedagogy appropriate for voicing and exploring the hitherto unexpressed perspectives of women and others must be collaborative, cooperative and interactive. It draws on a rich tradition going back to Paulo Freire, John Dewey, and even Socrates, of involving students in constructing and evaluating their own education. It assumes that each student has legitimate rights and potential contributions to the subject-matter. Its goal is to enable students to draw on their personal and intellectual experiences to build a satisfying version of the subject, one that they can use productively in their own lives. Its techniques involve students in the assessment and production, as well as the absorption, of the material. The teacher is a major contributor, a creator of structure and a delineator of issues, but not the sole authority.

This essay will first describe some sources of such an interactive pedagogy as it applies to women's concerns — namely, the needs and characteristics of women students, the nature of research on women and recent changes in the scholarly disciplines. It will next explain some components of this pedagogy as they may be practiced in classrooms. Finally, it will examine some further possible implications of interactive learning and teaching for women students, and for students as a whole.

Women students in the classroom

Women by now are over half the undergraduate population (Perun, 1982). Presumably they receive the same education and have the same college experience as men, including access to all college facilities, courses, and activities. Outside and inside the classroom, however, their experiences are very different from those of their male counter-parts. College is a male-dominated hierarchy in which male professors hold social and intellectual sway over other males (their students and disciples) and females in many subordinate roles (their wives, secretaries and female students and disciples). Female professors are fewer in number (even in all-women's colleges they are seldom a majority), usually lower in status, and do not command a similar 'retinue' (see Rich, 1979, p.137). In this regard, of course, college life reflects accurately many aspects of life in the society at large. Thus women students not only lack enough role models of women as scholars, but are faced with women in a variety of traditional, subordinate, and demeaning roles even as they are presumably enjoy-ing equal educational opportunities and status.

We are most concerned here, however, with the classroom setting. How are women, and women's experiences, devalued *inside* the class-room? Paulo Freire and others have described oppressed peoples in traditional and authoritarian societies as being denied their own voices and experiences by the imposition of the single dominant worldview of 'the oppressor' as the only reality. In the traditional model of education that Freire portrays, the teacher (representing the oppressor) is the sole authority and the 'Subject' (capitalization as original) of the learning process; he chooses the content which the oppressed students passively accept. In essence, he makes deposits of predetermined information into the empty vaults of the students' minds (see Freire, 1970, p.59). The application of this concept of 'banking education' to women in modern American society is striking.[1] Men in general have often been described as the 'subject' for which women are the 'object.' More importantly, women are silenced, objectified and made passive through both the course content and the pedagogical style of most college classrooms.

First, academic disciplines ignore and distort the experience of women as a group by structuring their concepts and subject-matter around male-derived norms. Second, however, the dominant peda-gogical style of most classrooms discriminates against women's experi-ence and participation in a variety of ways, all of which reinforce female passivity. Professors — male and, sometimes, female — tend to call on women students less in discussion, to ask them less probing questions, and to interrupt them more often. They make more frequent eye-contact with men and are more attentive to male questions or comments (see Thorne, 1975, quoted in Hale and Sandler, 1982, pp.7-9). On a deeper level, classroom discussions (as well as lectures) are usually conducted so as to reward 'assertive speech,' competitive 'devil's advocate' interchanges, and impersonal and abstract styles — often incorporating the generic 'he' (*ibid.*, pp.9, 10). These modes of speech, while perhaps not inherently 'masculine,' seem more natural to men in this culture; women tend to be more tentative, polite, and hesitant in their comments and thus are taken less seriously by teachers. Women who try to be more assertive face a double bind, for they are perceived as 'hostile' females rather than as 'forceful' men. Perhaps as a result of this treatment, as well as the subject-matter, women college students as a group are simply more silent than men. Like Freire's 'oppressed,' they do not speak up; their experiences, their interpretations, their questions are not heard as often.

What are the implications of this analysis for interpreting and changing current classroom practices? At the root of the problem of awakening women students is a recognition of the central validity of their own perceptions in choosing and interpreting their education. In order for the oppressed to be liberated, according to Freire, their experiences under the oppressors must be raised to the level of personal consciousness, recognized and affirmed. Then teachers and students can be equals in a cooperative search for understanding about the experiences of people in their world (Freire, 1970, p.67).

In this light we can begin to see the primary importance of the inclusion of women's perspectives in the subject-matter disciplines. But we can also reexamine women's patterns of classroom participation and see them as cooperative and constructive, rather than non-assertive and hesitant. Common patterns of competition and argument in discussion came not only from 'masculine' modes of speech, but from traditional notions of learning, wherein we search for objective truth and the single 'right answer' rather than for shared and comparative conclusions about multiple experiences. In fact, Hale and Sandler, in their research on college women's classroom experiences, intimate that 'feminine' styles might be more conducive to a notion of discussion as a 'cooperative development of ideas' rather than as 'competition from the floor.' They describe women's tendency to end questions with a questioning intonation, encouraging the next speaker to elaborate. They quote findings to show more class participation by both sexes in courses taught by women, although women teachers are not immune to the discriminatory practices we have been describing (Hale and Sandler, 1982, p.10).

Simply in terms of classroom interactions, then, we can suggest that teaching practices which stress cooperative rather than competitive participation may encourage more women students (and more students) actively to question and examine the implications of the material they are learning for their own experience and their own lives, thus better addressing their educational needs and priorities. (For a specific description of a graduate course in sociology using such methodologies, and its effects on students, see Nelson, 1981.) Some components of such an interactive pedagogy are described below; I wish now, however, briefly to indicate several ways in which interactive teaching practices are related to both methdology and content in the field of Women's Studies.

The nature of research on women

In every scholarly discipline wherein the female experience has been explored, the new scholarship on women has challenged not only the scope, the content, and the conclusions of the field, but also the research methods by which the knowledge in the field has been derived in the first place. Scholars concerned with women have evolved, not coincidentally, a methodology which reflects the nature of the information they are now seeking and also the kind of teaching practices described here. This methodology involves a conceptualization of knowledge as a comparison of multiple perspectives leading towards a complex and evolving view of reality. Each new contribution reflects the perspective of the person giving it, each has something to offer. This methodology replaces the search for a single, objective, rationally derived 'right answer' that stands outside the historical source or producer of that answer. Instead, it aims for the construction of knowledge from multiple perspectives through cooperative problem-solving.

What are some components of this 'interactive' research methodology? As said above, in every scholarly discipline concerned with human behavior, generalizations about 'man' have hidden women's experiences — which have often been different, even opposite. Thus, women's roles have been demeaned, ignored, privatized, and/or made the exception. Men have been the subjects of the actions, women the objects. If women's experiences are to be equally represented, then, we must locate and describe these experiences, analyze them, and give them theoretical and conceptual frameworks. Since prior frameworks have hitherto reflected only male perspectives, however, Women's Studies challenges the validity of any *single* 'objectively derived' framework within which to describe our experiences. There are 'woman's' version and 'man's,' but also the versions of 'old' and 'young' women, 'old black women' and 'young black men,' and so on. In this regard, we must acknowledge the subjectivity of the researcher, and the role of his or her perspective in the construction and interpretation of knowledge. We must also replace a search for one universal truth or explanation with a search for shared meanings, for comparative approaches, for what any one of many perspectives has to offer (or challenge) the others.

Thus the study of women calls for a research methodology that acknowledges the multiple contexts within which knowledge is produced. In fact, as Marcia Wescot says, such a methodological approach 'converges with the interpretive tradition in the social sciences . . . Social knowledge is always interpreted within historical contexts, and truths are, therefore, historical rather than abstract, contingent rather than categorical.' Why does the study of women imply such a methodology? Because 'the (traditional) concept of the human being is only the man writ large . . . The *specificity* of the knower is only revealed when women become subjects of knowledge, because women are not identified with the abstract human being but with particular deviations or negations of this abstracted universal' (Westcott, 1979, pp.422, 426). In other words, Women's Studies as subject-matter reflects the particularistic, historical and contextual nature of all our conceptualizations of human society. To study women as *subjects*, equal to men, is to recognize that human experiences are multiple and must be multiply interpreted.

A similar conception of methodology has been applied to the natural sciences as well. While acknowledging 'objectivity' as the goal of scientific method, Longino (1981) argues that scientific observations are, in fact, dependent on theoretical formulations which often compete with each other to explain the same facts. Therefore, 'there is no independent field of facts (for recourse); scientists work within logically independent and incomparable world views determined by their paradigms.' Given such disagreement, she reformulates the notion of science as 'something practiced not primarily by individuals but by groups.' Again, knowledge is conceived as the accretion of mutually critical perspectives, each reflecting 'background beliefs which can be articulated and subjected to criticism from the scientific community' (*ibid.*, p.191).

In another context, Catherine MacKinnon (1982, p.537) also argues that women's experiences outside the male paradigm allow them to critique the existence of any single paradigm:

> Feminism does not see its view as subjective, partial, or undermined but as a critique of the purported generality, disinterestedness and universality of prior accounts. Aperspectivity (or objectivity) is revealed as a strategy of male hegemony ... Power to create the whole world from (a single) point of view is power in its male form.

The worldview expressed in the traditional disciplines, calling itself universal, in fact only reflected the experiences and purposes of one group, giving them an exclusive power over the definition of knowledge which was denied to everyone else. Going further than Westcott and Longino, MacKinnon then asserts that feminist method, by legitimizing the study of women's experiences, gives women a new means of understanding and coming to terms with their own personal condition. 'Feminist method,' she says, 'is consciousness raising; the collective critical reconstitution of the meaning of women's social experience, as women live through it.' It could also, presumably, include men's experience, as men live through it, if handled in collective and consciousness-raising fashion. In either case, knowledge should be defined, interpreted and created so as to empower different groups of people to understand (and improve) their own lives.

As we have already seen, Freire's concern is for oppressed peoples (males); his approach to consciousness-raising is through pedagogy, not research. Yet he raises similar concerns. In defining the terms of his pedagogy, he calls for a search for 'generative themes' that describe the relations between men and their world. He says that such themes cannot be found 'in men, divorced from reality, not yet in reality, divorced from men ... [they] can only be apprehended in a man-world relationship.' In this search, research, teaching and learning all become part of the same educative process. Teachers and students become 'co-investigators' both in the discovery of knowledge and the frameworks that give it meaning. Because of this integral relationship between knower and known, 'the methodology proposed requires that the investigators and the people should act as co-investigators. The more active an attitude men take in regard to the explanation of their thematics, the more they deepen their critical awareness of reality and

. . . take possession of that reality.' Answering the charge that the
people, because searching for personal meaning, will destroy objectivity,
he echoes Longino: 'The same objective fact could evoke different
complexes of generative themes in different epochs.' (Freire, 1970,
pp.97-8). Giving students the tools to discover themes for themselves
will allow them to understand reality on their own terms. Like Mac-
Kinnon, Freire is concerned with knowledge for social change: once
able to name, evoke and describe their oppression, people will act to
transform it.

Thus, for many scholarly researchers, the study of women involves
a major methodological shift. They are moving away from the traditional search for objectivity and towards a multilayered and comparative construction of social realities. In this search they acknowledge
their own subjectivity, even as they try to transcend it by listening
to, and drawing on, the experiences of others. To go back to the
classroom with this perspective is immediately to recognize its relevance
to interactive pedagogies, which draw on students' experiences not
only for their own learning, but also to enrich the interpretation and
materials of the discipline itself.

The scholarly disciplines and Women's Studies

Another source of pedagogical change implied by the new research
on women is the change in the scholarly disciplines themselves and,
therefore, in the content of course offerings. The new scholarship
on women has begun to alter the standards of judgment, the concepts
and the generalizations in almost every discipline, by enlarging the
scope of experiences to be included. While a discussion of all these
changes is obviously beyond the scope of this article, we can briefly
examine the pedagogical implications of such changes in two disciplines
— history and psychology. In history, attention to women has been a
means of examining social history and of studying 'ordinary people's
lives, both in the public and private spheres. Feminist scholars attempt
to examine all aspects of human society as engaged in by both men
and women: the family, popular culture, the workplace, and religious,
philanthropic, and educational institutions, as well as politics and
laws. Even the study of politics has changed; the social roots of political
movements are explored in the motives and goals of reformers and
their followers.

Obviously, the inclusion of women's lives has in itself a liberating effect on the education of female students. They are not learning 'the history of man' while being denied the knowledge of any history of their own. But because woman have been not only an ignored but an oppressed group, to describe historical experience from the perspective of female lives is to liberate women (and men) students in another way. If history is not only the story of 'great men,' then students can use and critically evaluate it to locate themselves as 'ordinary people' in historical time and place. They can explore the popular roots of historical change and development in terms of their own position in society. For example, they can investigate the histories in their own families, examining particular occupational and gender roles to illustrate wider social trends. Pedagogically, a history which includes the experiences of women calls for a multiplicity of perspectives and experiences in the past and the present which students can explore.

In psychology the impact of the new scholarship of women has also been profound. The equation of male psychological development with the 'norm,' particularly for Freud and his followers, left women inherently inferior (and silenced), because of their lack of assertiveness, individuation, rationality, and 'objective' standard of moral judgment. The recent work of Chodorow (1978), Gilligan (1982), and others, however, has given us a picture of 'normal' female development as differently staged, toward different ends, than that of males. In these models, the interpersonal and responsive qualities of females are conceptualized not as 'inferior' and failed struggles for a (masculine) autonomy, but as particular strengths. Gilligan, for example, speaks of a female network of caring relationships to complement the hierarchies of moral choices based on male notions of abstract justice (Gilligan, 1982, chapter 2).

For educators, this psychology does more than describe a new perspective. The research illuminates and legitimizes female behavior in classrooms and elsewhere. For example, women in our culture, socialized differently from men, quite often have different speech patterns and ways of expressing themselves. We can say that some of these patterns, such as the hesitation mentioned earlier, come from actual (and perceived) powerlessness; they might also, however, come from a regard for other points of view. In either case, women's modes of expression are not 'less articulate'; they are different. The new psychological research also challenges the whole concept of what behaviors and attitudes constitute 'normal' or healthy development, in much the same way as the new historical research enlarges the concept of legitimate history. In both subjects, the range of legitimate, permissible, and valid experiences expands not simply from one or two, but from one to many. Instead of women as 'inferior' men, or blacks (and black women) as 'inferior' whites, we can perceive and articulate varieties of psychic health in a variety of situations. Third, some scholars have attempted, while exploring the differences between men and women, to locate areas of similarity and complementarity as well. Lifting the rigid mantle of contemporary sex-role socialization and gender identification gives us all an expanded emotional and intellectual repertoire. Again, the implications for pedagogy of these changes in the discipline of psychology are obvious. Students, in being encouraged to relate psychological insights to their own experience simultaneously learn and evaluate psychological theories (and their empirical basis), and can contribute to their ongoing formulation. An interactive and cooperative pedagogy, drawing on all the available perspectives in the class, is therefore not only appropriate but necessary.

Components of interactive pedagogy

The needs of the students, of the research process, and of the disciplines themselves thus all require an interactive pedagogy for the treatment of women's experiences. While women students (and many men) have been silenced in college classrooms, a new process of relating subject-matter to student needs and interests depends upon the active participation of all students, particularly women, whose experiences (and voices) have until recently been considered illegitimate. Such a process also draws on the 'female' modes of collaborative, rather than competitive, interaction. Researchers have turned away from a competitive search for the one best theory or explanation of phenomena (which can then be 'taught' to students) towards a collaborative, evolutionary and complementary approach (which can be opened up to include student views). In addition, the content of major disciplines is being reshaped to accept multiple viewpoints as equally valid, particularly those which have been unexpressed and suppressed before. Therefore, student contributions can enrich interpretations in the discipline as well as in their own learning.

What are some concrete and practical aspects of this 'interactive' pedagogy? How does subject-matter presentation change? What are some roles and activities of the teacher and student? How can classes be structured? What issues and problems need further discussion?

Subject-matter presentation

A subject-matter that denies or contradicts a student's own experience can still be absorbed in several ways. Students may 'learn' it on its own terms, without expecting the content to have any personal relevance or meaning. For instance, many have memorized historical facts and dates, and even used them appropriately in essays, without ever having experiential reference-points for these facts. A second mode of reception is that of misunderstanding. A teacher may describe a law as 'progressive,' a certain family as 'middle class,' or a person as 'depressed.' In each of these cases, students may 'understand' these words in a different sense from the one the teacher intends, and thus perhaps misinterpret course assignments and presentations. In either of the above examples, the traditional lecture approach leaves no room for clarification. Obviously, the more distant the students' own experience from the subject-matter as defined by the teacher, the more difficult and alienating this lack of understanding will be (as in women's exclusion from male-derived norms and concepts).

However, training in all disciplines involves the study of unfamiliar terms or terms used in discipline-specific ways. Thus, if we want our students to construct both an accurate and personally meaningful version of our subject-matter — one that can be discussed and built on with the teacher and each other — we must begin with the construction of a common vocabulary and language among teacher and students. Too often we assume that students attach the same attributes to key concepts as we do. In our formulation, we often use one term which is unfamiliar to students to describe another unfamiliar term — leaving them confused and reduced to rote memorization and passive learning (see Maher and Lyman, 1982). Teachers can begin classes by asking students for their *own* meanings for key terms, and then using these in the definitions of new ones. For example, students in an educational psychology class are asked to evaluate the concept of 'intelligence' as it relates to IQ testing. To prepare for this discussion, they write an essay entitled 'How Smart I Am' to express their own experience of this loaded and controversial concept.

For Paulo Freire, this act of naming our experiences is a crucial step in the awakening of the consciousness of the oppressed. The essence of dialogue is the 'word.' By constructing common names and meanings for their realities, people describe and activate the world for each other — and, in so doing, may change it. Once armed with the concept of 'exploitation,' for example, they can begin to define its features and interpret them: 'Dialogue is the encounter between men, mediated by the world, in order to name the world' (Freire, 1970, p.76). In our terms, *women* need to name and describe our world, to differentiate its terms and meanings from those of male experience, if only to see our commonalities as well. (For example, is 'depression' different for women than for men? How can the two forms be described and compared?) Until teachers explicitly work toward constructing a commonly understood language in their class-rooms, the subject-matter concepts will be alien to some students' experiences.

A more fundamental change in subject-matter presentation involves making explicit connections in course topics among the three levels of theory, research, and the students' (and teacher's) own observations and experiences. As students explore different explanatory models for data discussed in courses, they learn that the validity of any strong theory comes from its ability to explain aspects of both learned about and personally experienced reality. They also learn some ways in which different perspectives, including their own, help to determine what data is used and considered important. Thus Bunch (1979) has students compare personal solutions to set discrimination issues with those of feminist theorists. In my educational psychology course the students (all female) contrast a new model of female moral development (Gilligan, 1982) to the more traditional approaches of Kohlberg, Piaget and others. They analyze their own thinking in relation to these theories through class discussions of moral dilemmas. In so doing, they are able not only to challenge a previously held norm, but also to reassess the universal applicability of all such stage theories to explain human development.

In another course, students examine sexism in schools — the con-troversy over girls and math, discriminatory tracking and counseling practices, and classroom interaction patterns that favor boys. They compare research findings to classroom observations and to their own experiences as females in school. They look at explanatory models for this discrimination from feminist and non-feminist schools of thought. (For example, are girls' minds genetically different, or socially programmed for different interests?) Relating theory, research, and experience in this way, they can begin to think of ways schools might serve not only girls, but a wide variety of students perhaps previously ignored or demeaned by the imposition of a single academic norm.

The roles of teacher and student

Beyond such new treatment of subject-matter topics described above, there are several related ways of transforming our pedagogy to reflect the collaborative and interactive nature of the new scholarship on women. If this work has legitimized the study of ordinary lives from multiple perspectives, and made explicit the connection between the framework of the knower and what is known, then students and teachers can use their own experience in the creation, as well as the illustration, of course topics. One way to do this is by the use of the 'self as subject.' Student educational autobiographies in education courses and family trees and family history in history courses are examples of this approach. In one education course, students analyze the significance for both women's roles and the education profession of the fact that most teachers in America have been women. (See, for example, Grumet, 1981.) In a related discussion of their educational family trees, students in one class found that *every* grandmother who worked was at one time a teacher. This common background, besides giving these education students a strong sense of historical identification and persisting societal norms, also encouraged them to re-evaluate their own possible choice of teaching as a career. Central to this inclusion of the self as subject, however, is the teacher's acknowledgment of his or her perspective as, of necessity, a partial one as well. Instead of presenting all course topics and materials as objective truth, the teacher must be explicit about his or her rationale behind the choice of readings, issues and so on.

There is here, as we have said above, an admitted 'intersubjectivity of meaning of subject and object . . . the questions that the investigator asks of the object of knowledge grow out of her own concerns and experiences' (Westcott, 1979, p.426). Westcott and others see this dialectical relationship between self and material as particularly powerful for women studying women, because 'knowledge of the other and knowledge of the self are mutually informing . . . self and other share a common condition of being women.' However, this paradigm may illustrate any exploration in which aspects of personal identity illuminate the subject-matter — whether workers studying workers, Italians studying Italians, and so on. The interpretation of particular masculine experiences as generalized truths has denied such insights to many groups. Students and teachers using the 'self as subject' can call up and legitimize a variety of hitherto unexplored experiences and themes. (The validity and power of self-examination, and explicit subjectivity, in contributing to a personally meaningful education has also been recently explicated by many modern curriculum theorists. See, for example, Freire, 1970; Greene, 1975; and Mitrano, 1981.)

A second way of empowering students as experts is to use the notion of the 'self as inquirer.' Here, more than in other modes of teaching, we are asking our students not only to answer questions, but to pose them; to become creators and constructors, as well as learners, of knowledge. We can assign them topics to pursue in which they take a particular interest (once again being explicit about the connection between knowledge and knower); their research can then be challenged and enriched by each other's contributions and perspectives. Such assignments can make individuals or groups responsible for constructing components of the course: in a government course, for example, students can research and present the policies of a particular party, country, or pressure group. Or assignments can illustrate or examine course theories: as mentioned above, student field observations in elementary schools can test presumed differences in boy/girl behavior raised in education and psychology classes. Thus, student research into the experiences of particular groups can build on and/or transform theories or hypotheses introduced in class. Such research gives the material personal importance for students, as well as enriching the discipline itself.

The structure of classes and courses

This consideration of students as 'subjects' and 'inquirers' involves, however, the serious inclusion of their contributions in both the presentation and the structuring of our courses. Thus, in interactive and democratic teaching modes the most common form of communication is discussion, not lecture. The teacher (or student) raises a problem from the readings; students explore its meaning and ramifications, relate it to their own experiences, consider solutions and so on. The teacher may have been responsible for the selection of the reading and the framing of the problem, but the discussion legitimizes the experience of all in analyzing it. Hence, both teacher and students can play the role of both experts and learners.

In conducting discussions, teachers need to encourage students to listen and react to each other's statements, and to put student comments on the board for emphasis. To gain maximum participation, discussion on specific topics can be arranged in small groups, with results reported to the class as a whole and emphasized by the teacher. In general, habits of inferiority and passivity, of looking to the teacher for the answer, have to be deliberately challenged to be broken. We can be explicit that a course relies on student contributions and formulations, but we must also arrange classroom discussion so that this reliance is genuine. With women students (especially silenced) and Women's Studies (until recently not considered a legitimate field of inquiry) such new patterns should be particularly emphasized.

Differences among students are often an issue in ongoing class discussions. Some students are more vocal than others: for example, males tend to volunteer more answers than females. Females, and quieter students, need to be explicitly encouraged; to be called on when not volunteering and to be placed in small groups where participation may be easier. Students with differing perspectives may also actively disagree. They may not see each other's perspectives as mutually reinforcing, but as conflicting — which is sometimes the case. For example, in a recent Women's Studies case, working-class white women and upper-middle-class black women argued extensively over the relative weight of class and race in female oppression. Each group had both personal experience and evidence to support their position. More specifically, as Davis points out, 'feminist' students whose consciousness has already been raised may feel uncomfortable with their more traditional sisters. 'However "advanced" their intellectual and emotional grasp of feminist issues, [they] often lack empathy with or respect for the hard choices and important conflicts of traditional women' (Davis, 1981, p.8).

For differences and divisions like these (and again such differences can come up in any classroom where multiple perspectives are discussed), the teacher can function as a 'simultaneous translator . . . hearing and giving back in other words what another person has just said, and presenting an explanation in another language which will illuminate the issue for a second group without alienating the first' (*ibid.*, p.9). In such discussions, the prior creation of common definitions for terms and a common language for the group is particularly important. If all agree on what 'social class' means, then unnecessary misunderstanding can be avoided. Furthermore, the teacher can both model and explain the rationale for her translating activities. A more complete view of the world does not come from dichotomizing views into 'good' or 'bad,' 'right' or 'wrong,' but rather using them to build a more complex picture of the problem. This stance does not, and should not, minimize conflict or disagreement: it clarifies it and seeks to put it in a larger context. In addition, students can also be taught to listen to, and to translate, each other's languages and concerns. In this way, they may replace their own search for 'right answers' with a critical understanding and evaluation of their own and others' perspectives.

Second, courses can be structured so as to depend on, and draw from, student research as an integral part of the course work itself (rather than scheduling 'oral reports' at the end). Several students can read and comment on each other's papers before they are presented in class, so that the students can lead a discussion of the paper. Students can research topics that illuminate and build on course themes; such topics can become an integral part of the course syllabus (as in history via family trees, or psychology via biography and autobiography.) A related teacher responsibility may be to train students in the appropriate research and writing skills for successfully completing such assignments. Depending on the level of the students, teachers may hand out guidelines for research papers, for the use of the library and so on. Teachers can also encourage students to help each other on projects. Students may be put in cooperative groups for research as well as discussion purposes (see the work of David and Roger Johnson, 1975).

Related issues

Classes and courses can thus be deliberately structured to build on, and encourage, active student (and teacher) involvement in a collaborative learning enterprise. Other issues and considerations arise, however. There are differences *among* students, to which we assign relative value in the form of grades. Grading policies vary and are controversial.

An interactive pedagogy may imply that students grade themselves, or are involved in the process by which criteria for grades are set. However, teachers who wish to retain these powers of grading can be explicit about the criteria they themselves use. Written guidelines for conducting discussions, for research papers and for projects, as mentioned above, can function as checklists of evaluative criteria which are actually applied to student work. Many teachers also allow rewrites of papers after comments are discussed.

Finally, a word about large classes. This essay has assumed group sizes appropriate for dicussions. In classes of forty, eighty, or more, can we use interactive pedagogies? Outside of lectures, students can be divided into reading and discussion groups, or task forces for particular assignments and projects. The teacher can occasionally take class time to meet with these groups, and can schedule student-led presentations and discussions, as well. However, the structure of the university, in which large lecture courses are a dominant mode, is a paradigm for the traditional concept of knowledge as a fixed store of information and expertise to be pumped into passive student minds. The content of this knowledge has been masculine experiences, standards, and worldviews; its form is oppressive and exclusive. Even were the content of lectures in this mode to be replaced with a 'Women's Studies' content, it has been the thrust of this essay that such *forms* of both research and teaching must be changed to reflect the existence of multiple experiences of the world.

Conclusions

This essay has described some features of a classroom pedagogy to fulfill women's needs as students in relation to classroom treatment of the new scholarship on women. The elevation of female concerns into our consciousness and our curriculum has demonstrated the falsity and incompleteness of previous worldviews. It has imposed on us a search for multiple truths and perspectives, and showed us the integral connection between knower and known. Women's Studies has specifically challenged the teacher/expert-student/novice dichotomy by the inclusion of personal experience, private life, and popular history in our subject-matter — how can we simply 'tell' people about their own lives?

However, throughout this essay there has also been an attempt to link the lessons derived from the creation of a 'feminist' pedagogy to the consideration of pedagogy in general. The powers of creating and dispensing knowledge in our universities are at base only reflections of, and continuing guarantees of, powers in our social institutions at large. Both control over our social institutions and control over our education have been in the hands of white upper-class and middle-class males. Movements for equal voices in the universities, on the part of minorities and women, have always paralleled, supported, and been supported by, movements for social and legal equality in the wider society. Thus, there is a clear connection between the women's suffrage movement and the earliest female PhDs, the civil rights movement and Black Studies, the struggle for the Equal Rights Amendment and the new scholarship on women.

The pedagogical implications of this relationship are several. An interactive and democratic approach to knowledge and to pedagogy is appropriate for all oppressed groups seeking consciousness of their own past and future aims and identities. Men, too, can learn to think and learn 'like women.' Second, those forces against a realization of full equality in the wider society have their counterparts in the university. It is of course misleading to view the proponents of 'objective' science, 'great books' and traditional expertise simply as mouthpieces for the political status quo. However, the exclusivity of their hold on the definition of 'worth-while' knowledge must be actively challenged, rather than ignored.

The implications of a full implementation of the educational approaches outlined here are profound. First, we need to conduct research into both interactive and traditional classrooms, dealing with both Women's Studies and traditional subject-matters. What effect does the study of women's experiences in particular have on the cognitive development and personal confidence of female students? Do interactive pedagogies promote greater self-realization than the traditional lecture mode? How does the active involvement of the students with the subject-matter affect the meanings they give to their education? We need studies that further explore both the nature and the effects of the teaching practices outlined above. (For reviews of the current status of research in Women's Studies and teaching effectiveness see Boxer, 1982; and Porter and Eileenchild, 1980. Porter recommends 'an approach to research and evaluation that acknowledges the interaction between students, teacher and the subject matter and seeks to establish relationships between multiple variables that obtain in teaching and learning.') However, there are also implicit assumptions here about the value of interactive teaching and the inclusion of female and minority experiences as a framework for designing courses in all disciplines.

We want to educate women (and men) to a realization of the full worth and legitimacy of their own experience, as well as that of others. But can we really imagine a society that takes female voices as seriously as male voices, black voices as seriously as white ones, working-class voices as seriously as managerial ones? Inside the classroom we can dismantle, disperse and democratize the powers of knowledge and the means of acquiring it. However, we also need to examine explicitly the dimensions of the society our students will enter. A recent essay on Women's Studies and the academic disciplines pointed out that 'we especially gain from [the new work on women] many tools for understanding American life, so that we need not perpetuate the tenacious falsehood that in our culture any individual can do whatever he or she wants to do' (MacIntosh, 1982, p.31). We need to explore the wider political implications of our democratic pedagogy — what it shows us about both our society and the kind of society we desire. Otherwise it will indeed continue to be the case that 'Women's Studies' are peripheral, and not as important as those 'great books' which allegedly prepare us for life in the mainstream.

Notes

1   The relevance of Freire's work for women is ironic because Freire never mentions women. He uses 'people,' sometimes, but usually discussed men: 'It is not surprising that the banking concept of education regards men as adaptable, manageable beings' (Freire, 1970, p.60).

References

Boxer, Marilyn (1982), 'For and About Women, the Theory and Practice of Women's Studies in the United States,' *Signs: Journal of Women in Culture and Society*, vol. 7, no. 2, summer, pp.661-95.
Bunch, Charlotte (1979), 'Not By Degrees,' *Quest*, vol. 5, no. 1, summer, pp.7-18.
Chodorow, Nancy (1978), *The Reproduction of Mothering*, Berkeley: University of California Press.
Davis, Barbara Hillyer (1981), 'Teaching the Feminist Minority,' *Women's Studies Quarterly*, vol. 9, no. 4, winter, pp.7-9. Reprinted as ch. 22 in the present work.

Freire, Paulo (1970), *Pedagogy of the Oppressed*, New York: Continuum, 17th printing, 1981.

Gilligan, Carol (1982), *In A Different Voice, Psychological Theory and Women's Development*, Cambridge, Mass.: Harvard University Press.

Greene, Maxine (1975), 'Curriculum and Cultural Transformation,' *Cross Currents*, vol. 25, no. 2, summer, pp.175-86.

Grumet, Madeleine (1981), 'Pedagogy for Patriarchy: The Feminization of Teaching,' *Interchange on Educational Policy*, vol. 12, nos 2/3, pp.165.

Hale, Roberta, and Bernice Sandler (1982), *The Classroom Climate: A Chilly One For Women?* Project on the Status and Education of Women, Washington, DC: American Association of Colleges.

Johnson, David, and Roger Johnson (1975), *Learning Together and Alone*, Englewood Cliffs, New Jersey: Prentice-Hall.

Longino, Helen (1981), 'Scientific Objectivity and Feminist Theorizing,' *Liberal Education*, fall, pp.187-95.

MacKinnon, Catherine (1982), 'Feminism, Marxism, Method and the State: An Agenda for Theory,' *Signs: Journal of Women in Culture and Society*, vol. 7, no. 3, spring, pp.515-45.

MacIntosh, Peggy (1982), 'Warning, the New Scholarship on Women May Be Hazardous to Your Ego,' *Women's Studies Quarterly*, vol. 10, no. 1, spring, pp.29-31.

Maher, Frances, and Kathleen Lyman (1982), 'Definitions of Social Studies Concepts: A Precondition for Inquiry,' unpublished paper, December.

Mitrano, Barbara (1981), 'Feminism and Curriculum Theory, Implications for Teacher Education,' *Journal of Curriculum Theorizing*, vol. 3, no. 2, summer, pp.5-85.

Nelson, Randle (1981), 'Reading, Writing and Relationship: Toward Overcoming the Hidden Curriculum of Gender, Ethnicity and Socio-economic Class,' *Interchange on Educational Policy*, vol. 12, nos 2 and 3, pp.229-42.

Perun, Pamela (1982), *The Undergraduate Women, Issues in Educational Equity*, Chapter 1, 'The Undergraduate Women, Theme and Variations,' Lexington, Mass.: D. C. Heath, pp.3-14.

Porter, Nancy, and Margaret Eileenchild (1980), *The Effectiveness of Women's Studies Teaching*, Women's Studies Monograph Series, Washington, DC: National Institute of Education.

Rich, Adrienne (1979), *On Lies, Secrets and Silence*, New York: Norton.

Thorne, Barrie, and Nancy Henley (1975), *Language and Sex, Difference and Dominance*, Rowley, Mass.: Newbury House Publishers.

Westcott, Marcia (1979), 'Feminist Criticism of the Social Sciences,' *Harvard Educational Review*, vol. 49, no. 4, November, pp.422-30.

4

Women's Studies: a knowledge of one's own

Janice G. Raymond

The traditions of women's knowledge have not been passed on in the halls of academe but rather in the halls of obscurity — in oral tradition from mother to daughter; in women's writings whose authors created in isolation and who, as Virginia Woolf said, had neither '500 pounds nor a room of . . . [their] own'; and in extant journals recently exhumed as part of the present archeology of women's knowledge. In contrast to other erased, enslaved, and excluded traditions of knowledge, Women's Studies does not possess the past of a cohesive and self-conscious community. There is no history of a women's community which is comparable to, say, the Jewish community and which for Jewish Studies became its center of intellectual vitality. Indeed, one of the problems in doing Women's Studies is that women have been segregated from each other to the point of not even existing in the relatively unifying conditions of a diaspora.

To be more precise, there have been various women's communities (about which most women know very little) where women came together to teach and to learn — e.g. witch covens, convents, native American women's lodges, beguinages and women's support networks. Yet these have been so separated from each other in space and in time that it would be hard to speak historically of the women's community as one might speak of the Jewish community. As women have traditionally lacked self-definition, women have also lacked group identification.

It is not sufficient to remark that the university is a new locus for Women's Studies. One must realize that the university has been hostile to women and Women's Studies, so much so that what has evolved has been, for all theoretical and practical purposes, 'Men's Studies.' This interdisciplinary conglomerate of academic culture has consciously kept women not only out of the classroom,[2] but out of the curriculum as well. It has made the male the normative student and the normative subject of study.[3] 'Men's Studies' has spawned a definition of woman as Other, where women have been studied mainly as derivative and relational beings.[4] Feminists note the ludicrousness of sections in bookstores labeled as 'Men's Studies,' when the whole world of what has passed as systematic knowledge has been given over to the study of men.

Given the history of the university, women and women's knowledge have, at best, had an uneasy relationship to it. While women need its degrees, its resources, and what is worth while of its expertise, women also need much more. Women need the knowledge and the understanding of our own truth. By constituting itself as an autonomous discipline in the university, Women's Studies is founded on the premise that this truth can be found in the academic excavation of female literature, traditions, identity and values. Ultimately it states that the myriad manifestations of female existence are worthy of study in the most rigorous and organic way.[5]

Separation versus integration, or integrity versus assimilation

The university is a highly assimilatory institution, and one of the recurring dangers that Women's Studies faces in its quest for residence in the academy is immediate or gradual assimilation. Two positions have characterized the debate about the location of Women's Studies in the university — what have been called the 'integrationist' versus the 'separationist' or 'separatist' postures. This debate is not peculiar to Women's Studies, but the reality of separatism as applied to an autonomous and self-defined Women's Studies program impinges, in quite a different way, on the dominant male academic ethos — more so than, for example, a separate program of Irish Studies. For women to assert the need for an independent Women's Studies program raises, for men, the specter of the varieties of female separation from the personal to the political. Without necessarily intending it, the proponents of a separate Women's Studies program or department have raised the issue of female separatism — an issue that pervades any woman-centered reality from an all-female meeting to the philosophical position of abortion as a woman's right.

As the academic debate has been cast, separatists seek to organize the field in autonomous programs or departments of Women's Studies. They follow the conviction that Women's Studies is an entity in itself; that it should be studied as a unit rather than scattered throughout all the other traditional disciplines; that, as a whole, its content, while interdisciplinary, is greater than, and different from, the sum of its parts; that there is a relationship between the content of the knowledge about women and the concepts and methods employed in acquiring such; that a change in content effects a change in method; and the women's knowledge defined as Women's Studies can and should change the quality of students' lives.

So-called integrationists are represented as organizing women's knowledge primarily in established academic disciplines. Advocates of this position claim that only when Women's Studies permeates the 'mainstream' of the curriculum will the mainstream change and be more woman-centered. Separate Women's Studies programs or departments are discouraged as ghettos which will be impotent as centers of intellectual change and development. Furthermore, proponents of this position claim that separatism equals segregation. The integrationist's primary commitment is to traditional methodology and disciplinary departments, not so much to the content of what is studied, and much less to the spiritual quality of students' lives.[6]

There are two main issues to address here. One is the issue of placement: how and where should Women's Studies be located in the university? The other is the power of language to generate reality, and indeed even to generate what lies behind the arguments as they are worded and framed by the debate. Let me start with the question of placement.

If separate Women's Studies programs are opposed because it is feared that women's knowledge will be segregated out of the mainstream of the curriculum, and thus the curriculum will never change and be more woman-centered, what is one saying about the separateness of traditional academic disciplines and the power they have accrued by evolving separate academic territories? Did opponents seriously argue that political science, for example, would be segregated out of the mainstream of the curriculum when it was constituted as a separate discipline? Opponents may have argued against separate disciplinary status on other grounds and for other reasons. I would speculate, however, that such antagonists did not maintain that philosophers, sociologists, and economists would stop dealing with issues of political science if it became a separate discipline and department. Whatever one thinks about the fragmented state of disciplinary activity and the over-specialization and fetishizing of knowledge by departmental structures and boundaries, one would have to acknowledge that separateness, in traditional academic departments, has conferred power, not siphoned it away.

If impact on other fields is the genuine concern of the integrationists, then the logical argument to be made would be just the reverse. It is highly unlikely that traditional disciplinary content and methodology will change in a more woman-centered direction until Women's Studies is autonomous and self-defined enough to make a true impact on such disciplines. Religion departments would not be doing sociology of religion, for example, if there had not emerged a self-defined and autonomous discipline of sociology which determined its own content and methods.

What is it about separatism that is positively assessed when undertaken by the now traditional disciplines (as in the separation of sociology from psychology) yet negatively defined as escapist and ineffectual when sought by Women's Studies? To answer this, one must return to the deep philosophical nature of this debate and ask more about the charged reality of female separatism. I agree with Marilyn Frye:[7]

> Feminist separation is, of course, separation of various sorts or modes from men and from institutions, relationships, roles and activities which are male-defined, male-dominated and operating for the benefit of males and the maintenance of male privilege — this separation being initiated or maintained, at will, *by women*. (Masculist separatism is the partial segregation of women from men and male domains *at the will of men*. This difference is crucial.)

In my opinion, what lies behind the integrationist stance, on the part of men and many women, is the fear that men will no longer have access to women, or that they will have access only on a controlled and limited basis. 'Access is one of the faces of Power . . . The slave who excludes the master from her hut thereby declares herself *not a slave*.'[8] In the context of Women's Studies, what so-called separatists are saying is that traditional male content and methodology ('Men's Studies') will have access to the field only in so far as they are relevant to the body of knowledge now developing in Women's Studies. On a more immediate and existential level, men may fear lack of physical presence and access to women students. They know, on some level, that students, in rejecting the male mentor, will become the daughters of educated women, and the mentors themselves of other future female students.

Not only access, but definition, or naming, is another aspect of power. It is here that language generates reality. In the integrationist versus separationist debate, a fundamental reversal of language and definition has taken place on many levels, including the terms which name the debate itself. First, the opponents of separate and autonomous Women's Studies programs and departments may emphasize a fear of 'segregation' and the desirability of 'integration.' The spoken objection is that the separateness of a Women's Studies program will segregate it from other centers of power. Yet it is never acknowledged that segregation is always a state of existence that is imposed by a dominant group, institution, or ideology. As a corollary, integration is a state that a powerless group seeks out itself. However, in debate over the form and location of Women's Studies, it is the dominant group (men) and those (women) who identify with its values, that is pushing integration. Separation at our own summons is quite different than imposed separation at someone else's 'advice,' which would be tantamount to segregation. If what the integrationists want is to protect Women's Studies from segregation, they might give more thought to the *de facto* segregation that gave rise to the need for Women's Studies (in any form) to begin with. What I am suggesting, then, is that the integrationists' model of integration is, in effect, *assimilation*.

As Women's Studies courses are integrated into traditional departments and disciplines,[9] woman-centered values, content and methods are eliminated. The language of integration disguises the reality of assimilation. It reverses what is in truth happening: conformity to the dominant male ethos. An independent Women's Studies program, in so far as it is truly woman-centered in its content and method, asserts that women's traditions and knowledge will not be integrated out of existence. Within the context of the university, such a program may be forced out of existence for alleged political or financial reasons (e.g. a budgetary cut that targets the most vulnerable programs or departments in a financial period of 'no-growth'). Yet this is a far different situation from obliteration by traditional academic assimilation. The budget cut can be fought for what it is — quick and coercive extermination; it is much more difficult to attack, or even to recognize, slow and 'voluntary' euthanasia.

Finally, there is a reversal of meaning in the very words (separatism versus integration) which have framed the debate. Separatism is not the right word to describe the deepest levels of this controversy. What a separate and cohesive Women's Studies program seeks is its own *integrity*. As I have argued elsewhere, the word 'integrity' means an original unity.[10] In contrast, the word 'integration' connotes a putting together of parts, a mixing of one part with another, in order to complete that which is supposedly incomplete. If separatism ultimately means integrity, then what Women's Studies as an independent, autonomous discipline seeks is its own original unity — a unity of content and methodology, a unity of its own traditions and values, and the unity of asking its own questions which in themselves constitute a whole disciplinary endeavor. If separatism ultimately means integrity, a separate Women's Studies program asserts that the nature of women's knowledge is organic, systematic and *unto itself*. Women's Studies is the 'discipline' which searches out this original integrity of women's knowledge.

The religious dimension of Women's Studies

What is the nature of teaching and learning in Women's Studies? The integrationists would emphasize that commitment is primarily to traditional method and to traditional boundaries of disciplines. They would stress that Women's Studies courses and content be integrated into the established fields in order to illuminate some aspect of the sciences or humanities, for example.

Feminist teaching and learning, defined as Women's Studies in an autonomous framework, measures its integrity, in part, by its ability to communicate living feminist values in a socio-political context. Knowledge about women should help the student to locate herself within a tradition of which she is part and in which she presently exists. Commitment is encouraged to the content of what is studied, with a corresponding commitment to a change in method that is also deeply affected by content.

Many critics would see this latter emphasis as other than objective and as bordering on a political definition of Women's Studies. Yet I would venture to say that what is behind the fear of knowledge being 'politicized' is the perception of a lurking spiritual or even religious dimension. Women's Studies, in my view, does have a profound religious dimension, which goes beyond religion's identification with God, gods or religious organizations. It is religious in the sense that it raises questions of 'ultimate concern' or meaning for women's lives, aids and abets a conversion experience from female to feminist or strengthens the latter identity, and provides the words with which to articulate that standpoint.

I do not wish to quibble over the issue of calling these dimensions 'religious.' One might wish to argue that such matters are also the concern of psychology or anthropology, for example, as well as the concern of other fields. This, of course, is true, and I am not asserting that religion can be separated from many other aspects of learning and living. No definition of religion can state the necessary and sufficient conditions that neatly distinguish it from other areas.

For the purposes of this essay, and in attempting to explain further what I mean by the religious dimension of Women's Studies, I want to speak about religion in a most basic sense as it is derived from its accepted Latin root, *religāre*, meaning 'to tie' or 'to link.' As one author has commented:[11]

> Its role in human life is not to *add* something but to *unify* and to *direct* what is already there. The religious drive is . . . the contextual drive, as it were, manifested in all the others, the comprehensive drive through which they are related.

Women's Studies should help to tie women's lives together. It should make connections about female 'being-in-the-world' (*Dasein*), connections made perhaps for the first time. It should bring together those disparate and fragmented parts of female existence through systematic, comparative and historical reflection. Women's knowledge and understanding may not equal integrity, but they begin the journey to regain it.

In defining religion by reference to its etymology, it must be further noted that the Oxford English Dictionary states that the word is of doubtful derivation. By Cicero, it was linked with *relegĕre*, but by later authors, with *religāre*. Both Latin words, however, can be translated as 'to unify.' *Relegĕre* can mean 'to gather together,' 'to collect again,' and 'to read again.' A freer interpretation of this latter phrase might be to 'understand again' a knowledge that was once rightfully ours to begin with.[12] However, since over 60 per cent of the world's illiterates are women, and since women have been excluded from the world of texts in terms of both reading and writing, Women's Studies may well help women to read again.

Religāre, as stated previously, also means 'to tie,' 'to link,' 'to bind together,' and 'to unite.' As with many etymologies, however, it is not quite that simple. There are some problems. *Religāre* can also mean 'to bind up,' 'to tie back,' and therefore 'to constrain.' Historically, patriarchal religion has functioned to shrivel and to strangle women's creative power, to bind their very be-ing, and to tie them back by religious legitimations.

Since there are problems with the word 'religion,' there may be legitimate resistence to using it in describing the unifying function and 'ultimate concern' of Women's Studies. Again, I do not wish to quibble over words, but I am deeply aware that words do have power, and language does convey reality. Thus I do not consider this a semantic game, since people hear words in such different ways. On the one hand, many feminists will point out that not only is the word 'religion' a matter of doubtful and mixed etymology, but, more significantly, religion has been one of the ideological justifications for the historical oppression of women. What this criticism amounts to is the negation of any transcendent reality. In this perspective, transcendence is an illusion, or it is ultimately reducible to something else.

On the other hand, there are those feminists who would affirm a transcendent or spiritual sense of reality, but who would say that 'religion' or 'religious' are not appropriate words. They do not reject the transcendent force of women's knowledge. But they would suggest that other words — such as 'spiritual' or 'theological' — might more adequately convey such a force.[13]

To return to the further religious dimensions of Women's Studies, I will again invoke the image of the journey. For many women, feminist inquiry yields a network of meaning that transcends their past, their ordinary lives and their present. This knowledge begins a journey into another world which, as Mary Daly has described it, is 'about the journey of women becoming ... The radical be-ing of women is very much an Otherworld Journey. It is both discovery and creation of a world other than patriarchy.'[14] It is the perception of this knowledge as 'journey,' as 'more than,' and as 'Other' which imbues it with religious meaning. The transcendent possibilities of Women's Studies may be viewed as illusion or as 'really real' depending upon whether one transforms question into answer, absence into presence. For many women, what this knowledge communicates is promise and presence. Feminist be-ing goes beyond itself toward far-off be-ing. Many of us see women's knowledge as having revelatory power, and as an intimation of transcendence which, aside from grasping the mind passionately on an investigative level, transforms knowledge into culture, conversion and power.

Passionate teaching and learning versus objective scholarship

Professors who espouse the preceding view of Women's Studies are subject to accusations of 'preaching' and of using the classroom as a pulpit. I would contend that there is a vast difference between preaching and passion. The true aim of the teaching I have been describing is not to enforce feminist ideology but rather to *empassion* students with feminist knowledge. Inquiry is a profound passion, and the teaching of the male academy has most often left its female learners with a passionless knowledge, devoid of any deep commitment to its content.

Obviously, the boundary between preaching and passionate teaching is a thin one; one may argue that both are found on the same continuum. In this view, preaching is passion separated from its sources. However, I would add that objectivity is also passion divorced from its depth, and is a preaching of sorts. For professors are never really neutral nor do they ever merely teach. There are elements of advocacy conveyed by the questions and issues that are highlighted as primary or secondary, by those which are completely omitted from discussion, by voice intonation, and by the humor that is exhibited. Facts always bear meaning, and professors in many subtle ways impart this meaning.

In speaking about the place of Jewish Studies in a university setting, Jacob Neusner writes of teachers and students:[15]

Our students have rights, after all, and one of these is the right to be left alone, to grow and mature in their own distinctive ways. They have the right to seek their own way, as we find ours, without being pestered. We are not missionaries, but professors.

For Neusner, the missionary pushes, imposes, and coerces learning. 'There is a fine line to be found, an unmarked but dangerouly mined frontier, between great teaching and aggrandizing indoctrination . . .

The virtues of the professor are self-restraint and forbearance, tolerance and objectivity.'[16]

Again, to empassion is quite different from indoctrination, pro-selytizing, or academic fascism posing as feminist scholarship. Yet neither is it self-restraint, tolerance or objectivity. The conveying of passion means that in style, content, and method, the professor communicates that she cares deeply about what she is saying, that teaching and learning are living, and that scholarship is a standing-point on a journey that recognizes other different standpoints. Her own scholarship has a compelling cogency which should be contagious, not coercive. In one sense, the facts speak for themselves; yet in another sense, they do not. The speaker speaks them and thus also speaks *for* them. Those facts have a movement: their very articulation is their existence.

Thomas Aquinas pointed out that passion is essentially a move-ment which implies that 'the patient is drawn to that which belongs to the agent.'[17] Passionate scholarship has a drawing power which empassions students to care about their own learning so that the things they study become part of themselves. The scholar who tries to be dispassionate injures not only her own dignity but her own insights.

There is too much in the university which discourages passionate teaching and learning. It is virtuous for professors to remain outside emotional discussions, to manage them from the director's chair, to facilitate opposing points of view, to value neutrality and promote tolerance of all viewpoints, and to be committed to disciplinary boun-daries and methods. The virtues of a student are data gathering, proof-texting of all assertions, ability to take criticism well, and competence in one's chosen field. Rather than passion, the goal of a formal academic approach seems to be prediction and control. A good scholar has been encompassed by the definition of a good scientist.

I am not trying to drive a wedge between well-documented scholar-ship and passionate knowledge. They must come together. Both passion and scholarship are served by competence, criticism and consideration of other viewpoints.

It is true that we must not preach. But we must passionately teach. Scholars of Women's Studies are models of a particular sort of mind — a feminist response to the world of learning. We are deeply involved in the things we study. We cannot pretend we do not care. We look at our subject with passion because we are our subject. The basic attitude of the feminist scholar is existential.

It is true that we must not proselytize our students. But surely we have the responsibility to share with them that they have a proud tradition; but many women have gone before them who have asked compelling questions about the world, yet were never heard; that women have thought, have created, and have hoped; and that women have struggled under the most personally and socially stifling of conditions to become more than what they were. We may even teach our students that they are capable of thinking and doing the same.

The location of Women's Studies within the university is, in the final analysis, intrinsically allied with the quality of teaching and learning. An autonomous and independent Women's Studies program seeks its own integrity. This, too, is the aim of feminist teaching and learning in the academy — that teachers may teach and students may learn with a self-defined integrity.

The *kind* of teaching and learning that can occur within an autonomous Women's Studies program is perhaps the most important argument for maintaining Women's Studies as a distinct discipline. One may honorably wish to mainstream Women's Studies into the curriculum. However, what is often ignored is that mainstreaming also needs a base from which to proceed. Feminist teaching and learning is not a disembodied enterprise. The *communication* of feminist knowledge cannot be separated from its *context*. Where the context of teaching and learning has its own grounding, there too will the communication of knowledge be distinctly different from the mainstream.

Notes

1   Originally published in the *Union Seminary Quarterly Review*, fall/winter, 1979-80, pp.39-48. Reprinted with permission of the author.
2   From the founding of Harvard in 1636 to the opening of Oberlin in 1837, women were not admitted to a college or university education in the USA. Some colleges began to allow women entrance in the middle of the nineteenth century, and the major impetus for this was similar to pressures that are affecting the increased entrance of women into higher education today: economic. The second half of the nineteenth century was a time of dire economic need for many colleges due largely to shrinking male enrollments. Women were seen as sources of tuition that would permit colleges to continue operating. Moreover, as Burton Bledstein has written in *The Culture of Professionalism: The Middle Class and the Development of Higher Education in America* (New York: W. W. Norton & Co., 1978),

even after colleges and universities opened their doors to women, they did so with the aim in view of professionalizing the domestic, derivative and relational roles of women. The women's colleges (such as Vassar, Smith and Wellesley), especially, hastened to discuss and cultivate the so-called 'special aptitudes of women, as distinguished from those of men.'

3   Indexes of books are a rich source for revealing the non-normative position that women occupy in the 'larger' subject-matter of a particular book. For example, in *The Culture of Professionalism*, women receive three listings in a book of 354 pages: women 'in higher education,' 'magazines for,' and 'women as medical clients.' Bledstein's book would have been written quite differently if women had been an intrinsic subject of all of the chapter material. Course syllabi are another 'proof' of the non-normative position of women in the curriculum of the academy.

4   Simone de Beauvoir was the first to express this relational existence of women with a philosophical depth that, in my opinion, has been unsurpassed since the publication of her classic work, *The Second Sex* (London: Hart-Davis, 1971). She has written (p. xvi): 'Thus humanity is male and man defines woman not in herself but as relative to him; she is not regarded as an autonomous being . . . She is defined and differentiated with reference to man and not he with reference to her; she is the incidental, the inessential as opposed to the essential. He is the Subject, he is the Absolute — she is the Other.'

5   My essay is intentionally limited to the development of Women's Studies in the university. This is not to say that women's knowledge, and indeed Women's Studies, is not in process outside the university. As Adrienne Rich has written: 'even more is taking place outside it . . . it could be said that a women's university-without-walls exists already in America, in the shape of women reading and writing with a new purposefulness, and the growth of feminist bookstores, presses, bibliographic services, women's centers, medical clinics, libraries, art galleries, and workshops, all with a truly educational mission' ('Toward a Woman-Centered University,' in *Women and the Power to Change*, ed Florence Howe, New York: McGraw-Hill, 1975, p.16).

6   There is another position which hasn't been widely analyzed and which does not enter into the debate. Mary Daly has called this the 'maverick' position and when one researches the etymology of that word, one finds that it essentially means 'unbranded.'

The maverick contains elements of both the integrationist and separatist positions. Here the professor of women's knowledge teaches under the heading of a traditional discipline, yet makes all of her classes Women's Studies courses. They may appear in the course catalogue as philosophy, natural science, or sociology, but they are not confined by the boundaries of any of these fields. Thus the content and method of such courses *is* philosophy, for example, yet it is *not* philosophy as contained by the usual parameters of patriarchal thought.

The maverick or unbranded posture is, of course, risky business. Those who profess it may be confronted with the demand for conformity to both

their traditional disciplines and departments. The maverick hazards much
— her job, her professional reputation, her influence — and that is why this
position is not widely held and rarely lived out. Yet part of the definition
of maverick is the willingness to risk much or even all when conformity is
demanded.

On the negative side, the maverick may be subject to accusations of not
doing philosophy, for example, and of not performing her other disciplinary
duties. The professor asserts that she is doing philosophy, but her colleagues
may assert that she is not doing philosophy by any traditional methodological and content standards. No matter how demanding the creative process
is that she encourages in the service of really doing philosophy, no matter
how rigorous her standards and course requirements, she is labeled as doing
pop philosophy, fringe philosophy, or 'soft' philosophy at best. Thus she and
her work become marginalized.

On the positive side, both she and her students are doing 'philosophy in a
new key.' Functionally, they are separate while supposedly being integrated.
And, furthermore, the maverick escapes 'bureaucratization' on both sides —
that is, from the traditional department as well as from the emerging discipline of Women's Studies anxious to define itself and its methodological
turf. Also, because 'marginalization' brings with it a certain invisibility, the
professor is left alone and remains unbothered by the standards of traditional disciplinary activity. Her standards are self-sought and self-set. She has
the potential for a high level of creativity which in turn requires a high level
of individuality. Thus, the most significant advantage of the maverick
position is that it encourages creativity without being hampered by conformity to external departmental standards, whether these are generated by
the traditional fields or by Women's Studies itself.

The truly creative individual is not confined even by the standards of a
new field and realizes that Women's Studies can also develop paradigms
that stifle creativity. The maverick, in essence, is committed to the position
that women's knowledge should not be domesticated, even perhaps by
Women's Studies programs or departments; that such knowledge may be
tamed by focusing on the methods and boundaries of the field; that it may
be premature to define Women's Studies as a discipline since this may result
in making it into a field like any other field; and that it is a foreign land
which deserves exploration of the freest and most creative sort.

In the final analysis, the maverick is on the boundary of both the traditional disciplines and of Women's Studies. She sees women's knowledge as
not being circumscribed by programs or methods. She does not get self-
consciously obsessive about the boundaries of Women's Studies. Ultimately,
she is not concerned to develop *the* method or even *a* method of Women's
Studies.

7 Marilyn Frye, 'Some Reflections of Separatism and Power,' *Sinister Wisdom*,
   no. 6, summer 1978, p.31.
8 *Ibid.*, pp.35 and 37.
9 For that matter, why have 'separate' Women's Studies courses within traditional departments, since the logic of the integrationist position is to integrate Women's Studies content into traditional *courses* themselves?

10 See my book, *The Transsexual Empire: The Making of the She-Male*, Boston: Beacon Press, 1979, especially chapter 6, 'Toward the Development of an Ethic of Integrity.'

11 Michael Novak, *Ascent of the Mountain, Flight of the Dove*, New York: Harper & Row, 1971, p.5.

12 See again Raymond, *The Transsexual Empire*, chapter 6. Referring to dictionary definitions of integration and integrity, I write (p.163): 'Integration gives a certain validity to the parts themselves and to the process of putting those parts together. In contrast, integrity reverses this connotation and validates an original unity from which no part may be taken. Integrity gives us a warrant for laying claim to a wholeness that is rightfully ours to *begin with*.'

13 Both of these words are useful and point up other dimensions of women's knowledge as transcendent. Many feminists use the words 'spiritual' or 'spirtuality.' These are far more commonly used than 'religious' or 'religion.' Some would explain this preference by referring to the etymology of the word 'spirit,' literally signifying 'breath' but also meaning 'power' or 'energy.' Spirit is that which is the animating principle of life, indeed that which gives life to the physical organism. Others would say that to talk about the spiritual dimensions of Women's Studies is to put emphasis on the faculties of perception and reflection, signifying an integrity of intellect and mental powers, an active disposition and a vigor of mind.

I have not chosen to use the word 'spiritual' because I feel that the strength of its etymology and meaning, as described above, has been obscured by its more popular associations with spiritualism, supernaturalism and the occult. In response to this objection, many feminists would say that women's religious traditions have been branded as spiritualistic or occult by the dominating and male-centered religions as a way of reducing them to marginal or outlaw status. For example, Margaret Murray, a scholar of the witch movement in Western Europe, has remarked that divination, when done in the name of a deity of one of the established religions, is exalted as 'prophecy.' When done in the name of a so-called pagan divinity, it is termed 'witchcraft.' Thus women should reclaim our spiritual heritage by dignifying the word itself, and its roots in female-centred traditions, by breaking out of the old semantic context into a new meaning context.

Other feminists would argue that the word 'theological' is more appropriate, particularly if one is trying to speak about the transcendent dimensions of 'knowledge.' For theology has traditionally been defined as the science of the highest things and their nature and attributes. Thomas Aquinas identified theology as wisdom involving contemplative intuition and reasoning. Theology looked at things from the highest knowledge, reasoning from first principles to wisdom. Furthermore, the theologists looks at any subject that forms the content of theology with passion. She is not detached from her subject but is involved in it. The basic attitude of the theologian is commitment to the content she learns and teaches. It is in this sense that I will write, on pages 57-9, about passionate teaching and learning in the context of Women's Studies.

14 Mary Daly, *Gyn/Ecology: The Metaethics of Radical Feminism*, Boston:

Beacon Press, 1978, p.1.

15 Jacob Neusner, 'The New Setting for Jewish Learning: Towards a Theory of University Studies in Judaism,' The Bernstein Conference on Jewish Studies, University of Rochester, 22-24 February 1976, p.9.

16 *Ibid.*

17 Thomas Aquinas, *Summa Theologiae*, 1-11, 22, 2 c

5

The educational process of Women's Studies in Argentina: reflections on theory and technique

Gloria Bonder

The purpose of this paper is to contribute to the development of theory and practice on the process of women's consciousness-raising in the field of Women's Studies. I will begin describing the specific context and purposes according to which we have carried out educational-formation programs in Women's Studies, particularly those at the Women's Studies Center (CEM) in Buenos Aires. Then I will analyze the consciousness-raising effects of education-formation in Women's Studies. I will also outline some charactericstics of the process of consciousness-raising in Women's Studies such as: a developmental pattern; facilitating and inhibiting elements for consciousness-raising; and epistemological outstanding obstacles. Finally, I will make some technical suggestions about the coordination of education-formation groups in Women's Studies.

Women's Studies in Argentina is a very recent field of research and education. Its theoretical, historical, political and institutional idiosyncrasies differentiate it from the programs and objectives that characterize the development of the field in other countries.

Women's issues emerged as a theoretic-political research field for some academic groups in Argentina at the end of the 1970s. The first multidisciplinary seminar — Women's Place in Today's Society, which was organized in 1979 by the founding group of the Women's Studies Center in Buenos Aires represents the first milestone for the development of Women's Studies in Argentina. In order to understand the origins and further development of both the theory and practice of Women's Studies in Argentina, it is necessary to outline particular

socio-political, institutional and scientific conditions which characterize the country's recent history.

In 1979, Argentina was under a regime of military dictatorship
whose political, economic and ideological policies established one of
the most ill-fated periods in the country's history. It was an era of:
state terrorism, destruction of the national industries, closing of educational and welfare institutions, repression of dissident individuals
and groups, reduction of budgets for educational and social services,
severe censorship of the media, and so on.

The social movements which ordinarily produce the necessary
ferment to question the theory and practice in social science and
humanities were silenced or disappeared under the military regime.
The absence of an organized feminist movement can't be attributed
to this political period, although feminist groups suffered repression
in the same way as other social movements. Small feminist groups have
existed in Argentina since 1960, but they hadn't organized in a feminist
movement with strong political and ideological development before
the dictatorship. This situation may explain why Women's Studies
in Argentina has not developed in line with the political and ideological activity of the feminist movement in other countries (even
though Women's Studies in Argentina may indeed lead women to
a feminist practice at different levels and in different fields).

The academic research groups in Argentina, particularly in the area
of social and human sciences, are characterized by a high level of
scientific rigor, goals of theoretic and technical 'excellence.' All are
consequences of that cultural dependency which originated in Argentina's European cultural colonization (dating back to the very beginning of the country's educational history). Similarly, the reality and
illusion of social promotion by means of education gained acceptance
among the immigrants who began to populate the country in the last
century, and have determined a sort of 'educational perfectionism'
which characterizes Argentine professionals. This situation encourages
a very high valorization of scientific knowledge and scientific institutions.

Within this context, psychology merits separate consideration.
Psychology emerged as an autonomous discipline in the university
at the end of the 1950s and has remained the favorite choice of women
in the social and human sciences since then. I would like to stress the
importance of this fact as it relates to the particular nature and development of Women's Studies in Argentina: women psychologists and

women students of psychology are an impressive majority among the women who, as students, professors and researchers, are involved in Argentine Women's Studies. Within the field of psychology, it is also important to emphasize the weight of psychoanalytic theory and its contribution to Women's Studies.

Finally, because of the socio-political conditions described above and the destruction of educational centers at the university level, Women's Studies has developed in private institutions such as the CEM — a non-profit group which develops postgraduate Women's Studies programs. These programs obviously suffered from lack of economic resources and documentation. Consequently, we have had to postpone some important research projects, including those which contain a wide range of fieldwork. At the same time, however, our development was nurtured by the group's solidarity, born of a need for survival and resistance to the highly oppressive socio-political context.

At the crossroads of all these determinants, Women's Studies was founded. Its initial objectives were centered fundamentally on: legitimizing the study of women's subjects within social and human sciences; reconsidering existing practices and theories on women.

Education and consciousness-raising

The conditions described above determined that the CEM's first courses and seminars in Women's Studies had relatively traditional pedagogic characteristics. Thus, our first seminars (such as Psychology of Women, Women and Work and Women's Life Crises) were organized like any other contemporary postgraduate courses within a private social and human sciences institution for postgraduates. The only substantive differences were: the subjects that were considered; the bibliography recommended (mostly papers on feminist theory produced in the USA, England and France); the composition of the groups (exclusively women and coordinated by a woman professor, with few exceptions); the objective of critical reflection on the existing knowledge on women; confrontation between theoretic concepts and observations arising from our practices with women.

The formative and consciousness-raising processes produced within these groups — processes not determined at the beginning by an explicit goal of consciousness-raising — led us to evaluate some structural aspects concerning the formative education in Women's Studies.

I will begin with a distinction between the process of teaching-learning and the process of education-formation, particularly in regard to the subject's cognitive relationship to established knowledge. According to Anzieu[2] teaching-learning involves secondary psychic processes (psychomotor activities, diverse thinking processes). It requires the knowledge and manipulation of rules, training in certain disciplines of the mind and the body, and submission to the forms and rhythms of the taught knowledge. Education-formation for Anzieu concerns the subject at the level of its being within knowledge which is also that of its subjective meaning of knowledge. This distinction sets forth the operation of different cognitive processes.

Teaching-learning means conscious and pre-conscious logical-consensual processes which involve the adaptation of the students to the established cognitive contents and models. In the process of education-formation, subjectivity appeals to and is appealed by consensual knowledge on cognitive and emotional levels. Education-formation, then, is not a process of adaptation but rather an open dialogue between the subject and knowledge, a dialogue that involves distinct subjective levels of registration of consensual knowledge (conscious and pre-conscious registrations, structures of ideals and norms, imaginative and mythic productions, etc.).

In teaching-learning, knowledge presupposes an effect of censorship of the subjective characteristics, be these emotional or cognitive, in terms of the acceptance of the rules, while in education-formation, emotional and cognitive characteristics can be expressed and confronted with the particular characteristics of other subjects.

In teaching-learning, established knowledge is considered the model and therefore the guarantor of truth and giver of a code, in education-formation, the criterion of truth interlaces itself with the criterion of subjective and intersubjective sense and meaning. The personal and groupal code emerges as a result of this process.

Now then, in the formative seminars in Women's Studies, the question of 'being within knowledge' has a crucial importance for women. When one deals with knowledge and acknowledgment of women within the context of patriarchal knowledge (as is the case in Women's Studies) the problematic of being acquires a critical character, since this formation unavoidably leads women to the recognition of their silencing and objectification within knowledge and therefore their non-existence as subjects of that knowledge. Women in the process of education-formation will discover that in patriarchal scientific discourse they do not merely have a dehierarchized status, but fundamentally the position of 'the absent' and/or of the mirror-object of the 'old dream of masculine symmetry' as Luce Irigaray formulates it.[3] 'Women must painfully recognize that patriarchal knowledge operates as the master's discourse, where women are in the "position of a mute support.".[4]

The question of 'being within knowledge,' therefore, is crucial for women in formation because they cannot avoid having to recognize their position as object-slave of a scientific discourse which, while objectifying them, defines them as an object for another, the masculine subject, which finds through them its splendor as a transcendent subject. Women's consciousness — and, hence, what may be regarded as the nucleus of the self — reencounters in patriarchal knowledge its condition as a 'consciousness for another.' The association of women with Nature, which expresses itself in the omission of women from the socio-cultural environment, along with the restrictions placed on their bodies, their sexuality, and their ethics, is the basis of this objectification.

The objectification of women in knowledge is the alienation of women within scientific discourse since they have not established the objectifications in knowledge.[5] Therefore, a consciousness-raising process could not be avoided in our Women's Studies seminars, even though consciousness-raising was not foreseen as an explicit purpose in these seminars.

Joan Cassell[6] defines consciousness-raising as 'a subjective process which means becoming conscious of something one did not formerly perceive, raising something from the unconscious to the conscious mind, or to heighten consciousness of oneself or of a state of affairs.' On our side, we consider consciousness-raising in Women's Studies education-formation as a process which involves transformations in: cognitive and instinctual levels, in identifications, symbol-making and in social praxis. This process starts from, and finds its strength in, the representation 'women's group.' We agree with Joan Cassell that, even in education-formation groups in Women's Studies, the heart of the process of consciousness-raising — where women are called to learn, to ponder and to discover about women together — involves: the perception of women as a degraded group; self-identification with this group; the commitment to social and/or personal change, to the improvement of the position of women. These steps in consciousness-raising involve transformations on all levels of the subjectivity of women being educated in Women's Studies. There are, therefore, many cognitive and emotional obstacles to be overcome.

The process is complex and painful. It can be compared to a process of decolonization. These women discover they have been colonized by patriarchal knowledge and they think they have to make a cognitive and affective effort to recover codes of 'primordial women's knowledge.' The search for these codes is the basis of some of the utopias and myths women develop in those seminars. Education-formation in Women's Studies can also be compared with the process of alphabetization described by Paulo Freire[7] for marginal and oppressed groups. Women being educated pass through a process of appropriation, deconstruction and reconstruction of the language of science, in their search for an order of signification that might articulate different dimensions of their condition (traditionally dissociated by theoretical language — reason vs. intuition, knowledge vs. action, subjectivity vs. objectivity, etc.).

Education-formation in Women's Studies is a kind of scientific resocialization for women. As this process takes place in the groups of women involved in Women's Studies, our fundamental and theoretic challenge is to elucidate different stages of the process, its transformation, the facilitating elements and the obstacles of the process, so that we may construct progressive pedagogic strategies. In other words, in following Friere, we must be aware of the real or effective consciousness (Goldman) of women as an oppressed group faced with patriarchal knowledge, and the obstacles and distortions that social, cultural, institutional and subjective reality imposes on the establishment of the maximum consciousness possible. The process of education-formation enables women to confront how they had previously related to patriarchal knowledge, their 'solutions' and/or transactions with it, how they can begin to relate to scientific knowledge whilst including their own perspective, and to what extent it is valid for women to use existent knowledge.

I have observed three key stages of the education-formation process in Women's Studies groups which I have coordinated since 1977. I will call the first stage the 'encyclopedic stage,' the second the 'transitional phase,' and the third the 'dilemmatic phase.' These stages were always present in the groups I have coordinated. Each stage reflects the dynamics in the consciousness-raising process.

Encyclopedic phase

The women who began to be interested in Women's Studies in my country were consciously moved by intellectual curiosity and a certain uneasiness about their own experience as professional women in their everyday life and professional practice. When they began attending Women's Studies seminars, they believed themselves, and admitted to being 'uninformed, confused, ignorant in women's issues.' They expected to find guaranteed answers in established knowledge to satisfy their intellectual curiosity and to calm their uneasiness. They doubted or denied their own observations and experiences about themselves and other women, since these observations or experiences seemed to be 'unscientific.' They wanted to find *answers within science* for their uneasiness — either to calm it down or, sometimes, to legitimize it. To know everything, and to know more, became the group's overwhelming objective in this stage. The answers that theories provide on women's issues were timidly questioned. When women perceived mistakes or distortions in science, or its commitment to a patriarchal politics of knowledge, they tended to deny this evidence: they needed to save science as a valid point of reference and they feared losing their scientific tools. Truth must be in science. This is one of the most powerful obstacles in Women's Studies education-formation in this first stage.

The following descriptions characterize this stage of 'encyclopedism'. First, acceptance of science as the ultimate answer and privileged tool for reality's understanding, especially women's. Second, professional women believe scientific knowledge gives them a place as social subjects. A great intellectual voracity develops. Everything must be studied in order 'to know, and to exist' in scientific knowledge. Third, women develop a profound desire to be recognized by 'science' as an active part of its production. 'Being in knowledge' acquires the form of: 'To belong to knowledge is to therefore exist.' This creates a fanatic or bitter *deification* of established knowledge which motivates cognitive interchange in this first stage. A profound disillusion ends this stage. Women's oppression is recognized exactly where salvation was sought: in science. Scientific knowledge starts to be criticized while the valid point of reference is translated — the women's group dealing with Women's Studies.

Transitional phase

A formidable cognitive and emotional groupal process takes place in this stage. It deals with a kind of *regression and transgression* towards established knowledge in each woman. In this stage, 'being in knowledge' is expressed through a cognitive and emotional experience which follows the forms of what Donald Winnicott[8] has called 'transitional experience.' This term was employed by Winnicott to explain a stage in the development of the human infant where symbolization begins as a consequence of the process of discrimination between him/herself, and the mother. The transitional phase is characterized by shaping *a space between the subject and the object*. This space is found, created, invented. It corresponds to neither the subject nor the object. It is a potential space between the subject and his/her environment. The importance of this concept lies not only in the understanding of the earliest evolution of human symbol-making, but also in enabling us to understand the modes of cognitive process which are found at the base of cultural, artistic, mythic and religious creation.

By means of this framework, we are also able to understand social pathologies such as social over-adaptation and, in general, the alienation of subjects to dominant values and structures when the transitional space did not exist — either in personal or social relations. In this second stage, the women's group — as a symbol of 'being in knowledge' — enables the expression of transitional phenomena. For example, cognitive rules, such as discrimination between object and subject, rationality vs. emotion, intuition vs. conceptualization, passion vs. reason, singular vs. general, past vs. present, which were previously 'respected' in the encyclopedic phase, are reformulated now. Women's symbolic interchange in this phase is apparently chaotic, although in reality it is women's awakening to a cognitive revolution: education-formation in the women's group becomes for women the place for women's constitution as subjects.

Women's symbolic interchange seems to regress to an archaic stage. Women's discourses in this phase can be understood as an *associative flowing*: thought, emotion, humor, personal experiences, visions, memories, etc., all have an important and legitimate place without establishing conceptual limits. With words such as 'oppression,' 'discrimination,' 'love,' 'hate,' 'justice,' 'injustice,' 'freedom,' 'fear,' women express their rage and their joy as they start to understand women's social subordination, in general, and women's subordination to scientific knowledge, in particular. These words, as transitional objects, 'are bitten,' 'are spat,' 'are caressed,' 'are tasted.'

Joy comes with the discovery of an embodied word, with the possibility of voicing what they have had to repress, with the pleasure of talking among women within a context of scientific education. Women's Studies seminars become 'a place of initiation, a ritual party, an interlude which is provisional but prefigurative of a new society, a mark or emblem with which to identify oneself and differentiate oneself from those who have not experienced it.'[9]

All this leads to an explosive symbolic rupture that alters women's position of 'mute guarantor' of the masters' scientific discourse. Women become conscious of their previous mechanical reproduction of a code articulated by others — men who produced scientific discourse on women. There is a flowing relation between words and impulses. The semiotic function of language prevails, such as Kristeva defines it,[10] 'the pre-symbolic and trans-symbolic relationship between infant and mother.' This semiotic interchange is the basis of the dimension of meaning in knowledge in this stage. A groupal illusion is created: the existence of a primordial feminine knowledge once lost and now recovered. This illusion leads to the formulation of a utopia. Women are going to build scientific knowledge from women's perspective. They want to affirm their views through science, so as to become subjects in science. This intellectual ambition usually finds a powerful obstacle: essentialist and naturalist definitions of the feminine. That is, the revindication of women's perspective in knowledge may be reabsorbed by the traditional attributes of the feminine: irrationality, intuition, sensitivity, subjectivity, etc. The myth of a 'feminine nature' is always ready to spread its seduction during this phase. At this point, it becomes absolutely necessary to analyze women's subjective needs to support this myth: this analysis cannot be avoided in Women's Studies education-formation if our purpose is to develop women's consciousness as much as possible. At the end of this second phase, women usually arrive at a common conviction: the need of creating new paradigms in the knowledge of reality, and including women as subjects. They also come to a fundamental question; what principles of reality can their objective be based on?

This vital problematic can be understood through Rossana Rossanda's words,[11] when referring to women's search for a different principle or identity. She described this problematic as the recurrent oscillation between two temptations: that of identifying the self in the separate sphere which has been imposed on women but which has become their life experience over thousands of years, be it called the area of sensitivity, of body experience, of the emotions, of non-violence, of sweetness, of an idealization of woman's sexuality, of motherhood . . . or if not, rejecting this identification . . . because it is born in some way as a projection of the identity of 'The Other,' of women as 'a complementary fantasy of masculine sexuality.'

This dilemma expresses itself in the process of consciousness-raising in education-formation, when trying to put women's perspective in science.

The question that arises is: how do women want to change science? Incorporating values, meanings and forms of knowledge that have been their experience for centuries? Or rejecting any 'feminine' value, meaning, or form of knowledge because it is the product of women's subordination?

Rossana Rossanda compares the problematic of women's consciousness-raising as a group with the formation of class consciousness for exploited people. She asks: 'How can a class (or in our case, a gender group), defined by its alienation or its dispossession, its reification, its reduction to a commodity, become an active subject of a revolution, an active principle of a society based upon different values?' In other words: how can women propose a new principle of reality?

Dilemmatic Phase

In this third stage of education-formation, all these questions bring forth a conflictual practice.[12] On one hand, theorizing within the framework of the logical and methodological categories of science is for women in formation a kind of 'draingage of feminine materiality' from their own words. It supposes an effect of censorship of the transitional processes of the previous phase. Only literature and/or testimonial language seems to fulfill the symbolic requirements for articulating this explosion of feminine subjectivity in knowledge. On the other hand, the choice of this language leaves women in formation with a bitter feeling of defeat in the face of the power of the established knowledge. Women also want to continue expressing themselves in scientific language, using, for the comprehension of women's issues, methodologies, concepts and logical processes previously established. This gives place to a kind of bilingualism or multi-lingualism in women's interchange within the group and in their future projects referring to women's issues.

When dealing with certain subjects such as women's sexuality, women's language, power, women's subjectivity, women's relation with time and space, etc., the 'choice' of one form of language and knowledge or the other, becomes critical and gives place to a dilemmatic situation. This moment cannot be avoided in this stage of the process of education-formation in Women's Studies. Some women decide to develop different projects — such as literature or arts (as a private project) and scientific research (institutional projects). However, most women attending Women's Studies seminars do not feel satisfied with the results of their personal choices. The link between women and theoretic knowledge is a problematic one.

We agree here with what R. Darcy de Oliveira set forth: 'The analysis of the relationship of women to theoretic knowledge must become in itself one of the objectives of women's education-formation.' How can we bring this analysis to the *experience* of education-formation in Women's Studies if our purpose is not only teaching theoretic contents on women's issues, but also enabling women fully to develop their 'being in knowledge'?

At this point, let me suggest the use of a groupal technique which has been developed by Enrique Pichon Riviera[13] in Argentina. It is called 'technique of operative groups,' and has been used in this country since the 1960s, primarily in the field of education and institutional psychology. Pichon Riviere developed this technique from his experience in the coordination of groups and his research referring to group dynamics. The technique is similar to those used by Kurt Lewin in social laboratories and in the application of group psychology to the educational field.

I will briefly point out some fundamental principles of this technique, important for the coordinator in the educational group. The coordinator, as a co-thinker in the group, has to:

1 evaluate the participants' previous intellectual and experiential knowledge;
2 stimulate the circulation of knowledge among the participants;
3 question whatever seems to be 'obvious,' that is, what is shown

to be 'natural' and self-evident;

4   promote the constant dialectic of knowledge, experience and action;
5   help the group to support the collective truth over the individual one;
6   analyze with the group the subjective, social, cultural, and political obstacles in the education-formation process in Women's Studies;
7   encourage the group to understand the dilemmas and blind points of the cognitive group praxis.

In sum, the point is to consider education as a 'group maieutic.' This process develops as a conceptual, referential and operative spiral for Women's Studies' instrumental appropriation of knowledge, transformed in and by the subjective and intersubjective groupal processes. How can we develop this groupal pattern?

I will point out some elements of a pedagogic strategy which I have personally found useful for coordinators. It is important to consider that groupal interchange develops at different levels.

1   *The manifest guide-task*.[14] The learning or investigation of the programmed issues.
2   *The latent guide-task*.[15] The subjective and intersubjective, cognitive and emotional processes of an oppressed group facing the established knowledge about women and the social reality.
3   *The group dynamic*.[16] This is constituted by three elements.
     (a)   Information, formal and informal commentaries, readings, summaries, etc., expressed by the group and the coordinator. This is called 'group existing elements.'
     (b)   Interpretative interventions of the coordinator. This helps the group understand the dilemmas, obstacles, blind points, prejudices, anxieties or fears of a group facing knowledge.
     (c)   A new group dynamics that emerges from stages (a) and (b).

The pedagogic process must take into account the following steps:

1   pre-work: groupal exchange of previous knowledge about the subject in question;
2   new knowledge;
3   analysis of manifest and latent *dilemmas* that emerge with the

confrontation of previous and new knowledge;

4 evaluation of the resulting protosynthesis, called 'problematics';
5 analysis of the resulting problematics;
6 formulaion of personal and groupal research projects in relation with the newly discovered problematics.

These steps have to continue following this spiral pattern if our purpose is to stimulate women towards a process of continuous formation in scientific knowledge.

We do not consider these techniques as 'solutions,' but as technical and ideological contributions to a pedagogical process in Women's Studies. We believe Women's Studies must become a space where women can test, confront, and evaluate all forms of knowledge relating to women's issues and social reality as a whole. The question of women and scientific knowledge remains central — and unresolved. Will women's perspective in science build a new science? A different science? A feminine science?

Notes

1 This essay was originally written as a talk to be presented at the National Women's Studies Association Convention, June 1983.
2 Didier Anzieu, *El Grupo y el Inconsciente*, Biblioteca Nueva: Madrid, 1978.
3 Luce Irigaray, *Speculum de l'autre femme*, Les Editions de Minuit: Paris, 1974.
4 Julia Kristeva, 'Women's Time,' *Signs: A Journal of Women in Culture and Society*, vol. 7, no. 1, autumn 1981, pp.13-35.
5 Catherine MacKinnnon, 'Feminism, Marxism, Method, and the State: an Agenda for Theory,' *Signs: A Journal of Women in Culture and Society*, vol. 7, no. 3, pp.515-44.
6 Joan Cassell, *A Group Called Women: Sisterhood and Symbolism in the Feminist Movement*, New York: David McKay, 1977.
7 Paulo Freire, *Pedagogia del Oprimido*, Siglo XXI Editores: Argentina, 1971.
8 D. W. Winnicott, *Realidad y Juego*, Granica Editores: Argentina, 1982.
9 Rene Kaes, 'Los Seminarios "Analiticos" de Formacion: Una Situacion Social Limite de la Institucion,' in *El Trabajo Psicoanalitico en los Grupos*, Siglo XXI Editores: Argentina, 1978.
10 Julia Kristeva, 'El Tema en Question: El Lenguaje Poetica,' in *La Identidad*, Ediciones Petre: Madrid, 1981.
11 Rossana Rossanda, *Las Otras*, Editorial Gedisa: Barcelona, 1982.
12 R. Darcy de Oliveira, 'Le Rapport des femmes au savoir théorique: une

interrogation pédagogique,' Ginebra, July 1982. Presented at the Conference on the Research and Teaching about Women, organized by the Simone de Beauvoir Institute, Concordia University, Montreal, Canada.

13   Enrique Pichon Riviere, *Aportaciones a la Didactica de la Psicologia Social*, *El Proceso Grupal*, *Grupos Operativos y Enfermedad Unica*, Editores Nueva Vision: Buenos Aires, 1975.
14   E. C. Llendo, 'El Trabajo con Grupos Operativos,' Universidad de Buenos Aires, Facultad de Filosofia y Letras.
15   *Ibid*.
16   Pichon Riviere, *op. cit*.

PART TWO

Transforming the disciplines

6

Feminist pedagogy as a subversive activity

Robert J. Bezucha

Feminists on college campuses today face a dilemma. Given the remarkable growth of Women's Studies departments and programs, as well as the explosion in the number of courses for and/or about women, a good argument can be made on institutional grounds for consolidating what has been gained. Budgets, hiring and promotion clearly must become the order of the day, just as in, say, the Spanish department or the American Studies program. It is an unpleasant truth, however, that in spite of the recent successes, feminism has found the going rougher in the academy than most feminists once optimistically predicted. At many schools, moreover, there has been little or no progress at all. Why is this so? And what can be done about it? Theoretical and tactical reassessment is also going to be necessary.

Resistance to feminism comes, in large part, from the fact that it seeks to undermine one of the most powerful and deeply held sets of distinctions drawn in Western thought and society: the separation of the public, the impersonal, and the objective, on the one hand, from the private, the personal, and the subjective, on the other. Most of us who teach have literally been taught to think and act that way. As a result, it is commonly accepted among our colleagues that the cultural patterns associated with appropriate behavior in public – the prescribed objectivity and impersonal affect of a teacher in a college classroom, for example – are somehow 'male,' even when the instructor is a woman. Conversely, subjectivity and self-expression are deemed inappropriate outside the circle of home, family and friends, because the private sphere is strongly associated with 'female' activity. Teachers of such notoriously 'soft' subjects as art, music and literature are permitted some measure of exception, but by and large we are all expected to live by this pedagogic code. Our unwritten work-rules as teachers are part of a larger social text.

Feminist pedagogy is a subversive activity because it challenges these established notions of teaching and learning from within the academy itself. It also poses a new question about theory and practice for feminists themselves. The volume of scholarly production, the quality and frequency of meetings and conferences, and the broad network represented by the National Women's Studies Association and other organizations make it certain that many persons will continue to ask *what* we should teach our students. The time has come, therefore, to begin to ask *how* we should teach them, as well. My recent experience indicates that the two questions can no longer be separated, at least not by me. The purpose of this essay, however, is not to add to the growing body of male confessional literature: rather, it is to describe and reflect on a specific teaching experiment. If we think of feminist pedagogy as a 'project under construction,' what follows is a report from one of the apprentice carpenters.

Historians such as myself are often accused of having an obsession with details, but in the case of my encounter with the 'what' and 'how' of feminist pedagogy, a sense of chronology and setting is probably necessary for understanding where I feel I succeeded and where I know I have more to learn about a new subject and a different way of teaching. These particularities may also help the reader to make better sense of my reasons for believing that women's history should be taught as an integral part of the past.

Amherst College, an elite liberal arts college in Massachusetts, had been a bastion of male education from its foundation in 1821, until the admission of women as transfer students in 1975, and as freshmen in 1976. When I joined the history department in the fall of 1977, the trauma brought about by what my colleagues referred to as 'the co-education debate' was highly apparent to anyone who chose to see it. Many alumni were angry with the president and faculty for 'ruining' their college. Justly proud that the faculty had mobilized and convinced the board of trustees to reverse its initial negative decision about co-education, the majority of male professors readily accepted the external consequences: an increase in the size of the student body, co-ed dormitories and, eventually, fraternities, physical education classes and team sports for women, the employment of women administrators in the office of admissions and the dean of students' office. They even agreed in principle to the necessity for more women faculty members. Good liberals know how to change with the times, particularly when Harvard, Yale and Princeton have done so already. Many of these same men became stubborn, anxious, or defensive, however, at any suggestion that they reconsider either the content of their courses or the way they conducted their classrooms. 'After all,' they reasoned, 'we've been teaching students from Smith and Mount Holyoke [two nearby women's colleges] for years. Why should we do anything different now?' By this measure, few of them contested the official received wisdom that co-education was an instant 'success.' From their point of view, it was.

When I arrived at Amherst, women professors (approximately twenty out of 150, two of them tenured) were swamped by committee assignments and student demands. I had seen this phenomenon elsewhere and understood it as simply a result of numbers. More troubling was the fact that many women colleagues openly complained that they felt embattled and unwelcome. While I had no reason to doubt them, the stories they told me about the place were so foreign to what I was encountering as a male professor with tenure that it sometimes seemed as though we were talking about two different institutions. When some of these women resigned without bothering to stand for a tenure review, their male colleagues by and large refused to acknowledge the meaning of their gesture: initially, each was considered to be a 'special case,' and I recently heard it said that they were a 'weak' group. For the most part, Amherst's new women students quickly learned that the way to get by was to keep your mouth shut and to try to embrace the male ethos of the place. Once the pioneer generation of transfer students had graduated, it seemed that most women students were quiet about campus conditions because they felt they were getting just the sort of education they had come there for: they were learning how to succeed in future careers. Their parents, after all, had told them all about tuition bills. The faculty members, students and administrators who supported the fledgling Women's Center in those early days deserve special credit for refusing to accept the reigning piety that women were lucky to be at Amherst at all, and that to think or say otherwise lay somewhere between ingratitude and outright deviancy.

It is likely that I would have merely continued to lend a sympathetic ear to all this had it not been for two unexpected events. During my second year at Amherst, the members of my department met to discuss a proposal to change the major requirements in history. 'How can we approve this report,' I asked, 'since it doesn't even mention the fact that we are now a college for men and women? With everything that's been published in the past few years, doesn't a history department have a special obligation to think about this?' The response was startling. 'How in the world are we going to teach about women's role in American diplomatic history?' a senior colleague (and Amherst graduate) joked. There was widespread chuckling around the table at his cleverness and, presumably, my stupidity. The only woman present (untenured and a specialist in East Asian history) looked anguished, but remained silent. The report was adopted as it stood. For the first time I had not only witnessed but also experienced the sort of behavior previously described to me by women colleagues in other departments. That the gibe came from one of the most sincere supporters of the co-education decision made it all the more confusing. It also made me mad.

Let me make it clear that I had not earned any particular right to ask the question. My courses were still organized around the equation: History = What Men Have Done in Public: and my greatest scholarly achievement was a book about the revolt of the silk-weavers of nine-teenth-century Lyon which dutifully noted the fact that half of them were women, and then neglected to explore its significance. Books and articles have since been produced which show me things about the subject that I never saw were there; most of these works, need I add, are by women. My teaching style, furthermore, had not changed much since I went to Northwestern University as an assistant professor in 1968, where I used to drive by the International Headquarters of the Women's Christian Temperance Union and kid about burning it down because I couldn't buy a six-pack of beer in dry Evanston. It never occurred to me then that Frances Willard's old house might contain an important archive of the women's movement. A decade later I was still a 'male' teacher, but I had heard and read enough about women's history to know that someone ought to mention it at the department meeting. I took my authority from friends like Natalie Zeamon Davis and Joan Wallach Scott, whose personal enthusiasm for women's history signaled to me that something important was happening to my own discipline. The only problem was that I myself had no idea how to bring this important research on the history of women into the classroom. As a teacher I didn't know how to parry my colleague's barb. And where was I going to learn? Certainly not at Amherst.

The second unexpected event was a telephone call from Elizabeth Fox-Genovese a year or so later inviting me to attend a conference sponsored by the Organization of American Historians and The Fund for the Improvement of Post-Secondary Education. I was being asked to comment on a set of teaching packets for a survey course on modern European history prepared by a group of specialists in women's history. A part of me leapt at the opportunity since, for example, I'd be able to learn how Carolyn Lougee taught the eighteenth century at Stanford, but another part resisted for fear of making a fool of myself. One of the editors of this book suggested that I talk with Joyce Berkman, who teaches women's history at the University of Massachusetts at Amherst. She described the theoretical debates at the most recent Berkshire conference and then told me in an hour some of the teaching strategies it had taken her years to develop. I left for the meeting grateful for her generosity and also for the confidence she had given me. Once there, I had the opportunity to discuss what I had been seeing in my own department with other historians, women and men, and to hear about their experiences and ideas. Now that I was getting some possible solutions to my classroom problem, I needed the opportunity to try them out. I didn't have to wait long.

Shortly after I returned from the conference, laden with copies of syllabi, bibliographies, documents, and lecture and discussion plans, the chairperson asked me to inaugurate the senior seminar, which had just become part of the major requirements. Here is the course description I wrote and submitted to the department for inclusion in the catalogue:

The purpose of the senior seminar for majors is to address history as a scholarly discipline, a profession, and a part of the liberal arts curriculum. Although the seminar topic changes every two or three years, the course method remains the same: theoretical, historiographical, and comparative. The course this year will examine the impact that recent scholarship on the history of women has had on the received ideas of what constitutes American and European 'history' as it is written and as it is taught. Members of the seminar will read secondary works, use primary sources, and have the opportunity to meet scholars currently active in women's history. Enrollment is limited to senior history majors for whom it is required.

This was approved without opposition. My colleagues, to their credit, let me prepare for and teach this departmental course on my own terms. I am not certain, of course, how many of them hoped I would succeed with it.

What I did know at the start was that if I were to stand any chance of changing the received ideas of our students I would have to confront a sequence of four pedagogical problems. First, I had to overcome the ingrained resistance at Amherst to any required course, much less one on women. Second, it was probable that at least a majority of the members of the seminar would also enter the room on the first day convinced that the seminar's topic was either trivial or a marginal field of specialization; I would, therefore, have to demonstrate the legitimacy of women's history by showing them how it called into question much of the theory and practice of the entire discipline. I wanted them to recognize its centrality to their chosen college major field, even if they never encountered it until the start of their senior year. Between a quarter and half of the class would also be beginning honors essays, so there was still time to influence the work of our most intellectually ambitious students; if I got lucky, I might get all of them to rethink something they already thought they knew. To achieve that, third, I needed to expose and examine the intellectual and social constraints which determine the way that history is taught and learned in most classrooms. If all this were to mean anything to them, finally, I had to make it a personal experience. I wanted to convince them that if you like studying history in the first place, studying women's history or the history of women is an exciting experience — not only because of the fine work that has been produced recently, but also because of what so obviously remains to be done. I proposed to accomplish this through a series of seminar visitors (persons actively writing and teaching in the field elsewhere), and by requiring as the semester's only formal assignment that each student choose a subject in women's history or the history of women, report on it orally for the benefit of the other seminar members, and submit a written essay by the end of the term.

This teaching strategy appears more clearly reasoned on paper now than it actually was in my mind as I prepared for the first class meeting in the fall of 1981. In theory, I knew that I had to set a clear tone and direction from the start: in practice, however, I became so nervous about entering a new realm that I unconsciously slipped into one of the most comfortable postures of 'male' pedagogy: at the moment I sat down in front of the students I became *an expert in the field*. They were all familiar with this style of teaching, to be sure, but it is likely that I unwittingly precipitated a near-disaster by acting that way.

The assignment for the first of our thirteen two-hour sessions was Susan Moller Okin's *Women in Western Political Thought* (1979). With her feminist analysis of Aristotle, Plato, Rousseau and John Stuart Mill before us, I began by asking why there have been no great women political philosophers. As my own answer, I read aloud three short passages. The first was Virginia Woolf's imaginative and tragic tale of Shakespeare's 'wonderfully gifted sister' from *A Room of One's Own*. The second was from the final book of Rousseau's *Emile*, where he comments on Sophie's ideal qualities ('A perfect man and a perfect woman should be no more alike in mind than in face . . . The man should be strong and active; the woman should be weak and passive; the one must have the power and the will; it is enough that the other offer little resistance'). The third was an anonymous piece I had found in a recent issue of the Smith College alumnae magazine:

> According to a newspaper clipping dated about 1910, 'Miss Ethel Puffer, assistant in psychology at Harvard is a recognized member of the University faculty, but her name is not printed in the catalogue for fear that *it would create a dangerous precedent*.' Miss Puffer was the youngest member of her class at Smith College, and after a few years of teaching at her alma Mater, went abroad and studied under Professor Munsterberg, now at the head of the department at Harvard but then lecturing at Freiburg, Germany. He is reported as saying that Miss Puffer is his most brilliant and most thorough disciple.

The students responded sympathetically to Virginia Woolf's prose — not only because she was a great writer, but also because a room of one's own has become a pious concept at elite colleges. Some of them were clearly disturbed by the quotation from Rousseau, however. At the same time as his blatant misogyny disturbed them, they resented having to hear what seemed an attack on a Great Man. But they were angry and embarrassed by the case of Miss Ethel Puffer. (As evidence of this sort accumulated during the semester, one male student later told the class, 'For the first time in my life I feel like a villain and I don't know what to do about it.') Then, as if on cue, the discussion turned to their own experiences with co-education at Amherst. They were bringing the course home and, as valuable as that was for the moment, I had to make certain that it didn't stay there too long. This wasn't going to become a Bull Session.

Turning again to Okin's book I asked about the status of women in the Western tradition of political philosophy. I directed the discussion in terms of four fundamental premises: (1) the premise of family primacy, which links the state to the family, not the individual, as the basic unit of political society; (2) the premise of gender dualism, which links the stability of the family to the sexual division of labor; (3) the premise of the public and the private sphere, which links men with activity as citizens outside the household and women with activity as mothers and managers within it; and (4) the premise of patriarchy, which links men with political power and legitimacy and is the logical result of the first three premises. It is too simple to dismiss Rousseau as a sexist, I argued, because his ideas about Emile and Sophy stand in a long tradition which asserts that patriarchy is essential to the survival of civilization.[1] I further pointed out that history shares the premises of political philosophy because it (history) emerged in its present form as an academic discipline in the nineteenth century with the activities of the state as its principal subject and the records of the state as its primary source of information. In order to illustrate this theoretical observation we ended the class with a discussion of the implications of J. H. Hexter's 1946 review of Mary Beard's *Women as a Force in History*. In this, he contended that historians are concerned with describing and explaining change, and therefore women are not a legitimate subject for study because they have not played much of a role in bringing it about. 'We know what is mainly behind those trends and developments and movements . . .' Hexter wrote, 'For better or worse, it was men.'[2]

I was elated after the initial session by the conviction that I had already accomplished several of my pedagogical goals. The students had taken notes during my explication of Okin's evidence and no one seemed willing to defend publicly Hexter's position as being intellectually valid. I thought I'd gotten past the hard part, but I couldn't have been more mistaken.

The second session rapidly degenerated into a power struggle between me and several male members of the seminar. Whenever I tried to initiate discussion they would resist my leadership by joking and chatting, and generally trying to create an atmosphere around the table to reflect their attitude that this course was irrelevant to their education. The harder I sought to be serious, the more they pulled against me.

Finally, one of them (now enrolled in a prestigious law school) became so obnoxious that a black woman in the class slammed her fist down and said, 'I get the feeling that some of you don't take what's going on very seriously. Well, I do. This course is important to me, even if it's not to you. So, talk to *me* about it or shut up!' Her intervention saved more than just that day. Although anonymous letters were later sent to the dean complaining that I had violated a college rule by convening a seminar after the official end of classes in order to complete student oral reports, such hostility and anxiety were never on open display again. More importantly, I had learned a lesson about teaching and I needed to reflect on it.

Male authority in the classroom is highly problematic when the subject is women's history. Although our knowledge and powerful position make it relatively easy to attack the received ideas of under-graduates, it is fruitless to think that The Professor can compel them by the force of evidence and logic alone to accept a radically different vision, particularly when it challenges culturally defended, deeply personal aspects of their own lives. As seniors, my students were both completing a period of separation from their parents and beginning to face adult choices in a society which their parents had helped to create. Who was I to them? Did I represent the Good Father, or the Bad Father, telling them what to do and think? Until I understood what some writers on feminist pedagogy have suggested — that the classroom activates unconscious parental models in students and teachers alike — I might recite the facts all I wanted, but I could *teach* them very little.

Before the seminar began, I had been worried that some of the women students would contest my right to present the subject at all. Instead, they were tolerant to a fault during the first year. Even when I was ill-prepared and clearly responsible for a poor session they continued to smile, worked hard, and never complained except about their rebellious male classmates. I had underestimated the influence of the patriarchal tradition at Amherst. That is why in the second year, when a woman student objected to my identifying the historian Dorothy Thompson as 'the wife of E. P. Thompson,' I was at first embarrasssed at my gaffe and then delighted to realize that I was no longer con-sidered beyond criticism. Until then, like Good Daughters, they had been protecting me from my own mistakes.

I am convinced that the change was in part the result of a process of demystification. Once a group of seniors had taken a required course on women's history and lived to graduate, the students following them were more relaxed about the entire experience. So was I. No longer feeling that I had to command respect for my authority, and having learned that it probably wouldn't produce the results I sought, I retained the course's formal structure but adopted an alternative pedagogical approach.

During the second year, I took pleasure in admitting my amateur status as a teacher of women's history and poked fun at the omissions in my own scholarship. The class erupted with laughter when I told about the confrontation the previous year; they had all heard the story through the grapevine and were relieved to have me mention it. Overall, I tried to convey my personal sense of how difficult and potentially rewarding it is to try to relearn something you think you already know. I made it clear that, in my own case, it was necessary to catch up in my own field, modern European social and cultural history. I cannot be certain how it felt to the students, of course, but from my point of view the atmosphere was entirely different. Without a mantle of authority around me for protection against my own uncertainty, the prior aura of classroom competition (common at Amherst and many other places) dissolved and disappeared. One element of the demystification process, I think, came from meeting the seminar for several evening sessions around my dining-room table. With the telephone ringing and my children and their friends going in and out of the house, the class became familiar with the fact that I was someone's actual father and, therefore, could not be its Father, Good or Bad. Simply stated, I changed the signals and the class responded. Although the semester had its high and low points, like any other, I have never taught a course where the students have been more considerate and cooperative with one another.

Other men who already know enough about Women's Studies to have raised a hand in a department meeting, and who, like me, would not know what to suggest next even about their own classes, may already find it appropriate to support hiring more women, particularly those whose work is about women. This strategy is a kind of 'sideline' feminism for those of us with tenured positions, however. It allows us to continue doing what we are doing, as we have been doing it, while a minority of mostly untenured women colleagues do the hard part. I am now convinced this is not enough. Let me explain why in terms of my own discipline.

The impact of women's history and the history of women has been minimal on most undergraduate courses in American and European history. This is particularly true for survey courses, our first (and often only) occasion to tell young men and women what the past is about and why it is important. Perhaps we choose a more enlightened textbook and give a lecture on the suffragists here, make a reference to Rosa Luxemburg there, but not much else has changed in the last ten years. I think Gerda Lerner once gave the reason when I heard her describe this approach as 'the feminist cocktail: add women and stir.' It has proven such a weak drink because it is made from a 'male' recipe. The time has come, therefore, to *integrate* women's history with the established male curriculum, and to do so with the intention of eventually subverting the primacy of the state as the sole subject important enough to be taught to all of our students, as the basic structure of the traditional survey course. It is not enough to offer separate courses on women's history for those students who wish to enroll in them, although these courses shou'' be encouraged where they already exist and created where they do not. What is also necessary is a basic, personal commitment from 'sideline' feminists to do something about our own teaching. We need to learn how to break the old pedagogic codes and how to overcome the received ideas of our earlier training in order to find ways to talk to our students about a past where the public and the private are equally valid parts of human experience. This is going to take time and it won't always be easy, as I am learning for myself.

Nevertheless, one individual willing to change the content of his own courses can be an influence on others in a department. Last year, after our Senior award was divided between a male and a female student, each of whom had written an honors essay in women's history, some of my colleagues started dropping by to chat about bibliography in the field. And this year the same person who once joked about my question in the department meeting volunteered to take over the Senior Seminar. He then went off to attend the Berkshire Conference on Women's History.

My own experience also suggests that 'sideline' feminists should go beyond issues of curriculum development and become aware of the new thinking on feminist pedagogy. Had I done so from the start, I might have avoided the near-disaster with the seminar the first year, and would certainly have improved both years of the course. I now know, for example, that if that pack of resistant male students was ever going to accept the validity of the semester's topic, the Bull

Session I headed off about co-education at Amherst was probably necessary and valuable. I was courting disaster by insisting that we maintain the public/private distinction in the classroom when the logic of the material itself argued against it. Perhaps others can be spared such an avoidable mistake.

'Sideline' feminists can benefit from the wisdom and experience of large numbers of women who have much to tell us from their work in Women's Studies. But we must understand that once we change *what* we have been teaching as historians, *how* we teach history will also be called into question. I know I became (for myself) a better and (for my students) a more effective teacher after I started to surrender the mantle of 'male' authority in the classroom.

Let us return for the remainder of this essay to a discussion of my senior seminar on the impact of recent feminist scholarship on the received ideas of what constitutes American and European 'history' as it is written and taught. I want to comment on some concepts and methods of the course which may be useful. I found it tactically effective, for example, to reexamine a series of 'big events' — the sort that every history major knows something about — in order to illustrate how work in women's history refracts the discipline's established vision of the past, and to show that it does so in complex ways. The purpose of each session was to deconstruct the Renaissance, the French Revolution, or the Industrial Revolution as uniquely 'male' experiences and to attempt to reconstruct them as part of an integrated past of men and women. In each case we discussed how taking account of the experience of women alters our perception of the shape, meaning and significance of the 'big events' themselves. Take, for example, the case of the American Revolution.

Many students initially assume that the central purpose of women's history is to discover 'notable' women and restore them to their rightful place alongside the famous men of the past. They have, in other words, a 'male' view of history, and lack a sense of the historical consequences of patriarchy. Helen Vendler goes to the heart of the matter in her review of Harvard University Press's biographical dictionary of *Notable American Women, 1607-1950*:[3]

Before you can become a Notable Woman, if you have followed the usual social patterns and married in your twenties, you have to suffer adversity: you find your husband dead of a bullet wound, 'an apparent suicide,' and learn that your family's fortune is 'utterly

spent'; or your husband dies after confinement in an Italian laza-
retto, leaving you with five children; or you are widowed at twenty;
or you get married at 14, are divorced at 19, and are left with a child
to support; or your four children all die successively in infancy;
or of your 12 children only three live beyond their 33rd birthday,
and of these, two die insane — these events, and the psychological
convulsions following them, enough to destroy most women, force
certain souls into an even more constructive effort, and a Notable
American Woman is born.

It is hard to think of a work at once more encouraging and
depressing than this collective of some thirteen hundred life stories.

I have found that by using Vendler's cross-cutting insight as a gloss
on Mary Beth Norton's *Liberty's Daughters: The Revolutionary Experience of American Women, 1750-1800* (1980) students quickly begin to
see the extent of the domestic realm largely hidden from sight in their
other history courses. Norton takes them into a world they previously
knew only through Betsy Ross and Dolly Madison. Whether or not
you start with the same 'big event' as I do, the strategic purpose should
be the same: to help students learn that the public and the private share
a history.

We should not be impatient if at first some of our students think
studying the domestic realm is dull by definition: they only know
what we've been teaching them. An effective way to demonstrate
the excitement in the field of women's history is to assign a particular
piece of work and invite its author to discuss it with the class. This
involves planning and money, but it also provides an opportunity
to watch someone else work with the class and to ask questions about
teaching and scholarship. It can have unexpected benefits, too. The
week after Joan Scott talked with my students about how she and
Louise Tilly came to write *Women, Work and Family* (1978), I asked
how they had reacted to having her as a teacher. 'I wanted to put
myself up for adoption,' was the response of one of the men. There
is an essay on feminist pedagogy in that remark alone! Another kind
of visitor is the historian who doesn't consider himself or herself an
expert in women's history, but whose writing takes account of the
history of the domestic sphere. John Mack Faragher, for example,
has come to talk about writing the history of rural America, and Diane
Owen Hughes shared her work in progress on the relationship between
Renaissance laws regulating public dress and portraits of the Madonna.

Joyce Berkman also helped me a second time by coming in to discuss teaching women's history and how she began her work in the field. For those whose institutional resources do not permit such a celebrity list, even one lecturer on campus in a semester is worth the effort.

After 'big events' and flesh-and-blood historians have helped the class to accept the revised definition of 'history' required to do women's history, students need to learn that it is not a monolithic enterprise. This is one way to point them to journals like *Signs* and *Feminist Studies*, where they can look at the debates about women's culture and women's politics. There is probably no better way to learn what something is about than to listen in while those who do it talk to each other about it. As we discuss our positions, and those of our colleagues, be sure to ask the students where they stand on some of the intellectual issues involved.

Finally, have as many students as possible write some women's history for themselves. My situation was ideal for this: a required seminar with bright students, an adequate library and an archive — the Sophia Smith Collection — in the next town. The most important ingredient is not the setting, however; it is motivation. Use your office hours to meet with students individually and in groups, asking them to define a topic that comes out of their previous experience and/or interest in history, and advising them how to go about finding the right material. They can also be sent to members of the local Women's Studies network for help. In any case, don't confine them to the library. Projects where students interview women members of their own family and family friends about the Second World War or the 1950s, for example, can be a place where they start to connect the past with their current lives. The first year, the most recalcitrant member of the class read *The Feminine Mystique* and interviewed his mother about her life as a housewife. Another, in the process of applying to rabbinical school, wrote about the lives of seventeenth-century Jewish women by using *The Memoirs of Gluckel of Hamelin*. We all know that our students work harder on something they are personally interested in.

There is no doubt in my mind that my experiment with women's history and feminist pedagogy has been worth the effort. It has improved my eligibility really to *teach* students after nearly twenty years in the business. I even got a reward for it. This year, one person concluded her essay by writing, 'Not only has the senior seminar helped us understand relationships between theory and practice, it has opened new doors for understanding ourselves via liberation from received ideas.' The next step for me is to apply what I learned from the experience in my other courses.

Notes

1   These premises are part of Benjamin R. Barber's review of Okin, which appeared in *The New Republic*, 1 March 1980, pp.37-9.

2   Hexter is cited in Dale Spender (ed.), *Men's Studies Modified: The Impact of Feminism on the Academic Disciplines*, Oxford: Pergamon Press, 1981, p.55. This volume is a good place to start reading whether you are an historian or a biologist.

3   Vendler's review was published in *The New York Times Book Review*, 17 September 1972, pp.1, 18-19.

7

Teaching mediation: a feminist perspective on the study of law

Janet Rifkin

Introduction

Several years ago, I became intrigued by the possibilities of using mediation for resolving a broad range of interpersonal and intergroup conflict. My interest was generated by my frustrations and uneasiness as a law student and then as a Legal Aid lawyer. In those capacities, I had seen first hand how the formal legal system offers at best limited possibilities for resolving conflict, and how the adversarial arena so clearly exacerbates the underlying dispute. It also became clear to me how, in so many instances, the courtroom process and setting can skew a conflict by transforming the dispute between the parties from a private argument into a 'legal' issue[1] quite different from the original problem.

My attraction to mediation was also tied to my experiences as a teacher of law in an undergraduate setting. In this context, I realized that the mystique of law limits students' ability to think about conflict in other than legalistic terms. This became particularly apparent in teaching a course on 'Women and the Law,' a class in which I approached law as both a symbol and vehicle of male authority. From this perspective, I urged the class to see litigation and legislation as reinforcing the male paradigm of law, rather than as altering the basic gender hierarchy. Although the students were intrigued by my approach, they were not willing to relinquish the notion that law can lead to social change and can advance women's rights. The basic question the class had for me was: what alternative did I offer if I rejected litigation as an appropriate means of redressing women's oppression?

In all my courses, I was also confronted by another arena of resistance. As a teacher of law, I was explicitly rejecting the pedagogical approach of the professional law school, where the professor, using the 'Socratic method,' reinforces traditional notions of authority and hierarchy in the classroom and plays 'mind games' with the students in the name of legal reasoning. In my classes, it was clear there were no 'right answers' nor was I willing to be that removed 'expert.' I encouraged dialogue, emphasizing class discussion as much as written work. Although most students clearly enjoyed these classes, certain questions continued to arise: why wasn't I willing to give out the answers they thought I had? Why was I teaching law and not practicing? Would I recommend law school for students interested in social change? As a woman, what was it like to be a law student and a lawyer? These and other questions intensified as I more explicitly criticized and rejected the traditional pedagogy of law study — a pedagogy which supports and reinforces the male paradigm of law.

These experiences led me, finally, to put into practice my emerging theoretical critique of law as a limited mechanism for resolving social conflict in general, and women's issues specifically. The first step for me was to develop and teach a course in mediation and alternatives to the adversarial process. I became trained as a mediator, then founded and became the director of the University of Massachusetts Mediation Project.[2] Just as my experiences as a law student, a lawyer and a law teacher had led to my rejection of the traditional pedagogy of law study, teaching mediation now led to a fuller understanding of the substantive connections between law and patriarchy, and the ways that traditional pedagogy reinforces those connections.

Teaching about law through traditional, substantive law courses inevitably reproduces the typical law pedagogy. The ideology and content of these courses (embracing a patriarchal and social order) naturally gives rise to ways of teaching and studying that support traditional views of authority and power. The course on mediation, on the other hand, steps outside of substantive law to view law in a cultural and ideological framework — thus, the adversarial process is seen as but one of many ways of resolving social conflict. To use the traditional pedagogy in such a course would fundamentally contradict the theoretical perspectives of the class. Rather, the course in mediation explicitly rejects the male mode of law pedagogy and uses instead feminist pedagogical perspectives and processes.

Mediation: theory and critique

Mediation is a process of discussion, clarification and compromise aided by a neutral third party. The mediator has no powers of enforcement, and can succeed only by assisting the disputing parties in reaching a voluntary settlement fashioned by themselves rather than by a judge or other outside agency. The creation of consensus is the task disputants undertake with the mediator's assistance. Mediation takes place in an atmosphere of confidentiality, yet the conflicts which are being brought to mediation typically involve complex issues with broad social, political, or cultural significance.

Alternatives to the adversary process, programs offering mediation, arbitration, negotiation and conciliation are proliferating throughout the USA, Canada, Australia and Great Britain. These programs may be court-related or community-based; in either situation, however, the rationales for supporting their development and continued existence are very similar.

Mediating conflict as a substitute for litigating disputes has been justified by two basic rationales. First, many recognize that the formal court system is not suited to handling the range and number of disputes now being brought to it. Second, an understanding is growing that the adversary process itself is not suited to resolving the full range of disputes that occur between people. Some supporters of mediation, for example, suggest that the criminal and civil justice systems are arcane, myopic and frustrating to those who work within them, and inadequate for those served by them.[3] They claim, conversely, that mediation projects serve to facilitate citizen access to justice by processing cases rapidly,[4] by not requiring lawyers,[5] by holding hearings at times convenient to all parties to a dispute and by providing multi-lingual staff for non-English-speaking disputants. Furthermore, by providing opportunities to explore the underlying causes of disputes,[6] the potential for a meaningful reduction in interpersonal and social conflict can be enhanced. In addition, evidence has accumulated that disputants view mediation as a positive experience.[7]

While mediation is flourishing, it is not without its critics. It has been asked, for example, why informal systems purport to achieve justice in an unjust society when formal institutions cannot.[8] It has been argued that just as the image of formal law is enhanced by legal representation and procedural protections, informal processes — such as mediation — use other mechanisms to convey the *image* of equality without achieving *substantive* equality.[9] Critics further insist that compromise between unequals inevitably reproduces inequality;[10] that mediation limits and ultimately represses conflict;[11] and that the third-party mediator does not really care about the disputants — rather, the informal system simply reproduces and extends the relationship between the helping professions and the needy consumer of services, a paradigmatic form of domination in advanced capitalism.[12]

Others have suggested that the bureaucratic logic which supports state legality is as much a part of the process in informal and non-bureaucratic settings as it is in the formal court of law;[13] that the state, faced with fiscal crisis, achieves spending cuts by resorting to informalization, accompanied by appeals to popular participation, consensual social life, and the struggle against bureaucracy.[14] Some feel that mediation fosters the privatization of life — the cult of the personal — and denies the existence of irreconcilable structural conflicts between classes or between citizen and state.[15] Finally, the claim has been made that mediation is detrimental to the interests of women, who, being less empowered, are in need of the formal legal system to protect existing rights and through which to work for new legal safeguards.[16]

These critiques expand our understanding and evaluation of mediation and other forms of conflict-resolution in contemporary society. But these analyses are all predicated on the view that formal litigation leads to social change and that the 'lawsuit' is an appropriate, effective vehicle for challenging and changing oppressive social systems. In contrast to this view, I have argued elsewhere that[17]

> the real power of law is that by framing issues as questions of law, claims of right, precedents, and problems of constitutional interpretation, the effect is to divert potential public consciousness from an awareness of the deeper roots of the anger. At the same time, the paradigm of law as hierarchy and combat is reinforced as a legitimate mechanism for resolving social conflict.

Mediation has not been studied in the context of hierarchical and patriarchal law. The course I teach on 'Dispute Resolution' views mediation in light of a pervasive legalism which supports traditional authority-structures and reinforces the gender hierarchy in this society.

Teaching mediation: learning to think unlike a lawyer

The course entitled 'Alternatives to the Adversary Process' studies mediation (the main alternative considered) in the context of a theory of law which departs from those critiques which examine the dynamic between law and the state in contemporary liberal society.[18] Instead, the study of mediation views law from a feminist perspective. Examining mediation as a method of resolving conflicts illuminates the patriarchal nature of law and of law pedagogy. Patriarchal law is explicitly characterized by hierarchy, the adversarial approach, linearity and rationality: a paradigm in which reason is synonymous with rule, and the ideal of the 'reasonable man' is the fundamental frame of reference for making decisions.[19] In this context, litigation efforts on behalf of women are premised on the continued dominance of the official system, even while the gender and/or color of the officials may be changing.[20]

Teaching mediation allows a feminist analysis of law. But more fundamentally, teaching mediation — especially outside of a professional law school setting — makes teaching about law with feminist pedagogical processes possible. Indeed, professional law teaching has been antithetical to feminism and feminist pedagogy. The 'Socratic method,' at the heart of law school pedagogy, supports hierarchy, contention, combat and humiliation.[21] It is not possible, in fact, to teach law using traditional case-materials and simultaneously to challenge the paradigm.

The teaching of mediation offers substantive and pedagogical challenges to the traditional model of legal pedagogy. There are fundamental differences between feminist pedagogy and legal pedagogy. 'Feminist method is consciousness-raising: the collective critical reconstitution of the meaning of women's social experience as women live through it.'[22] Whereas legal pedagogy involves a learning process in which 'facts, issues, principles, reasoning and laws are learned without specific reference to behaviour or experience; where students are required to think in legal terms and to articulate problems and issues in the language of the law.'[23]

This course encourages the very questions which are anathema to traditional law teaching. Among these are issues currently being raised by some feminist legal scholars. Is liberal law, and the rationalistic linear mode of thinking of which it is a part, in some fundamental way male, and distinguishable from female 'contextual' thinking?[24]

Do women have a specific moral language which emphasizes concern for others, responsibility, care and obligation — as distinguished from male morality, which focuses on abstract notions of individual rights?[25] Do female and male engenderment generate different modes of thinking and discourse, and is it possible and useful to distinguish between them?[26] What explains the inequality of women to men? What is male power?[27]

These kinds of questions are not only outside the framework of traditional law teaching, they represent a challenge to the way of thinking that supports the basic structures of law in this society. By explicitly asking these and other questions, by supporting dialogue, and by challenging authority implicit in the law and in law teaching, a new pedagogy emerges which is essential to a new way of thinking about law. Whereas formal law reinforces the dominance of hierarchy and rationality supporting the traditional ideas of public and private,[28] mediation challenges these notions.

The course: 'Alternatives to the Adversary Process'

The course begins by critiquing the adversary process and demonstrating the connections between law and patriarchy. Using readings on this topic,[29] and on the operation of the courts,[30] we develop a framework to analyze the formal legal system. At the same time, introductory readings on mediation[31] allow the students to develop a comparison between mediation and resolution by adjudication. The following chart emerges from these discussions:

Adjudication	Mediation
public	private
formal	informal
strict evidentiary rules	no formal parameters — conversationalist
coercive	voluntary
emphasis on:	emphasis on:
conflict of interest	areas of agreement
value dissensus	points in common
win/lose — combative	compromise — conciliatory
decision-oriented	agreement-oriented

rule-oriented	person-oriented
professional decision-maker	community law volunteer worker
representation by lawyer	direct participation

After the readings and the discussions of them, staff members of the University Mediation Project, including student interns (who rotate every semester) develop and present a simulation of a mediated conflict based on a real dispute. This role-play demonstrates how mediation operates as a process of discussion, clarification and compromise, aided by third-party neutrals. The students see how a process can work in which the third party has no power except the power to persuade the parties to reach a voluntary settlement. Students further see how the mediation process involves the creation of consensus between the parties, in which people are brought together to discover shared social and moral values as a means of coming to an agreement. Finally, the simulation illustrates how mediation takes place in an atmosphere of confidentiality and how the conflicts mediated involve, under the surface, complex issues which may have broad social, political and cultural significance.

The demonstration of a mediation session and the discussion about it are examples of a pedagogy radically different in a number of respects from traditional law teaching. In traditional law pedagogy, the case-book is the emblem of the authoritative character of the law, and the 'Socratic method' mirrors and reinforces the structures of authority. The simulation embodies a contrasting way of thinking about conflict. The demonstrated mediation illustrates that conflict-resolution can be non-hierarchical and non-authoritarian, participatory and consensual.

After the simulation, we focus on mediator training and compare it to professional law school training,[32] the latter being an indoctrination process into the dominant ideology of law.[33] At this point, students who wish to, may be trained as mediators.[34]

The students are then asked to write a paper. Using the readings, they are asked to evaluate the simulation in the following ways: was the conflict appropriate for mediation? How does this mediation differ from formal law procedures? Was the mediation process fair? Were the mediators neutral and impartial? Such questions would be excluded from traditional law classes. In fact, questions about fairness are specifically excluded as irrelevant to a proper legislative inquiry into a problem.[35] The pedagogical approach in the mediation course shifts the emphasis to the female concerns of responsibility and justice, in contrast to the concern for individual rights[36] characteristic of the male pedagogy dominant in law school and other academic settings.

At this point, the class reads a number of critiques of mediation and discussion focuses on the issues raised. We consider, for example, how mediation can operate as a fair process in disputes where the parties are unequally empowered. Can disputes, for example, between merchant and consumer, landlord and tenant, or husband and wife be mediated? Or are the power imbalances too great? Does compromise between unequals inevitably reproduce inequality? Can mediation lead to justice in an unjust society? Can a process which has no due process guarantees provide justice for the less powerful party?[37]

As we ask these questions about mediation, we also examine the questions themselves. We discuss how the ways in which these reservations about mediation have been formulated reflect assumptions about law and power. We see that to ask these questions in these ways is in itself a statement. While our questions reflect real concerns, we have continued to frame them from the perspective that assumes that law is rational, hierarchical and focused on individual rights. It becomes clear at this point that as long as the questions about mediation are asked as traditional legal questions or are set in the context of the adversary system, they cannot be considered in other than legalistic terms. The real evaluation of mediation necessitates a rejection of the law paradigm itself, and the development of new ideological and pedagogical frameworks in which to consider these issues. Whether or not this is possible on a significant scale in our law-permeated society is a question which we discuss at length in class.

The final phase of the course focuses on a specific area of mediation. Most recently, this has involved a study of family-related mediation, including divorce, separation and custody, as well as parent-child and domestic-violence disputes. Each student is assigned a particular topic and is required to do an extensive research paper. In class, we continue to explore issues in these specific areas.

Mediation of domestic-violence disputes has emerged as one of the more controversial topics. Opponents of mediation here argue that women, the main victims, will be coerced in mediation, perhaps subtly, by their mate or by their mediators into either resuming an abusive relationship or forfeiting the financial rights they may have obtained in court proceedings. Our discussion of these issues has been enhanced by a guest speaker who is the chief county prosecutor for domestic-violence complaints. She is also a mediator for the University Mediation Project. As a strong advocate of the legal rights of battered women, and as a mediator, her position is unique. Her talk gives the students an opportunity to consider the ambiguities of this problem, and her openness about her mixed feelings toward mediating problems of domestic violence allows the students to see, first hand, how personal experience is not always consistent with a political analysis of an issue.

Again, we have an example of a pedagogy which departs from the mainstream teaching of law where ambiguous and morally complex problems are treated simply in terms of legal gamesmanship. In this class, we emphasize the moral questions and stress the ambiguous and uncomfortable aspects of the issues involved.

It is interesting that despite the speaker's support for mediation under certain circumstances and despite the empirical studies[38] of domestic-violence mediation programs (which suggest that mediation helps develop new ground rules between spouses and that women are not, in fact, returning to their husbands after mediation), the majority of the class did not feel mediation was appropriate for these kinds of problems. They felt similarly about using mediation for parent-child disputes where – based on obvious recent personal experience – they felt that parents had all the power, and mediation would not change that.

They had, however, a different reaction to divorce mediation. Although no student spoke about personal experiences in class when we discussed divorce, one-third of the papers on divorce mediation were based on the painful realities of being the child of divorcing parents. In all of these detailed discussions, the students concurred that mediation would have made the reality of divorce more bearable for them. Several mentioned the traumatic experiences in which they were forced to testify in court. Again, these final papers are a reflection of a pedagogy in which personal experience is viewed as a legitimate and important reference-point for scholarly work. Traditional law pedagogy rejects personal experience, and even the personal point of view, maintaining instead the illusion that reality can be evaluated from the point of view of rules, prior decisions of law and abstract notions of individual rights.

Conclusions

'Alternatives to the Adversary Process' is a law course in which the traditional authoritarian pedagogy is consciously and explicitly rejected. Instead, the course is taught from the feminist pedagogical perspective which emphasizes discussion of the moral issues involved in social and personal conflicts, which encourages student dialogue, and which views personal experience as a legitimate reference-point for scholarly reflection. In this framework, the teaching of law supports the development in the classroom of a critical analysis of traditional law, where the relationship between law and patriarchal power can be fully uncovered and understood. Studying the law from the perspective of mediation, where the pedagogy mirrors and supports the course content, offers the possibility for reexamining the operation of law in society.

Notes

1 Lynn Mahter and Barbara Yngvesson, 'Language, Audience and the Transformation of Disputes,' *Law and Society Review*, vol. 15, nos 3-4, 1980-1.
2 The Mediation Project began operation in February 1981. To date, ninety mediators have been trained. The mediators represent a cross-section of the population, including faculty, staff, students, and community members. Over 350 cases have been handled by the project. Of those cases which have formally been mediated, almost 80 per cent have successfully reached agreement. The types of cases that have been mediated include roommate problems, landlord/tenant conflicts, fraternity conflicts, sexual harassment disputes, family disputes, consumer problems and business partnership disputes. The University Mediation Project is supported by the university in addition to a small grant from a Massachusetts foundation. Disputes are referred to the project from all parts of the university hierarchy, through members of the local Bar, clergy, the Probate Court, and from increasing community awareness of the project.
3 David McGillis, *Recent Developments in Minor Dispute Processing*, National Institute of Law Enforcement Assistance Administration. US Department of Justice by ABT Associates under contract no. JLEAA 81378, p.10.
4 *Ibid.*
5 *Ibid.*, p.11.
6 *Ibid.*
7 *Ibid.*, p.12.
8 Richard Abel, 'Conservative Conflict and Reproduction of Capitalism, The Role of Informal Justice,' *International Journal of Sociology of Law*, 1981, p.248.
9 *Ibid.*, p.256.
10 *Ibid.*, p.257.
11 *Ibid.*, p.254.
12 *Ibid.*, p.260.

13 Bonaventure DeSousa Santos, 'Law and Community: The Changing Nature of State Power in Late Capitalism,' *International Journal of the Sociology of Law*, 1980, p.387.

14 *Ibid.*, p.389.

15 Abel, *op. cit.*, p.261.

16 See in general, National Council for Women and the Family, New York City.

17 Janet Rifkin, 'Toward a Theory of Law and Patriarchy,' in Piers Bierne and Richard Quinney (eds), *Marxism and the Law*, New York: John Wiley & Sons, 1982.

18 See generally R. Abel, *The Politics of Informal Justice*, vols 1 and 2, London and New York: Academic Press, 1981.

19 Peter d'Errico and J. Rifkin, 'Response to Zillah Eisenstein,' *ALSA Forum*, vol. VII, no. 2-3, September 1983, p.325.

20 *Ibid.*

21 See Scott Turow, *One L*, New York: G. P. Putnam's Sons, 1977.

22 Catherine MacKinnon, 'Feminism, Marxism, Method and the State: An Agenda for Theory,' in Nannerl O. Keohane, Michelle Z. Rosaldo, and Barbara C. Gelpi (eds), *Feminist Theory: A Critique of Ideology*, University of Chicago Press, 1982, p.29.

23 Meredith Gould, 'The Paradox of Teaching Feminism and Learning Law,' unpublished paper.

24 Ann Freedman, unpublished paper from the Conference on Critical Legal Studies, Camden, New Jersey. 1983.

25 See generally Carol Gilligan, *In a Different Voice*, Cambridge, Mass.: Harvard University Press, 1982.

26 Ann Freedman, *op. cit.*

27 Catherine MacKinnon, *op. cit.*

28 Jean Elshtain, *Public Man, Private Woman: Women in Social and Political Thought*, Princeton University Press, 1981, pp.4-5.

29 Janet Rifkin, *op. cit.*; and Diane Polan, 'Toward a Theory of Law and Patriarchy,' in David Kairys (ed.), *The Politics of Law*, New York: Pantheon Books, 1982.

30 Vilhelm Auber, *Courts and Conflict Resolution,' Journal of Conflict Resolution*, vol. 11, no. 1, 1967, pp.49-51.

31 Lon Fuller, 'Forms and Functions of Mediation,' *Southern California Law Review*, 44:305, 1971; Frank Sander, 'Varieties of Dispute Processing,' 70 F.R.D. 79.

32 Turow, *op. cit.*

33 Aleta Wallach, 'A View From the Law School,' in Florence Howe (ed.), *Women and the Power to Change*, New York: McGraw Hill, 1975.

34 To date, twelve undergraduate students have been trained as mediators. In general the mediators represent a cross-section of the community, including faculty, staff, graduate and undergraduate students and members of the surrounding communities.

35 Turow, *op. cit.*

36 Carol Gilligan, *op. cit.*

37 See generally Richard Abel, *The Politics of Informal Justice*.

38 Suzanne Goulet Orenstein, 'The Role of Mediation in Domestic Violence Cases,' in *Alternative Means of Family Dispute Resolution*, Washington, DC: American Bar Association, 1982.

8

Staging the feminist classroom: a theatrical model

Helene Keyssar

From the admittedly skewed vantage of Southern California, signs of radical change in the teaching and research that are the business of the academy appear on the watery horizon. After 100 years of carefully guarded separatism, a number of disciplines are cautiously beginning to speak to each other, and texts that were once considered the exclusive property of one field are now emerging as found treasures in others. Semiotics transports theoretical news from the sciences to the arts and back again; social scientists speak of a 'dramatistic' methodology; cognition captures developmental psychologists and computer experts; philosophers talk about movies; Freud and Marx are iterated in the same sentence. Of all these signs, the most vital is the persistent pressure of feminism on even the best-barricaded academic cells. And it is precisely in conjunction with feminist thought that politics may again find its legitimate route to the classroom.

It is in this context that I take Juliet Mitchell's[2] assertion — 'Feminism ... is the terrain on which a socialist analysis works' — to be an important cue to teachers and teaching. In the spring of 1982, I took this cue (with my own particular emendation) as the frame for a new course entitled 'The University of California: San Diego Feminist Theater and Video Ensemble.' Moving along similar lines to those elaborated by Mitchell in *Women's Estate*, my own research in British and American feminist drama had convinced me of the necessity of joining the personal and psychological emphases of radical American feminism with the analyses of work and class consciousness central to British socialist-feminism. In addition, I had some evidence and a good deal of conviction that theater was, in turn, an exceptionally fruitful terrain for feminism. During the same period that we have acknowledged the relevance of personal experience to politics, theater has recognized that the personal is theatrical. Perhaps more importantly, the kind of theater course I envisioned was one in which production was not just an object of discourse but a central and natural activity.

The key difference, then, between this and other courses I have taught was the joining of a feminist analysis with an actual engagement in production. The Feminist Theater and Video Ensemble's main tasks were to produce a script, a live performance of that script and a video production. But in contrast to instances where I have directed students in theater production outside the classroom, our assumption from the beginning was that the creation of a product was inseparable from understanding and changing the *process* of production. It would not suffice just to put on a show — even a show about women or about sexual politics. Our product had to reveal to the audience and ourselves a notion of work that transfigured images of women, and of men and women together; it also had to articulate alternatives to hierarchical, authoritarian, competitive ways of organizing work.

Ultimately, the title of this course is, or should be, a redundancy. If all theater, and especially theater in the model context of the classroom, does not spurn the impersonal, does not rebel against the tyranny of stars, directors and playwrights, does not fully embrace the worlds of women, then theater will soon die. And there will not be much significant mourning. It is also silly to have to call a feminist group an 'ensemble'; how else could one do feminist production work except as an ensemble? That the course was officially listed, however, as 'Women's Theater' does suggest the political significance of my own title. The class was not restricted to women as subject nor as participants, but, of equal importance, neither was the pedagogy neutral. There was no initial constraint on the students' modes of discourse or opinions, but judgments were to be made, and actions — including language actions — criticized, on grounds of challenging conventional power relationships between men and women.

It is a cliché of theater directing that once one has cast a show, everything is determined but the applause. This was not the case in the Feminist Theater Ensemble, but the structure I established for class enrollment did significantly shape the nature of the course. I initially limited the number of participants to sixteen, although I eventually admitted twenty students. These numbers are not arbitrary or magical but based on previous production experience. With more than twenty students, the social group inevitably fragments, and attempts at collaborative work on one project become chaotic. With fewer than twelve, it is more difficult to move to a critical stance: the group becomes more like a clique or consciousness-raising group and any struggle too easily threatens the structure of the whole.

From the beginning, I was determined that the course would not be restricted to theater majors: our purpose was not simply to do a particular kind of theater, but to exploit theatrical strategies as a means of exposing feminist issues. Technical competence in performance, design or camera-work was not irrelevant (some roles in each of these areas needed to be filled by people with prior skills), but it was important that participants learn from each other to respect the equal weight of different kinds of work and knowledge. Students who were well read in feminist literature might move the course forward at least as well as those who had held major roles in conventional theater.

I therefore opposed auditions, the usual practice for selection of students for theater production classes. Auditions for this class would have established a competitive framework and emphasized my role as distinct authority. Instead, I interviewed each interested student, asking each what she or he thought feminism was, what her/his skills were, why they wanted to participate in this course. Through these interviews and through public notices, I made it clear that men were welcome in the course. Although the campus has courses in 'Images of Women' and 'Women's History', no other course labeled itself as 'feminist,' and I wanted to make clear my own conviction that feminism was a coherent view of all of society — not just a female point of view about women. Since it is also the case that many feminist plays include male roles, the presence of men in the class would allow more flexibility in the choice of script and would more accurately reflect some of the concerns of feminist drama. The presence of men in the class would make certain kinds of talk more problematic, but that kind of problematizing seemed valuable. We ended up with fourteen women and six men, with the greatest number of students drawn from drama and communication and a few from literature, visual arts and political science. Two were graduate students; five were over twenty-five; two members of the class had children.

I awaited the choice of a script for production until the entire ensemble could participate in the decision. Although I knew that this would create practical problems and minimize my control, I did so precisely to undermine my own authority. The structures of both the classroom and theater production provide rich possibilities for a 'community of learners' and for the recognition of interdependence. Nevertheless, I have too often found myself in the contradictory role of saying to a class, 'This is your class,' and then handing them a syllabus and list of readings that greatly constrained what they could do. Since there was no way I could wholly counter their perception of me as teacher and director, I wanted at least to emphasize immediately that they would be pushed to make choices, that they usually assumed were beyond their control — and that they would do this together, as a group.

In the first weeks, I bombarded the students with scripts, instructing them to read quickly through as many as they could, to discuss among themselves the merits of each, and to come to class prepared to analyze scripts that particularly appealed. I did put limits around the material by what I had ordered and put on reserve: not only were all but one of the plays by women, but all were 'feminist' in that the playwrights' 'art was related to their condition as women.'[3] Four plays representing different modes of feminist drama were required reading: Viveca Lanfor's, *I Am Woman*, Caryl Churchill's *Cloud Nine*, Megan Terry's *Calm Down, Mother*, and Pam Gems's *Dusa Fish Stas and Vi*. Our conversations about these plays focused on form as well as issues: the sounding of women's voices as liberation from what Paolo Freire calls the 'culture of silence,' was one early focus; another was ways women talk to each other and about men; a third concerned attributes and definitions of male and female behavior as presented in drama.

During our first six sessions, held twice a week for two to three hours each, we talked in seminar fashion and then moved to exercises, particularized versions of theater games. Like many other contemporary theater people, I have long used theater games in acting classes and rehearsals; in recent years, I had paid attention to the sexual politics of these games. But I had few resources to draw upon for a specific and elaborate set of feminist theater games. I borrowed some from Caryl Churchill's descriptions of games used in the rehearsals for *Cloud Nine*, and picked up scattered hints from other feminist theater artists (including Megan Terry, Honor Moore, Lucy Winner and my colleague Robin Hunt.[4]

One of the more resonant games, modified from Churchill's descriptions, was a power game. The class divided in half so that one group was 'audience,' the other performers; they repeatedly alternated in these roles. Each performer received a playing-card whose number identified her/his quantity of power. I set up a simple improvisational context — a restaurant, a beach party, a bus stop — and skeletal roles to operate within that context. Each 'character' was to express her or his power in the situation according to the card received. The first time through, each participant retained her or his own sexual identity. The scenes were repeated, however, and the second time gender was determined arbitrarily by card color, not by personal identity. In this second attempt, performers had to determine behavior by their judgments of the relationship of 'number power' to gender power, the audience was to try to read who was male and female and how much numerical power each had.

More than the obvious resulted from this exercize. There was little ambiguity about the effects of gender-identification on power: a person assigned a card that determined her or him to be a woman with a '10' power consistently took less control of the situation than, for example, a person identified as a man with a '5' power. Social roles — whether one was a waiter or a customer — modified power relationships somewhat, but did not overcome the force of gender. Equally revealing were the ways in which participants chose to express power, dependent upon male or female identity. In the first trials of this exercize, stereotypical gestures of voice, physical aggression, manipulation, or choice of words tended to dominate the expressions of power. Once one group had witnessed another's performance, however, that group would try for more subtle and varied expressions of power or weakness: silence became a key weapon, as did wit and the placing of the body in more or less vulnerable positions. Still, it was difficult to escape clichés and everyone became troubled both about the ease with which 'males' took power, and about the limited repertoire of gestures for both men and women to express their status.

Some games were designed more specifically to examine these assumed models and conventions of male and female movement, voice and physical interaction. We looked at each other's walks, ways of sitting, ways of positioning ourselves in a group. In a variation of a familiar theater game, we mingled as a whole in a large, undefined space, greeting each other by saying our own names (or, in another version, the 'other's' name) and touching the other in any desired way. Afterwards, we talked about our observations — finding, for example, that a woman might gently touch another woman's hand or face, might hold another woman's hand in two of hers, but that men restricted their touches to other men to pats on the back or shoulders or a momentary clasping of upper-arms. Predictably, the most self-conscious physical encounters were between women and men and between men and men. Women and men never shook hands, often entirely omitted physical contact on greeting each other, or took on maternal or paternal roles: a woman might rumple a man's hair, a man might lightly touch a woman's dress-sleeve. In our discussion of these exercises, I recalled my observations of the very different public physical behavior of men and women in China, where it is commonplace to see adolescent and adult women walking hand in hand or arm in arm down the street, and nearly as ordinary to see two men arm in arm – but socially unacceptable for a man and woman to have any public physical contact. We reached no firm conclusions from these observations, but they were to become relevant later on in our rehearsals when we tried to expand our resources of physical gestures.

Other games were aimed at creating a sense of shared responsibility and at revealing ourselves as sexual beings. We employed transformation exercizes (developed in the 'new theater' of the 1960s and most fully adopted by feminist theater groups) to increase our ability to focus on each other, to respond exactly to what the other was doing, and to accelerate our ability to harmonize different rhythms. These games not only suggest the idea of change as a continuous process, but emphasize the reliance on the group to confirm and accept change. In one variation of a transformation game, participants form a cirlce, one member starts a simple sound-and-movement pattern, and all others must join in with the same pattern. As the game evolves, any member of the group can change the pattern such that it is a minor alteration of the previous gestures; everyone must pay attention to each other to participate in these changes. In a second step of the circle transformation, one member moves to the center, draws a second person from the circle, and uses the basic sound-and-movement pattern to create a dialogue. We focused these interactions on gender roles and erotic attractions, though the key point to the game was to discern and alter personal inclinations towards leadership roles. Much like in a seminar, where part of the teacher's task is to discern the slightest indication that a usually silent member wants to speak, the transformations, if successful, shift responsibility from those most ready to initiate, to those reluctant to lead. Here, however, it is not the 'teacher' but the group that is responsible for responding to its least aggressive members.

'Talk' games also helped to establish trust and shared understanding. Going completely around the circle of the class, we would ask, 'Tell us something you know about women (or about men).' The calculated series of such questions continues: 'Tell us something you like about women (men).' 'Tell us something you don't like.' 'Tell us something you want to (don't want to) tell us.' Another word game, called 'forced choice' embodies the notion of language as an activity, but also can reveal sex-role-related preferences in ordinary life. In this game, participants line up, half on each side of a room, in an arbitrary division. Paired terms — chocolate ice cream, vanilla ice cream; beer, wine; sister, brother — are called out by any member of the group, and all must move (or remain) to the side of the room associated with either the first or second member of the pair. No one can remain in the middle, and the rapidity of movement or steadfastness indicates the clarity of the choice. Because the whole group is involved in the act of choosing, the vulnerability of each person's revelation is reduced. And as in any of these games, the most basic rule from the beginning is that anyone can drop out of the game whenever she or he wishes, without any negative response from the group. This rule is central to differentiating between a therapy group and an ensemble.

While some of these games continued throughout the rehearsal period, the necessity for them diminished within about three weeks, a period that coincided with a beginning of a sense of recognition of individualities and with the choice of a script. The piece that emerged as everyone's preference was *Cross Country* by Susan Miller, a work particularly appropriate to a feminist endeavor because both its story and its structure concern the attempt to establish a distinctly female point of view. Susan Miller is a playwright and intended *Cross Country* to be performed as theater, but she deliberately wrote the 'score' such that, on the page, it resembles a short story more than a script. It thus demands participation in the shaping of the play. This had two advantages for our group and for any feminist ensemble: it removed from our midst the ghost of the playwright-as-authority, and it allowed us to make our own improvisations and writing an authentic production activity. Miller's narrative describes a woman writer-teacher who develops from frustrated dependence on a job and husband she can no longer tolerate to the discovery of an autonomous self. The play provided a strong base without confining our work to the fulfillment of the playwright's vision. *Cross Country* emphasizes women's friendships and displays a critical yet comic version of men and women's relationships. These features met the basic concerns of the group and provided space for the injection of the varied past experiences and fantasies now apparent among us.

Perhaps because we were able to recognize the generosity in the form in which Miller's script has been made public, the task of casting the production was surprisingly easy and uncompetitive. After ascertaining how many of the group now wished to perform (the number was greater than it had been at the beginning and included a half dozen people who had never been on stage), I consulted with those most interested in writing, and together we devised a division of roles that would enable each person who so desired to participate fully in performance. This was a critical step because it necessitated significant intervention on my part as 'teacher' and because it meant some manipulation of Miller's narrative. Two reconstructions of the text were involved: all minor characters were conceived of as male and female choruses from which specific individuals would emerge, and Perry, the central female character, became two women – one of whom would present her narrative, objectified voice and the other of whom would play the more dramatic, Perry-as-present subject. At the end of the play, these two characters would merge, and the woman playing the narrator would join the female chorus. This division was in fact not so much a transformation of the given text as it was a retention of the double voices apparent in Miller's narrative, voices that in drama would conventionally be merged into one role.[5] The creation of a two-voiced Perry not only dispersed attention and responsibility, but suggested a subversive, polyphonic voice similar to that described by Julia Kristeva in her discussion of Bakhtin.[6]

The playwriting subgroup and I described the roles to the potential cast and sent them home to contemplate which role each thought most appropriate to her/his interests and abilities. We had already read through the narrative script a number of times; each member of the group had heard her/his own voice speaking a variety of roles. How much of the result was the luck of well-distributed desire, how much a matter of good tools of self-analysis and cooperation, I cannot say. When the class returned, though, no two people were in conflict over any one role and each asked for a role that was entirely appropriate and possible. More than one woman in the group was willing, perhaps even eager, to play the non-narrative Perry, which still remained the most demanding role in the play-to-be. Yet all yielded easily to the member of the group who asked for that role with clear conviction and who had both substantial performance experience and the relevant personal experience of having a child. No try-outs were ever, therefore, called for, and the elimination of this highly competitive moment in production meant that rehearsals began in an ambiance of mutual support.

The rehearsal period, which extended through the next five weeks of the course, was at once more fertile and more conflict-ridden than the first stage of initiation. We agreed upon divisions of labor, with non-performers taking major responsibilities for writing, video production, design, publicity, assistant directing and stage management. While the necessity of such divisions was accepted, however, the separation of the whole into task-forces provoked immediate and resonant fear that the ensemble would no longer function as a whole. There was also a genuine concern that a hierarchical evaluation of kinds of work would become embedded in our endeavors. I was particularly committed to eradicating the persistent division in theater between actors and 'technicians,' a structure that too frequently leads to an assumption that the performers are fragile and vulnerable, yet all-important — and that everyone else is there to support them. Although this has been a concern of many contemporary theater ensembles, it is a particularly crucial area of reconfiguration in a feminist context. To accomplish social change, work often considered trivial must be acknowledged as significant. Some reversal of normal orders of dominant and subordinate cultures was already built into our structure by the very fact that only three of the six men in the group were performers. Nonetheless, the possibility loomed large for either infantilizing the women as egocentric stars or simply switching roles without challenging their meanings.

The group's response to these problems was a covenant that while each person would have major and minor responsibilities, everyone would participate in at least two aspects of production. The method by which we would create final scripts — one for live performance, one for video — was also intended to sustain integration. Each night for the first three weeks of rehearsal, we would improvise from predetermined paragraphs and patches of dialogue in Miller's piece; those not performing at the time would comprise a dramaturgical subgroup whose task it was to discuss the strengths and weaknesses of the improvisations with me and the performers and then to record what they had seen and heard, amending and structuring the raw material into more formal scenes. The 'writers' were to display their findings to the group as a whole every few days, so that everyone had a chance to criticize the script in process. At the same time, those preparing for video production would observe rehearsals and shoot sketches of the rehearsal process both because of the inherent value of such footage and to ensure that the video production concept was strategically consistent with the ensemble's sense of its overall performance strategies. Finally, we established a rule that each member of the group must attend at least two rehearsals a week, no matter what her/his individual responsibilities, and that we would all meet regularly once a week. (Not everyone, however, fully understood the importance of problematizing the division of labor, and many of our later controversies resulted from narrow and individualistically conceived definitions of tasks.)

It was at just this point in the course that the men enrolled began to express their discomfort with feelings of marginality in the group as a whole. The theater games and discussions of feminist plays and criticism had evoked from the women a rush of anecdotes of oppression, powerlessness and role-confusion, and our first improvisations toward a script accelerated that process. One of those improvisations was based on an interview between Dan, Perry's ex-husband and a reporter, who is seeking background for a story about Perry's new-found success as a writer. Susan Miller's score for this scene includes a painfully honest moment in which Dan says, 'Well, for a long time, I thought she was me.' Work on this scene, as well as subsequent ones that present the unraveling of Dan and Perry's marriage, gave the women in the class permission for expressions of their own rage at men. Ironically, this was true especially for women in the class who had, at the beginning, expressed their fears that the course would have a man-hating motif. A number of these women were now flipping back and forth in as yet unacknowledged or unresolved contradictions: it was not uncommon at this stage to hear the same woman refuse to come to a rehearsal on a given night because her boyfriend would not let her and then, a moment later, erupt at a memory of a man calling her 'chick.'

In part because they were on the outside of these eruptions, the men in the class became more quickly aware than the women that the class was becoming politicized. Almost unnoticed by many of the women, the men were growing increasingly silent during class discussions, although they were talking to each other after class and eventually sought me out — outside of class bounds. To their credit, there was little hostility in the men's distress, and no one was about to drop the class. But they shared a sense of being seen as the enemy, and most were grappling with the possibility that they *were* the enemy. They were caught and confused by a combination of shock, guilt and recognition in the stories they were hearing, and while they felt empathetic and privileged to be allowed to hear this 'women's talk,' their strongest feelings were of the displeasure of exclusion from a group in which they wanted to be full members.

These half-hidden tensions exploded unexpectedly in the second week of rehearsal in the context of a scene in which Perry asserts her power. She has just posted a note on her office door saying, 'I have gone to the South of France,' and then quickly replaced it with another that reads, 'Term papers not welcome here.' She has also drawn a crowd of students by tossing papers at random on the floor. Perry at first responds nonchalantly to the protests of the one male student who assertively enters her office, telling him pleasantly that an appropriate student response would be to rewrite the papers and 'make them better.' When he persists and escalates his protests in the language of threat and exploitation — 'Don't jack us off. Just don't' — she responds by aggressively putting her arms around his neck and kissing him. 'Now get the hell out of here,' she commands and, as he hesitates, she kisses him again, and then once more, saying, 'Go. Allez.' The scene ends with the young man's exit, but Miller directs: 'Not without [his] first touching her breasts. And then [he goes] not without considerable effort.'

To be fair, I should acknowledge that even without its sex-role reversals, this is not a readily accessible scene for students to play. The conflicts it engendered may have been exacerbated rather than reduced by the perspicacity of the woman playing Perry, who instantly understood her character's power and liberation in the scene and played the part accordingly with capricious joy. It may, in fact, have been her supreme control over the moment, even the very first time we tried it, that provoked her co-player's confusion. Whatever the direct cause, instead of approaching Perry hesitantly and literally 'touching' her breasts, the man playing the student strode towards her and fiercely, with overt erotic impulse, grabbed and held each of her breasts. The actress and everyone else watching were visible disconcerted; the man playing the role, however, was puzzled that I would ask why he had grabbed her that way. We explained that Perry had established herself as the source of power and control, and that what the 'student' was doing was testing her and a new set of rules, not assaulting or making passionate love. By reversing the rules of both student-teacher and male-female games, Perry had made herself mysterious and impenetrable; unless he were extraordinarily violent or crazy, the young man would no more grab her breasts and caress them than he would disfigure a painting in a museum. He might, however, fleetingly touch a painting — or a breast — to test its reality and to determine limits.

What at first might have been dismissed as a momentary difference of interpretation soon became a locus of sexual politics for the class. In subsequent rehearsals of this scene — deliberately postponed for a few nights — tension only increased. The man playing the role of the male student insisted on the correctness of his initial interpretation, essentially on grounds that 'no man would do otherwise.' The conflict was complicated by the presence in the ensemble of his female lover, a woman for whom I and others had unhesitant affection and respect. Hours of talk seemed only to plunge us deeper into a mire of misunderstanding and, even when I violated one of my own cardinal rules and demonstrated the kind of touch most of us felt appropriate to the moment, the actor responded with a different, but even more eroticized, gesture than previously.

Only gradually did we allow ourselves genuinely to hear what the actor was trying in words and deeds to convey: he could not imagine any response other than sexual arousal to the kisses of an attractive female teacher, and he could not project anything but aggression in response to a woman's exhibition of power. Our tendency to reduce his obstinance to a peculiar and personal sexism was wrong; we assumed, too facilely, that the man could leap into the role of the sexually exploited person — but everything in his experience refuted the possibility of such a role for a man. This is not to condone his understanding but to emphasize our disturbing insight that this was not an idiosyncratic situation or one that was to be overcome just by pointing out its problems. All of our attempts to 'enlighten' the male actor had been based on accounts by the women of incidents in which men in positions of power had made sexual approaches to them; other men in the group were troubled by the whole situation, caught between their empathy for their symbolic brother and their discomfort with what was starkly wrong. We were all reminded that parallels do not intersect, and for the actor to find some non-possessive, unconventional way to approach the woman's breasts, he had also to be able to imagine a world utterly different from anything he knew. We had asked the actor to think of himself in that moment as a woman, but that was insufficient: he had to conjure up a world in which women had power and used it, and in which men recognized that fact and were changed by their knowledge. Once we were able to admit the complexity of his task, the actor was freed to attempt affable imitation of what he thought we wanted, and that, in the end, was better than where we had begun.

Our next crisis involved a scene between two women and had the fortunate secondary effect of relieving the pressure on the men. The setting was the kitchen of Perry's best friend, Lois. Perry has come to announce an imminent breakdown, or, more likely, her imminent departure from her husband, her child, her job, this town. Lois reads this news as desertion — of *her*. I had known for some time that the scene was not working, but both actresses were so engaging and so self-critical that I had felt certain they would discover for themselves what was missing. They never did, however, so finally, at the end of one run-through, I asked why, in a scene where Perry says, 'My Lois, you're as basic as the day we fell in love,' neither woman ever touched the other. Their identical reactions could have slipped unnoticed into a slapstick comedy. Both women turned straight toward me with eyes wide open and mouths literally dropping. One of them then recovered sufficiently to articulate the obvious answer: did I, she asked, think Lois and Perry were lovers? 'Yes,' I answered, unhesitatingly. 'But how did you know that?' came the next question. I responded by returning to the dialogue in Miller's original score, but that meant that all of us spent the next three days confronting the desire to suppress the erotic components of this friendship between two women.

It is not difficult to imagine the conversations that ensued. Let it suffice to add here that, for a time, the results of my query were disastrous in terms of performance of the scene. One of the women players moved quickly to a view that the relationship between Lois and Perry was at the least sexually ambiguous: the other firmly resisted any possibility of a lesbian relationship but agreed, as a dutiful actress, to include a few physical gestures of affection. That, in turn, transformed a scene that had been poignant and committed to one that was so awkward it would have provoked laughter had the tension between the actresses not been so obviously acute. Then, one night, nearing our opening, we ran the whole play and suddenly the kitchen scene had a new integrity. Near its end, the two characters embraced with a rare and complex tenderness. Our sparse rehearsal space resonated with the respectful silence of the whole ensemble. 'What happened?' I brought myself, finally, to ask. 'Well,' said the woman who had been most resistant, 'I stopped fighting that line about falling in love. There was no good reason for them not to make love.'

One more major hurdle lay before us. In the middle of the rehearsal period, I had asked the ensemble to talk about the mode of presentation of a scene in which Miller calls for Dan, the husband, to appear naked except for boots and an umbrella. On paper, this moment was essentially comic, but there was an undeniable difference between reading about a man in this minimalist costume and seeing him thus on stage — especially if, as would be the case for the spectator, you were wholly unprepared for nudity. The actor playing the role immediately stated that he would do whatever the group agreed upon. With that clear, the minor worry about the inhibitions of our university audience seemed to me of less concern than the nature of this gesture in a feminist context.

The theoretical grounds on which to base this decision were sufficiently elusive that the group initially sought alternatives to complete nudity. As each suggestion was raised — a jock strap, wildly patterned boxer shorts, neutral white underwear, pajamas — it was rejected. Reading the ensemble's dissatisfaction with any of these solutions as a silent confirmation that the scene had to be played in the nude, the next time we rehearsed the show the actor found a natural moment on stage to remove his clothes, opened his umbrella, and continued with his lines. For most of us, this unanticipated unveiling made clear that the visual image had to be exactly what we saw before us. It was an epiphanic instant in which we understood that the strategy of the gesture was not to titillate the audience, but to overturn and clarify the common exploitation of the nude *female* body. Forced to regard the male nude body framed by an umbrella and boots, we recognized the inclination to objectify the man; we were also moved by his vulnerability, perhaps particularly because this was live theater. We are inundated by various media images of the nude or partially clothed female body that we pay only lip-service to its demeaning objectification: we are too calloused to acknowledge the vulnerability it implies. This was a subversive act that called attention to the inseparability of body and person in men and women.

Unfortunately, we were too ready to congratulate the actor and ourselves. In the next evening's pre-rehearsal discussion, two women in the ensemble exploded with rage at the previous night's 'exhibition.' They had, they said, been disturbed and surprised by the nudity itself, but they were even more distressed by what they felt to be a violation of trust and the will of the group. Since we had never explicitly agreed that there was no substitution for nudity, they had thought the issue was unresolved. Why had the actor not asked permission of us first?

The careful attempts of the rest of the ensemble to acknowledge and assuage this unexpected anger succeeded with one of the women, but not the other. The real problem, it became evident, was not a matter of the fact or theory of nudity, but of the feelings and fact of exclusion of one woman from the group. Among students possessing a range of familiarity with, and interest in, feminism, she had the most unpredictable responses to feminist principles. I had to acknowledge that we had thus colluded in creating a context in which this woman had not been fully involved in group decisions. Her articulation of this truth left us to face the unresolved issues. How does a group committed to collaborative production make decisions, particularly in the absence of an authoritative leader? What are the signs of consensus, and is consensus itself a necessity? If there is a 'party line' to which one member will never agree, does one cast that person aside? In a society where most classes are not like the one I have described and where many women are like the one among us who stood aside, what do we lose in losing these women? I ended the class, despite a real sense of achievement among most of the students, with a nagging suspicion that what we had accomplished — including the eventual success of the performance itself — was only a whisper in the wind if it could not touch precisely the kind of student who was least likely to elect such a course.

This is not to denigrate the possibilities of ensemble production for feminist teaching. On the contrary. What I, as teacher, took away from the Feminist Theater and Video Ensemble was a deep belief that the mode of working with students was as important to a feminist classroom as the texts we use. I will teach the Feminist Theater Ensemble again. More important, however, is the effect it has had on my teaching in other contexts — especially in large, introductory lecture courses. It is there that we need to begin — with peer-group criticism, collaborative writing, mini-productions in a variety of media — to train students to think together, so that they not only have the ideas of a feminist, but the means to become one.

Notes

1 Although I take full responsibility for both the narrative and the course described within it, I should here acknowledge that the Feminist Theater and Video Ensemble, and many of my reflections upon it, belong to all those who participated. I refrain from listing the names of the class members only because it is likely that some would wish to remain anonymous.
   Note: all Citations from Susan Miller's *Cross Country* are from the published version in *West Coast Plays*, vol. 1, Los Angeles.

2 Juliet Mitchell, *Woman's Estate*, New York: 1971, p.96.

3 Honor Moore, quoted in Phyllis Mael, 'Interview with Honor Moore,' (Los Angeles, April 1978), *Chrysalis*, no. 10, 1980.

4 See Helen Chinoy and Linda Jenkins, *Women in American Theater*, New York: 1981.

5 Although I did not know this until later, a colleague, Robin Hunt, had once made a similar division of Perry's role in a production she directed of *Cross Country*. (I should add here, too, that I was initially inclined to create three Perrys, but was persuaded by the ensemble that this would create too much confusion for the actors and audience.)

6 Julia Kristeva, *Desire in Language*, New York: 1980, pp.173-4 and pp.64-90.

PART THREE

Teacher as other

9

Pink elephants: confessions of a black feminist in an all-white mostly male English department of a white university somewhere in God's country

Erlene Stetson

I am an oddity. I fear the malady exists in me rather than in them. I take momentary solace in a poster glimpsed in my graduate years: 'Just because you are paranoid doesn't mean they are not out to get you.'

I am paranoid. I have a PhD that allows me a provisional stay. It has granted me five(!) keys. One allows me to visit the lounge area where I can meet others with a key. The second gives me access to the elevator. The third (the one I use most) lets me into the Y and Z enclosed space that is my 'office.' It has a number. Still another allows me to enter the English department office at odd hours. The last — the one I use least — allows me to visit the faculty women's club.

Given these signs, I cannot help but know that I have access. I know that somewhere some affirmative action goal has been met. That the fact of my five(!) keys proves there is no institutional exclusion — that the problem of admission is solved is obvious even to me.

But I want to enter. I walk down the long length of hall to get to my office that is next to a fire extinguisher that sits recessed into the wall. My office is smaller as a result of it. I tell myself that I shall start no fires and that I shall put none out. I also tell myself that it is a blessing and not a curse. When you are black and alone in an English department, the will to believe that someone cares is a strong one.

I open my door by placing the key in the diagonal slot opening. It works. I am always surprised when it does. I walk in where I see all the signs of some totally chaotic presence, my own. It is here at my desk, replete with an institutional perquisite of tape-holder and stapler, that I try to make some connection with research and teaching. It is here that, after having made my entrance, I struggle for parity.

My door is open. A young black woman passes — returns — reads the name on the card on the wall by the door. She doesn't know that my first name is misspelled and doesn't need to know.

A black woman wants to talk. I have no time, having just experienced some vague associative memory, the primal chord of the coercive pull of teaching, research and service. Her need hasn't the ring of any of these.

She confesses that she is looking for the black woman's movement. She is incredulous when I admit that I, too, am looking. She thinks I am the movement. She refuses to believe me when I tell her that I am not. I tell her of my longing to find it; the coherence. She is unconvinced. We are two black women in a white university. A black woman student and a black woman faculty experience each other. We face the fact of our alienation and disaffection.

Like the luckless Alice Hindman of Sherwood Anderson's *Winesburg, Ohio* we confess that we had better be careful or else we might do something awful. Ours is a poor wonderland. She leaves and I close my door.

There is one of me and many of them. Some days I easily see them turning into doubles and quadruples. They overwhelm me by numbers, their sheer duplication. Almost all are pipesuckers. The rest come with elbow-patches. These clichés are real! On these days it is not safe to do other than keep my door closed, my lights off.

When I emerge, they are there. Waiting. Civil. Civility is the curse invented by English department academics.

It is time to take the elevator down. One is already waiting. I dare not take a waiting elevator. It looks too much like a set-up. I want to go to the first floor. To get there I need to use my key. I hesitate. It is the thought that if it presumably could take me where I want to go, what would stop it from taking me where I don't want to go?

In my struggle for parity, I am told that my research boils down to a simple statement. Really? Wanting that coherence, thinking maybe I would hear it in the most unexpected of places, I eagerly ask what it is that all my research 'boils down to.' Desultorily, I am told the answer. It is that black women have been left out of the literary canon. The pipesuckers are not in jest. There is no humor in this place.

We sit in the women's faculty lounge. I am black and am told that

I am rising in the ranks and leaving a considerable number of castrated black males in so doing. I am, at the moment, giddy, happy and silently acknowledging to myself that it took several generations to put me here. The white woman administrator is speaking confidentially to me of her difficulties. She wants to be taken seriously. Apparently, she has no castrated bodies on her conscience and thereby has a right to feel that she is not taken seriously enough. She speaks of our need to establish a mutual support system. This I agree, but I miss a lot — due, no doubt, to the wine I am drinking. To emphasize her point, she bangs the table with her fist. She perceives an antidote, but all I can hear is her saying that 'Otherwise we haven't a Chinaman's chance.' I realize that I don't know who to fight anymore.

Notes

1   Originally published in *Sojourner: A Third World Women's Research Newsletter*, no. 3, November 1979, pp.1-2. Reprinted with permission of the author.

10

Is there room for me in the closet? Or, my life as the only lesbian professor

Judith McDaniel

I didn't know what to expect. I had never done it before: moved to a new job and community — and announced that I was a lesbian. I knew why I was doing it. I could think of no other way to live sanely. My announcement was the solution to a black depression that had felt like walking a tunnel with no light at the end. It was survival: the only way I could imagine facing a new life. I jeopardized no one but myself, I thought. I was going alone.

But I didn't know how to announce it. I went to my first faculty meetings. I taught my first classes. I assigned *Rubyfruit Jungle*. I wore a ring with a double woman's symbol, but almost no one noticed. A woman who lives with a woman lover is a lesbian; a woman who lives alone is single.

One of my students did notice. She came and sat in my office to talk about George Eliot, but the double woman's symbol she wore on a small chain around her neck spoke more eloquently than her words. We began to speak about our lesbianism, the problems of organizing and running a women's coalition on campus.

One afternoon during the first hectic month, two faculty women invited me to have coffee. Except for department functions, it was my first social contact. My students had told me that one of the women was a lesbian, but no one must know; the other, they said, was a feminist with a 'closet' boyfriend.

We spoke briefly about our work.

'Why did you leave your last job?' they asked.

'I was fired,' I said, 'with another woman. We were too "feminist."'

'Did you sue them?' one woman asked.

'It was difficult,' I said. 'We were both lesbians.'

My comment lay like something unpleasant in the middle of the table. No one referred to it. As our half-hour chat ended and we stood to leave, one of the women turned to me and asked angrily, 'Just where do you expect to fit into this community?'

'I don't know,' I responded. And I didn't. It was a question I would ask myself many times.

Not everyone responded with fear. My students asked me to come to their first women's coalition meeting, where we shared ideas and experiences. Another young faculty woman was there. She noticed my ring and began to speak enthusiastically about Charlotte Bunch's speech on lesbian feminism at the Socialist-Feminist Conference. She wondered whether I'd be interested in a feminist study group. We began to plan for the future.

At a formal dinner for the trustees and faculty, I sat across the table from a faculty wife who told me she was a feminist and — very confidentially — that more students didn't attend women's coalition meetings because of rumors that *lesbians* were in control.

'Oh,' I said, gesturing magnanimously with my wine glass, 'that's why I always say I'm a lesbian. It helps other women to know where I'm coming from politically.'

Her eyes glazed and her wine glass thumped on the table, belying her casual attitude.

'Oh, really,' she said, as her gaze cleared.

In the classroom I was less daring. An audience of one is less intimidating than a group of thirty. At the beginning of the semester, however, I had assigned *Rubyfruit Jungle* in my 'Introduction to Fiction' course — as an example of the modern picaresque novel. During the first weeks, as we struggled through Dickens and Virginia Woolf, I waited anxiously for a comment from someone who might have read the back-cover blurb announcing gaily that *Rubyfruit Jungle* was about 'growing up lesbian in America.' Not a word from my students. When the time came, I announced that *Rubyfruit Jungle* was due on Monday. I told them about the picaresque novel and Fielding and socially unacceptable or shocking behavior. And then I stopped. I couldn't say the word 'lesbian' in my own classroom. I spent that weekend in a panic. How the hell was I going to teach this book? What could I say about it? Was my own sexual preference relevant to teaching this novel? What would I say if they asked me whether I was a lesbian?

By Monday I had resolved nothing. I had spent all weekend preparing a class for which I was totally unprepared. I walked into the classroom, perched casually on the edge of my desk, and asked vaguely, 'Well, what did you think of *Rubyfruit Jungle*?' Responses ranged from 'best book in the course,' 'I loved it, 'she was so funny,' to 'weird' and 'it was perverted.' Now I had something to deal with; we worked intensely with the novel and the students' attitude for three meetings. At the end of our last scheduled class on the book, a woman raised her hand and hesitantly asked, 'Um, can I ask you, um, it may not, um, but . . .' Here it comes, I thought wryly, my moment of truth.

'Ask,' I said bravely, 'Is Rita Mae Brown a *lesbian*?'

'Yes,' I answered laughing, dismissing the class. 'Yes, for sure she is.'

Three years later, after many such encounters, I have begun to understand those feelings of fear and insecurity which I experienced in first teaching a lesbian work. The students I teach have been raised in a society that fears and hates homosexuals. When my students did not know I was a lesbian, and when the material we were dealing with made homosexuality a topic of discussion or reference, I was in an extremely vulnerable position. In talking about *Rubyfruit Jungle*, my students — assuming they were among a peer-heterosexual group — could easily have said things that were threatening and hostile to me.

What I feared then happened — in fact, this year. A student wrote a poem about how unfortunate it is that the pansy, a delicate and complex flower, has been so maligned. In discussing the poem, I assumed she meant that the flower and male homosexuals — those named for it — were maligned.

'No,' she said, 'isn't it awful to name faggots and queers after such a sweet flower?' I went numb. I stared at her, momentarily unable to speak. My impulse was to scream, to let her know that I took this affront personally. I knew I could silence her, if not change her mind. But *this* was what I had feared in that first class. I was personally assaulted, and whatever I did to correct her, I was still left shaken and raw.

'I will not allow those attitudes or that language to be expressed in this classroom,' I told her. But I did not say, 'I am one.'

I do my best teaching when I can assume that all of the students in my class know I am a lesbian. Whatever the particular focus of the literature we are discussing, I encourage students to bring their own experiences to the literature and to relate literature to their own lives. I need to be able to do the same, and my sexual preference is one important part of my identity and experience. When I introduced a course on the poetry of Adrienne Rich, it seemed natural in talking about her journey from daughter-in-law to lesbian feminist for me to identify with that process.

Within my wider social community, I gradually became identified as a lesbian – a free spirit, as it were. I had hoped I would find a lover in my new community. I had expected I would. I did not expect – and did not understand until much later – that I was a hot sexual prospect: a new dyke in town.

I also applied what I called Rule Number One: teachers do not become involved with students. At the time, it seemed a clear statement of intention to me – one that would make relationships with my lesbian students open, above board and simple. I believed if I stated my understanding of the contract between us, that would be sufficient. From the very beginning of my contact with students in this new job, I made Rule Number One an open subject of discussion.

Students seemed to think Rule Number One was funny. It usually came up in those conversations about male professors who had affairs with their female students. We all had opinions about such things. Mine was that power in such relationships was unequal, and I presumed therefore that the relationship was exploitative; hence Rule Number One, which I have never broken, I explained. Laughter. Insistence on exceptional relationships. Tension. And I did not realize that Rule Number One left unstated the most essential understanding of my relationship to these students: that an affair or the slightest implication of seduction would make me subject to administrative and possibly legal scrutiny of a kind rarely experienced by a heterosexual teacher.

By the end of the first semester, I had found a new lover – not in my own community, but within commuting distance. I had not told many women about her. When she moved in with me, I did not consider it a community project. My love life was my own, I thought. A student confided in me later that when my lover had appeared on the scene, her friend had seemed shaken, come late to class, and scribbled in the margin of her notebook, 'I'm going to commit suicide. J.M. has a new roommate.'

'Why did she do that?' I asked, puzzled.

'She told us she was having an affair with you,' my student answered.

'Did the other students believe that?'

'We did for a while,' was her reply. So much for Rule Number One.

Then I began to understand a confrontation with that student which had occurred mid-year. We had been working together on several projects. I had thought her a friend, until she walked into my office one day and announced that she couldn't work with me any more. I was exploiting her. I was a fascist. She was smiling. I looked at her, trying to decide between the expression of my fury and the efficacy of a low-key response. Could she be more specific, I asked, watching her tight grin. No. She had nothing else to say. Her attitude toward me the rest of that year was one of belligerent confrontation. The student had lost track of reality. In lying about our relationship within her own peer community, she had taken an enormous risk — a risk I didn't understand at first. But it was a response to tensions she must have felt in my openly lesbian presence on campus. In the beginning, I had not understood that I would create such fear and tension. I had thought coming out was something I would do by myself, implicating only myself.

I understand now that any woman who associates with me must somehow deal with what my lesbianism means to her. For a lesbian who dares not be exposed, associating with a 'known' lesbian is extraordinarily risky. For those who are not even 'guilty,' association can feel risky. A married faculty woman with whom I have worked closely confessed this year that she was afraid to be seen sitting with me in faculty meetings. It was not a feeling she was proud of, but she *was* afraid. Students who are unsure of their own sexuality are threatened: I am a role model who says it's OK to be a lesbian, implying a permission that can be liberating or terrifying. Students who are lesbian but have not come out publicly feel pushed to do so by my example, creating fear and tension. Originally, of course, I had expected only support from those who seemed logically to be my closest friends and community.

I don't think my example is a harmful one. Far from it. Even when it causes fear and tension. I believe that stress can create an opportunity for growth that didn't exist so clearly before. Difference needs to be recognized and allowed to exist. But I have no prognosis for my own success or failure, which in a college teaching career is measured by continued contracts and tenure. My work, much of which has a feminist or lesbian feminist perspective, will be judged by an institution which is by its very nature patriarchal and heterosexist. My open presence as a lesbian challenges many of the assumptions on which such an institution is based. And I will never know whether my work as a writer and teacher is being judged, or my lifestyle. One of my colleagues has told me that my work with gay studies is looked on benignly: 'I hope we're all open-minded here,' he said. Another specifically said my perspective as a lesbian feminist was 'too narrow for this department.' The teaching half of my professional life depends upon the continued support of an institution.

As the 'only lesbian professor' on campus, my visibility creates isolation. Within my department and college, I have no peers — no one who shares my personal or political view of the world. Dealing with the alienation produced by such a situation is consuming and exhausting, but the alienation of living a hidden life was far more debilitating to me. I don't really want to go back into the closet. It's too late. And too crowded. Living life in the open has been personally liberating and has felt enormously healthy. Not simple. Not without risk and challenge. But healthy.

Note

1   Originally published in *Heresies*, no. 7, spring 1979, pp.36-8. Reprinted with permission of the author.

11

A male feminist in a women's college classroom

Diedrick Snoek

Feminist pedagogy means teaching in the context of awareness of female oppression. My first exploration into what this might mean began in 1970, when a colleague and I combined our respective seminars into a single experiment that was to consider issues of character-formation in women as represented in fiction and psychology. We were convinced that such considerations were painfully absent from the curricula of our respective departments, but had to break a number of rules in setting up such a collaborative course: all new seminars were to be reviewed by a college committee which required long and closely argued justifications before approving such innovations; seminars were understood to represent the culmination of long and arduous training in a discipline — not new ventures into unknown 'interdisciplinary' terrain; and co-teaching, while not expressly forbidden, was thought to pose such insoluble issues of credit, grades and teaching-loads that it was in practice virtually unknown. All these circumstances lent an air of adventure to our undertaking that served to carry us through our own terror of not knowing what we were getting into. Only one thing was certain: we would not lack students.

The course plan was simple enough: we would read a number of works of English and American literature, carefully selected for the seriousness of their attempt to present women characters who had thoughts and feeling of their own, and juxtapose this reading with works on the psychology of women by such authors as Karen Horney, Clara Thompson, Simone de Beauvoir and even Helene Deutsch. The effects of this procedure turned out to be complicated and electrifying:

after a period of sullen silence and plaintive questioning about what they were to learn from all this reading, our students burst forth into a variety of forms of imaginative expression. They clearly regarded this as a course in self-exploration and began writing journals, short stories, poems and, above all, autobiography — without regard to their major discipline. We, in turn, found it increasingly difficult to 'control' the discussion, or to 'keep ourselves out of it'; we began to set aside periods of each class to consider the dynamics of the group itself in an effort to make our students more aware of the possible relation between their emotions and the way the class collectively handled issues of authority, participation, rivalry and intimacy.

As it happened, my collaborator was denied tenure in her department and took up a position in the experimental college of a neighboring university. We decided to continue our joint venture by offering the same course in both institutions — and wound up teaching two very different groups of students back to back. On Tuesday nights, we would meet psychology students who thought themselves avant-garde and feminist, and who were taking the course for credit in their major in my college (one of the renowned 'Seven Sisters'). On Wednesday nights, we taught a group of women who, while meeting in a room in the university's new women's center, were by no means sure they were feminists and had little idea how the credits they would earn for this 'experimental' course might affect their choice of major, vocation, or other future plans. They professed a general interest in the subject-matter of 'women' and expressed a good deal of doubt about themselves as students.

Despite our largely succcessful attempt to follow the same syllabus with both groups, the differences between the two classes were dramatic. The general studies group made friends in class, complained about the heavy reading-load, and followed our attempts to theorize with skepticism. But our discussions on Wednesday nights had an honesty and richness of response that kept everyone coming back eager for the next session. The students in the psychology seminar competed with each other for air-time, offered sweeping and sometimes insightful generalizations, seemed intent on proving the merits of a feminist point of view in understanding every author we discussed, but by and large resisted empathetic identification with the fictional characters we read about, avoided personal discussion, and formed few bonds with each other. We were well along in the semester before the turning-point came in this class. We were reading Kate Chopin's novel *The*

Awakening, beginning to explore connections between sex and power, when one of our students, haltingly but persistently, began to talk about the unwanted sexual attention she was getting from one of her (male) lab instructors. As I remember, we teachers had to resist several attempts by other students to ignore or silence her before the class as a whole began to respond. The style of this class remained intellectual and competitive, but previously silent students participated more and were more successful in bringing their own experience as women to bear upon the reading.

A second memory from this pair of classes deserves some mention here. My friend and I arrived one evening somewhat unprepared and found also that most members of the class had not really read the assignment. On the spot, we asked each person to pair off with a partner and to take turns telling the stories of their mothers' lives. Our intention was simply to focus on generational differences and to introduce some historical consciousness, but the exercize took much longer than we anticipated and clearly generated a high level of energy. When we returned to the group as a whole, our students insisted on sharing not their sense of history, but their excitement over unsuspected strengths they discerned in their mothers' life-stories. In so far as they were able to reconstruct these stories from family lore, hints and gossip, it also became evident that there were large gaps in what they knew of their mothers' lives. How is it, they asked, that despite vast differences between us in personality, background and relationship to our mothers, we *all* know so little about their lives after marriage?

Suspecting that their mothers' lives were at least as interesting as their own, several of the participants followed up this session with extended conversations with their mothers in order to discover more. And what discoveries came to light! One student of Greek extraction, for example, found that her mother's 'emigration' had come about when she decided, as a 17-year-old young woman, to walk out of her inland village to Athens. There she had embarrassed her city relatives in finding passage to the USA rather than endure the sexual harassment of an uncle. We repeated this exercize with less spontaneity but similar results in the other class and concluded, as teachers, that one's mother's life is a powerful entry into women's experience and serves to raise all the right questions about 'ordinary' lives.

This early experience taught me several things. First, it helped me to overcome the notion that being male somehow disqualified me from leading a class focused on women's experience. For that, I am indebted to my friend and colleague, Maurianne Adams. Her confidence and skill served to embolden me so that I could proceed on my own. Second, and perhaps more important, the whole experience seemed to underline the importance of exploring the personal relevance of the material we are considering. I began to see my task as a teacher to enable students to set aside their narrow expectations of getting 'the point,' 'mastering' the literature, or out-competing their fellow-students for 'the best grades'; instead, my aim is to empower them to discover their own point of view, their own voice and their common interests as women. Third, the experience of dealing with *fiction*, as well as with explicitly psychological theory and findings, confronted me with the painful task of sorting out the respective legitimations of scientific and humanistic scholarship and what my loyalty to them was: it ultimately served to liberate me from certain self-imposed restraints while discovering the parallels between the modes of analysis practiced in literary criticism and the psychological analysis of lives. After years of dealing with 'hard' data from surveys and experiments, I used my sabbatical leave to turn to the study of psychotherapy and became familiar with the necessarily tentative and constantly changing 'soft' data of autobiographical narrative.

Having broken out of the barriers imposed by my original training, I was ready, a few years later, to propose a course on adult development that would focus on women and to persuade my department to adopt it. Called 'The Study of Lives,' the course takes a decidedly life-historical approach and teaches theoretical ideas (and their limitations) through class discussion of 'cases.' The ideal case consists of a life-history narrative produced in the searching manner characteristic of psychological anamnesis. I was fortunate in my first classes to have access to a long and carefully done life-history that had been presented as a doctoral dissertation, because cases of this kind dealing with women's lives proved hard to find. Robert and Jane Hallowell Coles's two volumes of *Women of Crisis* proved to be helpful in that they narrate their subjects' life-stories with respect for the integrity of the subjects' own words. Other good material could be found in Sara Ruddick's and Pamela Daniels's *Working It Out*, because each contributor writes a first-person account of finding her true vocation.

The case approach provided a method excellently suited for empowering students in the classroom. I quickly learned to discipline myself to offer my own interpretations sparingly (if at all), and relied instead on the students' developing sense that even if the subject of the case was very different from themselves, they often possessed in their experience *as women* the means for imaginative identification. The fact that I often *felt* at some disadvantage in being a male also helped to diminish the students' initial tendency to rely on my authority in the discussions. There are no absolutely right answers in making sense of people's life-histories, only more or less plausible interpretations given the internal evidence of what the subject says and how she says it. The result is that the class must learn to search the text of a case in a collaborative process, in which one comment builds on another to enrich our understanding. My role is to ask thought-provoking questions, to listen well to what is said (I usually record the gist of each comment on the blackboard), and to keep insisting that all interpretations be checked against the subject's own narrative for corroborative or disconfirming evidence. Thus I use my authority as teacher to support the authority of the text.[1]

It did not take me long to learn, from journals and after-class conversations, that there are many things students wish to say for which the classroom does not feel safe enough. Indeed, I am well aware most of the time that there are things about my own reactions to the cases that I wish to censor or hide. I have learned, gradually, that sharing my own personal response to what is being said in the class, however haltingly or passionately, is an essential step in establishing safety. Keeping cool and in control, which is how I would like to be, prevents the hardest and most authentic questions from coming to the surface.

I work on breaking down the anonymity of the class early in the semester by asking each student to tell others what her class, ethnic and religious background is. I also ask each of us to identify one or more things in that background we take pride in or appreciate. Again, I must set the tone by going first. The first part of the instruction helps rapidly to establish that not everyone was brought up in well-to-do, upper-middle-class environments. The second part of the instruction confronts the mixed feelings of shame and pride with which most of us have been saddled by virtue of ethnic and class stereotypes. By gently insisting that all persons identify something in their own background they care about or identify with, we begin to undo some of the harm these stereotypes have done. I know that some teachers feel uneasy about distinguishing between appropriate and inappropriate self-disclosure in the classroom and would not want to use their authority to require such revelation. I do respect genuine refusals, just as I do not force myself to say things that make me too anxious in the particular circumstances. On the other hand, my experience is that most students greet the outcomes of this sharing with relief and pleasure. Perhaps in an 'elite' college like mine, the anxieties about how well one fits the stereotypic image of a student at one of the 'Seven Sisters' are more intense, and there is correspondingly greater relief in discovering how richly diverse the collective experience of the class is. The value of identifying ourselves with our backgrounds shows up later, in that students will sometimes make spontaneous reference to their own background to make sense of the point of view from which they have been thinking about the discussion.

In presenting what goes on in my classroom, I have spoken of it as a place in which the experience of women can be considered in the relative safety of peer discussion. What about the confrontation with hard truths about the misogyny, subordination and isolation that our society's gender system continues to impose on women? If all I have written so far implies that a male teacher can do some of the work that must go into the long process of making visible the experience of women, I do not wish to omit the difficulties and limitations in such a situation. It has been a fact, so far, that expressions of anger and despair — so characteristic of my women colleagues' experience with the feminist classroom — occur relatively rarely in mine. But anger at psychology's neglect of women is common. It is also a fact that while my students express gratitude and appreciation for a course in which the experience of women occupies a place of central interest, exploring their feelings as 'others' in a male-dominated society is still a rare occurrence in my classroom. Perhaps this has to remain the province of the woman-to-woman encounter that can take place mainly in the female-taught classroom. Students must unconsciously identify me with their fathers or brothers: for some, this means keeping me at a guarded distance; for others, that fact seems to be experienced as a relief and permission to enter a world of feminist concerns with a legitimacy of which they had previously been unsure. In both cases their emotional response remains somewhat muted.

Another factor is the self-doubt I feel as a male in the midst of a feminist revolution. At times this has intensified a certain timidity in voicing my convictions in the classroom and a constant self-questioning about how firm those convictions are. What do I regard as a society worth striving for? What are my feelings about, and relations with, other men? How can I feel pride in my maleness while noticing, restraining, and correcting my own chauvinist or comfortable assumption of privileges. I suspect my students know that I am struggling with such questions. Nevertheless, it still surprises me that so few of them question or confront me about it. I am constantly *expecting* more hostility than I do in fact encounter.

What I am doing also presents another hazard, a counterpart to that isolation of women who try to join the common world of men — those whom Adrienne Rich sees as being in danger of 'losing touch with . . . [their] real powers and with the essential condition for all fully realized work: community.' I think that any man who undertakes this work is forced to question deeply why he is doing it. While he may get a welcome hearing in the feminist community, as a man he remains an *ally* and cannot become, in any full sense of the word, a *member* of that community. This makes the male feminist doubly marginal: traitors to the common world of men and hangers-on to the newly forming world of women. For myself, I could not sustain this straddle without some powerful support of women.

Aside from the feelings of loneliness, though, there remains a lack of certainty about who one's audience is — and self-doubts. I think this situation points to a future in which feminist men must reclaim full membership among men and enter the battle for gender equality — not as advocates of women, but for their own and their sons' future.

'The source of any kind of virtue lies in the shock produced by the human intelligence being brought up against a matter devoid of lenience and of falsity.' Simone Weil's comment is a supreme expression of the encounter each good teacher tries to produce in the classroom, and its hoped-for outcome. I have always thought the job of the teacher more than that of facilitating (or compelling) the acquisition of knowledge. I have come to believe that feminism holds the key to all other liberation struggles: it is *male* culture that perpetrates the social forms in which inequality of gender, race and class are cast; *males* who are encouraged to compete for power in that system by exploiting their advantage in it to the maximum extent; and *males* who may reap the rewards of power, status and self-approval for a heroic life. As a man I also know how many 'losers' such a system produces and how fearsome are the sacrifices of self and wholeness demanded of those who play the game. It is a male fear and resentment of this situation, as well as pride and privilege, that hold men in place in such a social system. Women who free themselves — to the extent possible — from psychological and political bondage to the gender system constitute a powerful antidote to male despair at the world ever being otherwise.

I do not mean to sound too optimistic: I do not think that men's envy of liberated women or their secret hope for an end to their own bondage are enough to guarantee a successful outcome to the historical passage humankind is now trying to negotiate. To be whole people whose rationality is balanced by feeling, whose self-love is balanced by a care for others, who respect community and love our home on earth, we require those qualities of humanness that are more easily cultivated in the work of protection, preservation and repair assigned by the sexual division of labor mainly to women. It is not clear to me what circumstances — both inner and outer — will induce men to take up and share this work. I am, however, hopeful.

Note

1 While this is common in teaching literature, it is highly unusual in psychology to consider the implications of phrasing, juxtaposition of ideas, narrative tone and all the other 'literary' devices spontaneously adopted by those who try to tell their life-stories. It inevitably leads students to the question of *why* and *to whom* and *under what circumstances* the tale is told and whether it might be told differently to another person or at a different time. Far from regarding these as weaknesses of life-history data, I celebrate this as recognition of the complexity of self-identity and the value-suffused nature of all psychological data.

PART FOUR

Experience as text

12

Breaking silences: life in the feminist classroom

Nancy Jo Hoffman

It's evening. Women straggle into a large, musty room of the student services building of a state university in the Pacific Northwest. The majority wear American college fashion of jeans and shirts, but some in uniforms have come from work, others in dresses from the dinner dishes of their suburban homes. Their ages range from fourteen (the daughter of a class member) to fifty. Their backgrounds vary: a welfare mother at school supported by the Work-Incentive Program, several teachers and a librarian back at school for credentials, a quotient of women in their twenties enrolled full-time in the university, and several drop-outs from the elite college across the river. They are white, black, and Chicana.

Now there are about forty women and two men in several small groups chatting about *Ariel*, Sylvia Plath's book of poetry and our reading for the week in the course, 'Literature by Women.' We meet in small groups for an hour before this three-hour class because we discovered through the uncomfortable silences in our initial classes that it took more courage and confidence than most women could summon to speak aloud about literature into the expectant void. (Women enroll in such classes with extraordinary hopes — intellectual challenge, clarified identity, a new career — which makes talking even harder.) I, the teacher of the class, circulate from group to group; asking Gloria if she needs a phonograph to play her recordings of black women singers for next week's class; telling Kate why critics call *The Bell Jar* an autobiographical novel; reviewing an argument with Elena, who says she is sure I will be disappointed if I assign for

a final project 'a significant piece of work, a creation you care about.'
In Judy's group are several Plath devotees who have been my students
in a past course, 'Poetry and the Female Consciousness.' As a group,
they have taken the position that, in the final lines of Plath's 'Lady
Lazarus,' the poet intends 'men' to mean males, not all human beings
— a clue to Plath's self-consciousness about womanhood.

This week, Carolyn and Rose, who are particularly interested in
Joyce Carol Oates, assign the class some reading and writing on *The
Wheel of Love*, a collection of her short stories we'll discuss two weeks
hence. (As is usual for us, different students lead the class discussion
each week, after a planning session with me.) Before I have a chance
to speak, there are announcements — an abortion meeting, a time to
plan programs for Women's Studies, a decision on the place of our
brunch the next weekend. 'What we do in Women's Studies is eat,'
a student of mine once said. She was right.

I am in charge of the evening's discussion, having claimed with no
opposition that poetry is difficult, Plath extremely so, and that my
expertise might help. For in this feminist classroom, we say explicitly
that the teacher's power should be abandoned, but not her skills and
knowledge. I play a rarely heard recording of Plath reading 'Lady
Lazarus.' 'Don't let her get you,' I say — a remark which I will take
seriously a few minutes later. We listen: women close their eyes, hearing
the chilling, precise voice, the intonation of hatred. 'Play it again,'
someone asks. I do, and am jolted myself as I hear with puzzlement
Plath's flat, unironic tone as she counts off her suicide attempts: 'This
is Number Three/What a trash/To annihilate each decade . . .' I had
read those lines with sarcasm.

Informally, I set the stage for our discussion. Yes, this is a poem
which seems to grow out of Plath's numerous bouts with death and
certainly the title is a self-mocking reference to herself as one miracu-
lously reborn, like the biblical Lazarus rising from his grave. 'Was
Plath a Jew?' Carolyn asks Judy, our class expert on Plath's biography.
Picking up *Ariel*, she adds, 'Look at all those lines in the poem where
she says her skin is "like a Nazi lampshade," her face "a fine Jew
linen," those accusations that her remains consist of "A cake of soap/
A wedding ring/A gold filling."'

'Well,' answers Judy, 'it confuses me. Her father was not a Jew. He
was born in what is now part of Poland, though his name, native
tongue, and bearing were German. He died when Sylvia was eight —
during the time of Nazi Germany. She's sure got a woman's problem of

figuring out what he meant to her. All I can say is that she turns herself into a Jew because she feels like a victim of persecution. Not hard for a woman. Symbolically, the torturer, her authoritarian father, becomes a German.'

There is silence for a moment; we've talked about father-daughter relationships often. Finally, I remark, more personally, that I get angry with Plath, and with the poem, for although I gasp at the perfection of her isolation, and think the poem consummate art, I feel as though she is accusing *me* of being a Nazi, identifying *me* as a member of 'the peanut-crunching crowd' that troops in to watch her sensational recovery from death. As a woman, I react against her hatred of normalcy, the vortex of despair which is her home. I hear the end of the poem as a feeble curse against us all, not as a signal that she *will* control her own life by acting against men.

Around the room there are murmurs of surprise. 'I know about suicide,' says Maria, an older woman. 'You envy normal people who enjoy eating peanuts; you think it a waste to give up life. But there's a paradox. If you have no pain or pleasure of your own, then the risky bet with death is the only way to feel again. You're all wrong about the poem, Nancy,' Maria tells me specifically. 'She's not accusing you; she wants to feel you touch her, to have the world come back into focus.'

'It's a problem of confidence,' says another woman. 'She dislikes herself so much that she's sure that anyone seeking contact with her could only be enjoying her weakness.' The conversation continues, and as I listen I realize that many women are discovering that their own feelings of unworthiness make them suspicious of others.

The students have convinced me that my first reading of the poem was not accurate. Alexa, a student who knows me well, announces that I'm afraid of risk-taking, dislike violent emotion, and do not understand Plath's feelings of unworthiness.

'OK,' says Maria, who suddenly seems to take the discussion in hand, 'where are we? I think Nancy is right and so am I in terms of our own relation to the world. Nancy thought Plath cursed her; I thought I was standing right beside her and she called me closer. Actually, she does both at once, and that's why the poem's so frighteningly human.'

As for the image of the red-haired phoenix rising from the ashes to take her revenge on men, we agree that Plath does identify herself as Jew, woman and victim; her enemy as Nazi and male — but that here, male represents not masculine sexuality, but controlling power.

Plath's feeling of powerlessness, we do connect with womanhood and our discussion turns to the double bind of women. Like Plath, their upbringing forces them into the role of full-time, selfless wives and mothers, while their creative strength drives them to be full-time, self-involved poets. When 10.30 comes, we're exhausted. As the class splits up, I overhear Janet, a teacher and the mother of three, asking Rose to read her first short story; Maria, claiming with a laugh that it's time for some healthy egotism.

In most feminist classrooms, it is with difficulty that students and teachers find a comfortable mix between personal experience — the private world into which a piece of writing takes you — and the generalizations one wishes to make about writing, or the role of women. Though it is easy to say 'the personal is political,' or to claim that authentic feminist discussions must join together emotional and intellectual responses, or even obliterate such categories, our training as students and teachers has taught us to present our rational, objective selves in the classroom, and to reserve emotion for privacy and silence, or perhaps for a women's consciousness-raising group. In a Women's Studies class, we try to be both personal and analytic in a specific way. The consciousness-raising group question may be, 'Who am I?' or even, 'Who am I in relation to this poem, this novel, this psychology text?' But in the class I've just described, we did not want to know the details of Maria's suicide attempt, if indeed there had been one. If Plath asked her to examine her life, that was done in private. Rather, we encouraged Maria and trusted her to use her life-story in a disciplined way as an authority which could help us all understand 'Lady Lazarus.'

In a class later that semester, the use of personal experience has become a more natural mode both to discuss literature, and to begin changing one's life. The class has come to agree that although *all* women share *some* problems, the subtlety and severity of the limitations placed on a woman vary according to her background. We have been discussing two autobiographies — *The Diary of Anaïs Nin*, and Anne Moody's *Coming of Age in Mississippi*, the autobiography of a black woman who grew through adolescence during the civil rights movement of the early 1960s. We are reading the self-portraits with questions. How do women present themselves in the world? What are the sources of their self-knowledge? How do they relate to everything outside the self? We've suspended our schedule (which says

Lessing's *The Golden Notebook*) as everyone has felt a disturbing and unresolved conflict in the past week's discussion.

Some women are clearly partisans of Nin, writing journals of their own, and even corresponding with the great lady herself — who, amazingly, answers them. Others, mainly the older women and the minority women, have made Moody their female hero, an ordinary woman like them, a woman who acts in the world, whose identity is carved against the hostile white society in which she lives. Though we joke warmly, humorously, with Mary, an Indian woman married to a black man, we have reached the point of recognizing that we must go beyond the question, 'Do I identify with this writer?' to 'What does it mean if I don't identify with her at all?'

Delores and Linda, two Chicana women, start the class. Delores says, 'Listen to this passage. It's when Anne Moody is working in a New Orleans chicken-processing factory. Listen, and then you'll see why I get impatient with Nin's constant interest in herself.' Delores reads:

> I stood there reaching up and snatching out those boiling hot guts
> with my bare hands as fast as I could. But I just wasn't fast enough.
> The faster the chickens moved, the sicker I got. My face, arms,
> and clothes were splattered with blood and chicken shit . . . I shall
> never forget the slaughterhouse — the men pulling feathers from
> the bloody chickens . . . Grasping chickens by the neck and knifing
> them one after the other, their eyes sparkling with what looked to
> me like pleasure.

'This is concrete; this is real,' says Delores. 'When I worked in the fields, I was afraid of the angry, drunken men. I thought they'd kill me. There was no reason why they wouldn't.'

'I felt that as a poor Chinese kid,' says one of our two male students.

Sue, a young woman in blue jeans, who's been furiously hunting through the pages of *Diary III*, calls out, 'Listen to this passage. Nin has fears, too, but they're inside of her.' And she reads:

> We have our demons, and we let them destroy us or we tame them.
> If you cannot control your demons, whoever or whatever they are,
> you do harm to others. I found the way to cage mine, that was all.
> Anger, jealousy, envy, revengefulness, vanity. I locked them up in
> a diary. That may be why I so often dream that the diary is burn-

ing . . . If the diary burns, this demon will be on the loose again, not chained. Not contained.

'How like a woman,' says Bea, 'to chain one's demons, to be gracious, to be helpful, to turn anger against oneself.'

I, too, had been thinking of what the class fondly called the Nin-Moody split, and its implications for preventing white middle-class women and working-class women from ever understanding where their realities touched. I remarked to the class that the problem could be put in terms of external versus internal antagonists. Moody's fears, her strengths, her bent toward action, developed immediately in response to an external social order where tension between black and white was overt, treacherous, and unremitting, where there had been no time to identify demons within, for those with guns were on the outside.

'Wow,' interjects Bea, still thinking hard about the paragraphs she's just heard, 'that's why some of us thought a man could have written Coming of Age in Mississippi. We nice white girls are so used to analyzing everything psychologically, fighting battles in our heads, that we don't know what to do with a woman who fights society. I get it. Maybe a lot of Nin's demons were concrete; maybe they existed out there in the world and needed to be killed rather than chained. If she was worried about being vain, maybe she should have begun to look at how women get that way, rather than seeing vanity as a personal, moral flaw.'

'Yes, but don't forget,' cautions Delores, 'I never get any choice about being identified as a Chicana, and Moody has it coming to her just by being alive and black. Nin could have become an activist, but she didn't have to fight to surrvive.'

Now Delores directs a question at Bea and the other young white women — most of whom have grown up in the majestic Northwest landscapes, on farms, in small towns, where community values represented the best of America, and went unquestioned.

'Would you call your autobiography Coming of Age in the Northwest?' she asks. 'Would you write as though the Northwest were a hostile place like Mississippi?'

'Mine's called Spirit Flowers,' comes one reply.

'I wouldn't have before Women's Studies,' says Elaine, a woman who has just made her first foray into the community to speak to her mother's church group about the women's movement. 'In some ways, I'm envious of Anne. She and her friends knew the enemy; they *had* to learn to act against it. I never knew what was happening to me. Of course, my brother got to go away to college, not I. Of course, I'm scared of math, and my parents think I'm crazy to want to go to law school. Of course, I can't get angry at anyone, and end up patching up all the fights in our family. I didn't recognize until this year that because I was white, and pretty, and obedient, the social order had accommodated my growing up. If I couldn't be a tomboy, it wasn't because white people would kill me, or that I would be in danger. It was for some inner mysterious reason that the whole community understood and approved, but which I couldn't mention'.

'I guess that's why I'm fascinated by Nin — because she, like me, has the demons in her head, fears and conflicts for which no one has a name. If I were to write *Coming of Age in Salem, Oregon*, now, it would be a chronicle of white American girlhood. Society would be the antagonist. A certain amount of self-analysis is good, but Moody's showing me that changing your situation comes by *acting* to change it. I love Nin's style; I love her language. But I'm beginning to think she obscures concrete reality'.

And so it goes. Obviously, we could not reconcile conflicts between id and ego with conflicts between white and black, but we well-socialized white women did now comprehend that our socialization had shielded us from the cutting-edges of power relations between male and female, poor and affluent, minority culture and majority assumptions.

With an ironic turn, I mentioned Anne Moody's pattern of taking to bed with excruciating headaches after every few months of political struggle; I said jokingly that Nin could write a whole diary about one of those headaches. Delores spoke up, saying that she, too, suffered from terrible headaches — particularly since she'd become involved in organizing Chicano people.

'Maybe you need to think about how much tension you can take,' said Mary, who loved Delores, Nin and Moody. 'Maybe if Anne Moody had been more introspective she wouldn't have gotten sick; she would have known more about her own needs beyond the civil rights movement.'

'Think about myself?' said Delores, incredulously. 'I don't know how.' Our conclusions: that some of us would talk with Delores about what it means to be 'in touch with your feelings'; and that our next discussion would again raise the serious question of why the Nin partisans identified Moody's activism with unattractive male behavior. Could we define a feminist style of activism?

There *is* a feminist way of being in the world, and my students were beginning to discover it. For myself, the Nin-Moody discussion confirmed again what I had learned in my first Women's Studies class several years earlier — that there was much I could learn by listening to other women. In that first class, I had listened to my students, and we had listened together to Doris Lessing's voice in *The Golden Notebook*.

The students and I began to generalize from *our* personal experience, just as Lessing's women tend to. We began to sort out the validity of what others, mostly male, had *thought* our experience to have been.

I, for example, was inspired by Lessing's Anna, who is shown to be dissatisfied with her own writing. I began to admit that my own precarious self-image depended on masking a sense of intellectual inferiority, and that my self-doubt was in some ways engendered by aspects of a masculine style of thought which I could not, and now did not wish to, replicate. In short, like women students in my classes today, I discovered that when questions were real — 'concrete,' as Delores said – when the teacher was not abandoned as an isolated figure with an authoritative option on the Truth, I could use my mind quite adequately. When the Plath class challenged my interpretation of 'Lady Lazarus,' I had long since ceased to pine for airtight theorizing. I had grown comfortable with the materials of a feminist classroom — our books, our past experience and ourselves.

Note

1 Originally published in *Ms Magazine*, no. 2, September 1973, pp.49-50, and 84-5.

13

Black-eyed blues connections: teaching black women

Michele Russell

In Detroit, I am at the downtown YWCA. Rooms on the upper floors are used by Wayne County Community College as learning centers. It is 10 a.m. and I am convening an introductory Black Studies class for women on 'Community and Identity.' The twenty-two women who appear are all on their way from somewhere to something. This is a breather in their day. They range in age from nineteen to fifty-five. They all have been pregnant more than once and have made various decisions about abortion, adoption, monogamy, custody and sterilization. Some are great-grandmothers. A few have their children along. They are a cross-section of hundreds of black women I have known and learned from in the past fifteen years, inside the movement and outside of it.

We have an hour together. The course is a survey. The first topic of conversation — among themselves and with me - is what they went through just to make it in the door, on time. That, in itself, becomes a lesson.

We start where they are. We exchange stories of children's clothes ripped or lost, of having to go to school with sons and explain why Che is always late and how he got that funny name, anyway, to teachers who shouldn't have to ask and don't really care. They tell of waiting for men to come home from the nightshift so they can get the money or car necessary to get downtown, or power failures in the neighborhood, or administrative red tape at the college, or compulsory overtime on their own jobs, or the length of food stamp lines, or just being tired and needing sleep. Some of the stories are funny, some sad, some elicit outrage and praise from the group. It's a familiar and comfortable ritual in black culture. It's called testifying.

The role of the teacher? Making the process conscious, the content significant. Want to know, yourself, how the problems in the stories got resolved. Learn what daily survival wisdom these women have. Care. Don't let it stop at commiseration. Try to help them generalize from the specifics. Raise issues of who and what they continually have to bump up against on the life-road they've planned for themselves. Make lists on the board. Keep the scale human. Who are the people that get in the way? The social worker, the small-claims court officer, husbands, the teacher, cops, kids on the block. Ask: what forces do they represent? Get as much consensus as possible before moving on. Note there is most argument and disagreement on 'husbands' and 'kids on the block.' Define a task for next meeting. To sharpen their thinking on husbands and kids, have them make three lists. All the positive and negative things they can think of about men, children and families. Anticipate in advance that they probably won't have the time or will to write out full lists. But they will think about the question and be ready to respond in class.

Stop short of giving advice. Build confidence in their own ability to make it through whatever morass to be there at 10 a.m. the next day. Make showing up for class a triumph in itself. Because it is.

Try to make class meeting a daily activity. Every day during the week. Like language, new ways of seeing and thinking must be reinforced, even if only for half an hour. Otherwise the continuity is lost. The perpetual bombardment of other pressures upsets the rhythm of your movement together. No matter how much time you take with them or who they are, the following methodological principles are critical.

1 *Take one subject at a time* — but treat it with interdisciplinary depth and scope. In a variety of ways the women in class have been speeding. Literally, they will all either be on medication, be suffering from chronic hypertension, or be skittish from some street encounter. Encourage them to slow down. This does not mean drift — they experience that too much already. Have at least three directions in mind for every class session, but let their mood and uppermost concerns determine your choice. They have come to you for help in getting pulled together. The loose ends of their experience jangle discordantly like bracelets from their arms. You must be able to do with subject-matter

what they want to do with their lives. Get it under control in ways which thrive on complication.

2 *Encourage storytelling*. The oldest form of building historical consciousness in community is storytelling. The transfer of knowledge, skill and value from one generation to the next; the deliberate accumulation of a people's collective memory has particular significance in diaspora culture. Robbed of all other continuities, prohibited free expression, denied a written history for centuries by white America, black people have been driven to rely on oral recitation for our sense of the past. Today, however, that tradition is under severe attack. Urban migrations, apartment living, mass media dependency and the break-up of generational units within the family have corroded our ability to renew community through oral forms. History becomes 'what's in books.' Authority depends on academic credentials after one's name or the dollar amount of one's paycheck: the distance one has traveled, rather than the roots one has sunk. Significant categories of time are defined by television's thirty-second spots or thirty-minute features.

Piecing together our identity and community under these circumstances requires developing each other's powers of memory and concentration. When, as a teacher, one first asks women in class, 'Where did you come from?' you will get spontaneous answers ranging from: 'my mamma' and '12th Street' to 'Texas,' 'Africa' and 'Psych. 101.' They are scattered and don't know what question you are asking in the first place. Still, the responses say something about their associational framework. The most important thing about them is their truth. Build on that with the objective of expanding their reference-points.

Formalize the process. Begin with blood lines. Share your own family history and have class members do the same. Curiosity will provoke diligence and the abstractions of 'identity' and 'community' will give way before the faces of ancestry.

Historical narrative will be most difficult for the younger members of the class. Their knowledge of what it means to 'take the A-train,' for example, will in most cases be limited to hearsay or music. They relate to TV. Minimally, you want to get them to a point where they will enjoy evaluating all their contemporaries on *Soul Train* or the three generations of black women in *The Jeffersons* series in relation to all the family history of black people over the last fifty years that they have been discovering with other class members. To start that process, convene the class (as a field trip) to watch *Soul Train* and *The Jeffersons*. Then press for answers to the questions they ask all the time, anyway, when watching each other: 'Who does *that* one think *she* is?' In this setting, help history to prevail over personality.

Or begin with one photograph from a family album. Have each person bring it in and tell a story just about that one picture. Go from there. One eventual outcome of such a project may be to encourage black women to record these stories in writing, still an intimidating idea. Use a tape-recorder to ease the transition.

To help increase their powers of observation and their capacity for identification, have each woman sit, in a location of her own choosing, for one hour and record what she sees. It can be anywhere: a shopping mall, a beauty shop, a bar, restaurant, park, window — whatever they feel most natural with. Ride an unfamiliar bus to the end of the line and be alert to the community it attracts. Spend a week riding with domestic workers on suburban express lines. Record the conversations. Help women learn how to use the streets for investigation instead of exhibition. Have them go out in pairs and compare notes, bringing the results back to the group.

3 *Give political value to daily life*. Take aspects of what they already celebrate and enrich its meaning so they see their spontaneous tastes in a larger way than before. This means they will see themselves with new significance. It also imposes the responsibility of selectivity on the teacher. Embrace that. Apply your own political acumen to the myriad survival mechanisms that colonization and domestication breed into subject peoples. Remind them of the choices they make all the time.

No life-area is too trivial for political analysis. Note that a number of black women, myself included, have begun choosing long dresses for daily wear. In one class session, discussion begins with the remark that they're more 'comfortable' in this mode. What does comfort consist of? For those who are heavy, it means anything not physically constricting. For working mothers, comfort means 'easy to iron.' For the budget-conscious, 'easy to make.' For some of the young women in class, comfort is attached to the added respect this mode of dress elicits from brothers they pass on the street. For a Muslim grandmother, cleanliness and modesty are signified. For her daughter, also in the Nation, Africa is being invoked. The general principle which emerges is that this particular form of cover allows us greater freedom of expression and movement.

Don't stop here. Go from their bodies to their heads. A casual remark about wearing wigs can (and should) develop into a discussion of Frantz Fanon's essay, 'Algeria Unveiled,' in which he analyzes the role of protective coverings, adornment, camouflage, as tactical survival modes for women in the self-defensive stage of a movement. Help them to recall the stages of consciousness they've all experienced in relation to their own hair. When did they start to regard 'straightening' or 'doing' hair as 'processing' it? When did they stop? Why? If some women in the class still change their hair texture, does that mean their *minds* are processed, too? Read Malcolm on the subject. How do they feel about Alelia Walker in this context: the first black woman in America to become a millionaire for producing and marketing hair-straighteners and skin bleaches. Take them as far as memory and material allow. Normally, there will be at least three generations of social experience personally represented in community college classes. Try to work with it all.

Go beyond what is represented in class. Recall all the ways, historically, that black women in America have used physical disguise for political purposes. Begin with Ellen Craft, escaping from a Georgia plantation to Boston in 1848, passing as a white man. Talk about the contradictory impact of miscegenation on their thinking and action. Then connect this to class members' public demeanor: the variations they choose and the purposes at work. What uniforms do they consciously adopt? Focus on motive as well as image; make intent as important as affect, a way to judge results.

4 *Be able to speak in tongues.* Idiom, the medium through which ideas are communicated and organic links of association established (i.e. community) must be in black women's own tradition. When black women 'speak,' 'give a reading' or 'sound' a situation, a whole history of using language as a weapon is invoked. Rooted in slave folk-wisdom which says: 'Don't say no more with your mouth than your back can stand,' our vocalizing is directly linked to a willingness to meet hostilities head-on and persevere. Take the following description of a black woman 'specifying' by Zora Neale Hurston, for example:

Big Sweet came to my notice within the first week that I arrived . . . I heard somebody, a woman's voice 'specifying' up this line of houses from where I lived and asked who it was. 'Dat's Big Sweet,' my landlady told me. 'She got her foot up on somebody. Ain't she specifying?'

She was really giving the particulars. She was giving a reading, a
word borrowed from the fortunetellers. She was giving her opponent
lurid data and bringing him up to date on his ancestry, his looks,
smell, gait, clothes, and his route through Hell in the hereafter.
My landlady went outside where nearly everybody else of the four
or five hundred people on the 'job' were to listen to the reading.
Big Sweet broke the news to him, in one of her mildest bulletins
that his pa was a double humpted camel and his ma was a grass-gut
cow, but even so, he tore her wide open in the act of getting born,
and so on and so forth. He was a bitch's baby out of a buzzard egg.

My landlady explained to me what was meant by 'putting your
foot up' on a person. If you are sufficiently armed — enough to
stand off a panzer division — and know what to do with your
weapons after you get 'em, it is all right to go to the house of
your enemy, put one foot up on his steps, rest one elbow on your
knee and play in the family. That is another way of saying play
the dozens, which also is a way of saying low-rate your enemy's
ancestors and him, down to the present moment for reference,
and then go into his future as far as your imagination leads you.
But if you have no faith in your personal courage and confidence
in your arsenal, don't try it. It is a risky pleasure. So then I had
a measure of this Big Sweet.

'Hurt who?' Mrs Bertha snorted at my fears. 'Big Sweet? Humph?
Tain't a man, woman nor child on this job going to tackle Big
Sweet. If God send her a pistol she'll send him a man. She can
handle a knife with anybody. She'll join hands and cut a duel. Dat
Cracker Quarters Boss wears two pistols round his waist and goes
for bad, but he won't break a breath with Big Sweet lessen he got
his pistol in his hand. Cause if he start anything with her, he won't
never get a chance to draw it. She ain't mean. She don't bother
nobody. She just don't stand for no foolishness, dat's al.'

Talking bad. Is it still going on? Some class members do it all the
time. All know women who do. Some, with a concern for manners,
find the activity embarrassing. One woman observes that it's getting
harder and harder these days to find targets worthy of such invention.
Another, bringing in the prior comments together, says there's too
little audience for the energy it takes. Whatever our particular attitudes, we all recognize in Big Sweet a pistol-packin' mamma, conjure
woman, voice of judgment and reservoir of ancestral memory — all of

which are the bases of a fighting tradition also personified in Harriet Tubman, Marie Leveau, Sojourner Truth, Ericka Huggins. Discover the continuities in their words, acts and deeds done in their name. Emphasize how they transformed personal anger into political weapons, enlarged personal grudges to encompass a people's outrage. When words failed, remember how Aunt Jemima's most famous recipe, ground-glass plantation pancakes, made the masters choke.

Take the blues. Study it as a coded language of resistance. In response to questions from class members about whether feminism has ever had anything to do with black women, play Ma Rainey singing, 'I Won't Be Your Dog No More.' Remind them of our constant complaints about being treated as a 'meal-ticket woman,' our frustration at baking powder men losing their risables and of going hungry for days. Know the ways in which Peaches are Strange Fruit. Introduce them to a Depression era Bessie Jackson responding humorously, but resolutely, to our options for feeding ourselves when that period's diaspora forced us on to city streets. Two songs, written in 1930 and 1935, document our determination to be treated with the dignity of workers, no matter how we labored. They testify to daily struggles over the conditions of our labor, the urge to control turf and hours. The first is 'Tricks Ain't Walkin No More.' She says:

Sometimes I'm up, sometimes I'm down
I cain't make my livin around this town
Cause Tricks ain't walkin, Tricks ain't
    walkin no more.

I got to make my livin, don't care where I go.

I need some shoes on my feet, clothes on
    my back
That' why I'm walkin these streets all
    dressed in black
But Tricks ain't walkin, Tricks ain't
    walkin no more.
And I see four or five good tricks standin
    in front of my door.

I got a store on the corner, sellin stuff
    cheap
I got a market cross the street where I
    sell my meat

But Tricks ain't walkin, Tricks ain't
   walkin no more
And if you think I'm lyin, follow me to
   my door.

By 1935, when they got to her door, they found she'd gone into a new business. The address was the same, but the commodity had changed. She sang:

When you come to my house, come down
   behind the jail
I got a sign on my door, Bar-B-Que for Sale
I'm talkin bout my Bar-B-Que
The only thing I sell
And if you want my meat, you can come
   to my house at twelve.

Bring the idiomatic articulation of black women's feminism up to date by sharing stories of the first time we all *heard* what Aretha was asking us to *think* about, instead of just dancing to it. Let Esther Phillips speak on how she's *justified* and find out if class members feel the same way.

Be able to translate ideological shorthand into terms organic to black women's popular culture. Let the concept of internationalism be introduced. But approach it from the standpoint of a South African Miriam Makeba, an Alabama-born Big Mama Thornton or a Caribbean Nina Simone all singing Bob Dylan's 'I Shall Be Released.' Concentrate the discussion on each woman's roots, her place of national origin. Reflect on the history behind the special emphasis each woman gives to phrases such as: 'every distance is not near,' 'I remember every face of every man who put me here,' 'inside these walls.' Ask: what kinds of jails are they in? And what happens when we start acting to effect our own release? Devote one class session to a debate over whether it is an antagonistic contradiction for black women to use Bob Dylan's music as an expressive vehicle. Explore the limits of nationalism in this way.

The whole world is ours to appropriate, not just five states in the South, or one dark continent. Treat the meaning of this statement through Nina Simone's recreation of Pirate Jenny. Play the music. Know the history it comes out of and the changes rung: from *The*

Beggar's Opera, through Brecht and Weill's *Threepenny Opera*, to the Caribbean and Southern situations everywhere that Simone takes as her reference-point. Know the political history involved and the international community of the oppressed she exhorts to rise. Particularly notice the cleaning woman's role. Recall the rebellions of the 1960s, when Nina Simone was performing this song. We all lived through the rebellions, but how did we relate to them? At what point did class members begin associating Detroit with Algeria, Watts with Lesotho, the Mississippi with the Mekong Delta, America with Germany? Share your own experience and growth.

5 *Use everything*. Especially, use the physical space of the classroom to illustrate the effects of environment on consciousness. The size and design of the desks, for example. They are wooden, with one-sided stationary writing arms attached. The embodiment of a poor school. Small. Unyielding. Thirty years old. Most of the black women are ample-bodied. When the desks were new and built for 12-year-old, seventh-grade bodies, some class members may have sat in them for the first time. Now, sitting there for one hour — not to mention trying to concentrate and work — is a contortionist's miracle, or a stoic's. It feels like getting left back.

With desks as a starting-point for thinking about our youth in school, class members are prompted to recall the mental state such seats encouraged. They cite awkwardness, restlessness and furtive embarrassment. When they took away our full-top desks with interior compartments, we remember how *exposed* we felt, unable to hide anything: not spitballs, notes, nor scarred knees, prominent between too-short, hand-me-down dresses and scuffed shoes. They remember the belligerence which was all the protection we were allowed.

We talk about all the unnecessary, but deliberate, ways the educational process is made uncomfortable for the poor. Most women in class hate to read aloud. So we relive how they were taught to read, the pain involved in individual, stand-up recitation. The foil one was for a teacher's scapegoating ridicule. The peer pressure to make mistakes. We look back on how good reading came to mean proper elocution to our teachers — particularly elderly black spinsters, also in the church.

We remember that one reason many of us stopped going to school was that it became an invasion of privacy. Not like church, which was only once a week, an event you could get up for. School was every day, among strangers, whether you felt like it or not, even if you ran out of clean clothes for the ritual. Showing up was the hardest part. After that, it was just a series of games.

Then, of course, someone inevitably says, 'But here we are, back again.' Is that a joke on us? Is it still a game? What are we trying to do differently this time around? To answer those questions, have women devise their own criteria for evaluating the educational process they engage in with you.

6 *Be concrete.* In every way possible, take a materialist approach to the issue of black women's structural place in America. Focus attention on the building where we are learning our history. Notice who's still scrubbing the floors. In response to class members who pin their hopes for the future on 'new careers,' pose the following questions: how is a nurse's aide different from a maid? What physical spaces are the majority of us still locked into as black women who must take jobs in the subsistence and state sectors of the economy? Do we ever get to do more than clean up other people's messes - be we executive secretaries, social workers, police officers, or wives? Within what confines do we live and work?

Reflect on the culture of the stoop, the storefront, the doorway, the housing project, the rooming-house bathroom, the bank-teller's cage, the corner grocery store, the bus, hotels and motels, school, hospital and corporate corridors, and waiting-rooms everywhere. What constraints do they impose?

If we conclude that most of our lives are spent as social servants, and state dependants, what blend of sex, race and class consciousness does that produce? To cut quickly to the core of unity in experience, read the words of Johnny Tillmon, founder of the National Welfare Rights Organization in Watts, 1965:

I'm a woman. I'm a black woman. I'm a poor woman. I'm a fat woman. I'm a middle-aged woman. And I'm on welfare.

In this country, if you're any one of those things — poor, black, fat, female, middle-aged, on welfare — you count less as a human being. If you're all of those things, you don't count at all. Except as a statistic.

I am a statistic. I am 45 years old. I have raised six children. I grew up in Arkansas and I worked there for fifteen years in a laundry, making about $20 or $30 a week, picking cotton on the side for carfare. I moved to California in 1959 and worked in a laundry there for nearly four years. In 1963, I got too sick to work anymore.

My husband and I had split up. Friends helped me to go on welfare.

They didn't call it welfare. They called it AFDC — Aid to Families with Dependent Children. Each month I get $363 for my kids and me. I pay $128 a month rent: $30 for utilites, which include gas, electricity, and water; $120 for food and non-edible household essentials; $50 for school lunches for the three children in junior and senior high school who are not eligible for reduced-cost meal programs. This leaves $5 per person a month for everything else — clothing, shoes, recreation, incidental personal expenses and transportation. This check allows $1 a month for transportation for me but none for my children. That's how we live.

Welfare is all about dependency. It is the most prejudiced institution in this country, even more than marriage, which it tries to imitate.

The truth is that AFDC is like a super-sexist marriage. You trade in *a* man for *the* man. But you can't divorce him if he treats you bad. He can divorce you, of course, cut you off anytime he wants. But in that case, *he* keeps the kids, not you.

The man runs everything. In ordinary marriage, sex is supposed to be for your husband. On AFDC, you're not supposed to have any sex at all. You give up control of your own body. It's a condition of aid. You may even have to agree to get your tubes tied so you can never have more children, just to avoid being cut off welfare.

The man, the welfare system, controls your money. He tells you what to buy, what not to buy, where to buy it, and how much things cost. If things — rent, for instance — really cost more than he says they do, it's just too bad for you. You've just got to make your money stretch.

The man can break into your home any time he wants to and poke into your things. You've got no right to protest. You've got no right to privacy. Like I said, welfare's a super-sexist marriage.

Discuss what it means to live like that. What lines of force and power in society does it imply? A significant percentage of black women have had direct experience with welfare, either as children or mothers. In discussing 'how it happened to them,' all become aware of how every woman in class is just one step away from that bottom line. A separation, a work injury, layoffs, a prolonged illness, a child's disability — any one could put them on those rolls. It is a sobering realization, breaking through some of the superior attitudes even black women have internalized about AFDC recipients.

What other work do we do and how does it shape our thinking? Compare Maggie Holmes, domestic, Alice Washington, shoe-factory order-filler; Diane Wilson, process clerk from Studs Terkel's *Working*. Study what women just like those in class say about themselves. Although, as with everything, a whole course could be devoted just to analyzing the content, process and consciousness of black women's jobs, be satisfied in this survey to personify history so it becomes recognizable and immediate — something they participate in.

7 *Have a dream*. The conclusion to be drawn from any study of our history in America is that the balance of power is not on our side, while the burden of justice is. This can be an overwhelming insight, particularly in times of economic stagnation, physical deterioration and organizational confusion. Therefore, it is important to balance any discussion of the material circumstances of black women's lives with some attention to the realm of their dreams.

In all other areas of life, we can talk about struggle, organization, sabotage, survival, even tactical and strategic victory. However, only in dreams are liberation and judgment at the center of vision. That is where we do all the things in imagination that our awareness demands but our situation does not yet permit. In dream, we seek the place in the sun that society denies us. And here, as in everything, a continuum of consciousness will be represented.

At their most fetishistic, black women's spiritual dreams are embodied in the culture of numbers, signs and gambling. In every poor community, holy water, herb, astrology and dream-book shops are for women what poolrooms, pawnshops and bars are for men. Places to hang on, hoping for a hit. As Etheridge Knight has observed in *Black Voices from Prison*. 'It is as common to hear a mother say, "I gotta get my number in today" with the same concern and sometimes in the same breath as she says "I gotta feed the baby" . . . In some homes the dream book is as familiar and treated with as much reverence as the Bible.' In many homes, dream books produce more tangible results.

The most progressive expression of our dreams, however, in which mass liberation takes precedence over individual relief, and planning replaces luck, is occasionally articulated in literature. Sarah Wright provides such an example in *This Child's Gonna Live*. In that story of a black family desperately trying to hold on to its territorial birthright and each other in Depression Maryland, the most fundamental religiosity of poor black people is recreated, its naturalism released. The landscape is made to hold our suffering and signify our fate. Particularly in the person of Mariah Upshur, the faith of the oppressed which helps us to fight on long after a cause seems lost is complemented by a belief that righteousness can make you invincible. Colloquially speaking, all that's needed is for God to send the sufferers a pretty day. Then, children will be cured of worms, and land thieves will be driven from the community, the wind will be calm for the oystermen, the newly planted rye will hold and a future will be possible in a land of 'slowing-up roads' and death. That is, if we're deserving. What does 'deserving' mean? Discuss Richard Wright's approach to this subject in 'Bright and Morning Star.'

Relate the fundamental hopes and values of Mariah Upshur's dream to other belief systems through which people have been able to attain freedom. The concrete experience of people 'moving mountains' is communicated by the story of Ta-chai in the People's Republic of China. The triumph of vision, perseverance and organization over brute force to regain land is demonstrated in Vietnam and Cuba. Spell out the commonalities in all liberation struggles in this age which vanquish the moneychangers. Find examples in our own history where beginnings have been made of this kind. Make the Word become Flesh, so the new day that's dawning belongs to you and me.

As teachers, we should be able to explore all these things and more without resorting to conventional ideological labels. This is the basic, introductory course. Once the experiential base of the class-in-itself is richly felt and understood, theoretical threads can be woven between W. E. B. DuBois, Zora Neale Hurston and Frantz Fanon. Then bridges can be built connecting the lives of ghettoized women of every color and nationality. In the third series of courses, great individuals can be put in historical perspective; organized movements can be studied. In the fourth stage, movements themselves may arise. Political possibilities for action then flow from an understanding conditioned by life on the block, but not bound by it. And the beginnings of a class-for-itself may take shape. But the first step, and the most fundamental, should be the goal of the first course: recognizing ourselves in history.

Note

1   Copyright © 1976 and 1977 by The Feminist Press. From *The Women's Studies Newsletter*, no. 4, fall 1976, 7 and 8; and no. 5, winter/spring 1977, pp.24-8. Reprinted with permission of The Feminist Press, Box 334, Old Westbury, New York 11568.

PART FIVE

Theory as text

14

Suspicious pleasures: on teaching feminist theory

Joan Cocks

Twice in the course of my meanderings as a political theorist, I have come face to face with the question of what exactly theory is. On the first occasion I was still a graduate student, and I turned my gaze to theory itself out of sheer wonder at all it had taught me about the social world. How was it able to reveal dimensions of life of which I previously had been only dimly, or not at all, aware? These dimensions were sometimes like missing pieces of a puzzle, making sudden sense of what had perplexed me before. Sometimes they were like whole new puzzles, unexpected and surprising. I decided then that the special power of theory lay in its conceptual illumination of aspects of social relations that were invisible to the seeing eye. Typically, these aspects were invisible because they were never sense-data to begin with. Often enough, they also were invisible because they were so ugly in conventional moral terms, or so dissonant with favorite notions of the self, that they depended for their safe existence on being obscured from general view.

It was, I think, theory's access to secrets hidden from the senses and ordinary thought that made it exquisitely alluring to me. I was sure it must be equally alluring to others. Thus I was caught entirely off guard when, several years later, I walked in to teach my first feminist theory class. It took me several more years of teaching before I appreciated the full significance of the hostility to theory among the more politicized students: that not at all fortuitously, but for a very interesting set of reasons, the theoretical presumption itself had become problematic in the feminist context. What *was* clear to me right from the start, however, was the singularly stubborn resistance students showed to theory in courses on feminism as opposed to Marxism, liberalism and so on. In those other settings, their initial discomfort was no more than the uneasiness one might feel on meeting a stranger before that stranger becomes a friend. In a feminist setting, on the contrary, students tended to move straight from discomfort to aggressive antagonism. They were likely to accuse theory of active intimidation, manipulation, domination, hyper-rationalism, the evasion of feeling and — at the root of it all — an irredeemable maleness. What made things especially sticky for someone who, like myself, was enamored of both feminism and theory, was that the most radical writers we read each semester were themselves determinedly anti-theoretical, at least in overt posture. The most vocal students, the most radical texts, and the most militant members of the women's community being aligned on the other side, one had to fight for the space to think and speak theoretically inside the theory class, as well as out. The crucial battle was that of convincing students to suspend their participation in the refusal to theorize, in order to reflect on why that refusal had become so integral a part of the general ambiance.

These experiences in the classroom prompted the occasion for my return to meta-theoretical questions. In the pages that follow, I have set down my thoughts on the nature of theory, the obstacles feminism has placed in front of its own theoretical development, and the pedagogical difficulties such obstacles produce. Many of these thoughts have developed out of discussions I have had over time with my students. I originally had intended to write this essay in a style that mirrored the informality of our conversations. Somehow, I have ended up writing instead in theory's own tongue. How much was my use of this suspicious language dictated by the autonomous force of my subject-matter? How much by some perverse impulse on my own part? I will leave the answer to the reader's judgment.

The most celebrated delights in teaching feminist theory have to do with the immediacy, the intimacy and the urgency of its subject-matter. Intellectual inquiry very often requires that students grasp things at a distance from their own situation. The world into which feminist theory inquires, however, is directly their world. Students have bodies marked in language as physiologically female or male, and they know one gender or the other as the core, and sometimes the prison, of the self. They are, then, at once reflecting subjects and the most palpable proof of the system they are reflecting upon. This system, moreover, centers on physically and emotionally intimate relations which rivet the attention in a way in which other, less evocative dimensions of social life do not. Intimacy is, after all, the privileged domain of the body and the heart; it is suggestive of some of the most acutely felt moments of hope, desire, frustration, hatred, disillusionment and despair. It draws students in far more easily than they are drawn in to the study of, for example, bureaucracy, capital or the state.

But what makes the sex/gender system particularly compelling as an object of analysis is its permeation by power relations of a long-lived and far-flung sort. The dynamic of power and vulnerability makes distinctive appearances in economic mastery and servitude, in the symbiosis of colonizer and colonized, in erotic encounters where control and submission are not played out along male/female lines. It also emerges as the bond between masculine 'self' and feminine 'other.' The premise that men dominate women, in however partial or subtle or brutal a way, lends a certain urgency to feminist investigations. Students are quick to appreciate this urgency, and many respond to it by making a special commitment to one another and to their work. Such dedication is typical in Women's Studies courses and extraordinary in the academy at large.

The highly charged conditions feminist theory creates for itself mean that students are likely to respond strongly to it, and to situate themselves, whether as protagonists or antagonists, in the struggle to comprehend and transform gender relations. It is exhilarating for any teacher to provoke such engagement in the classroom. It is also profoundly disturbing. However knowing or jaundiced students may be, they have lives which are much less lived out than one's own, and there is something in showing them the underside of gender relations that is akin to a corruption of the innocent. The teacher can keep them intellectual company in that corruption, but the private rereadings they may do of their own pasts, and the personal dislocations those rereadings may induce, will, ultimately be, their own to suffer through. All of this is not to say that the teacher is left untouched by what she is teaching on her own account. To the contrary, it is impossible not to be moved by new revelations about an already formidable system of power, swept up in debates over the implications of that system, and needled by doubts about whether favored interpretations of it have been astute or committed enough.

But such pleasures and their accompanying agonies are familiar to anyone working in Women's Studies, and I have not chosen them as the topic of my essay. Instead, I want to address the question of why certain other pleasures in teaching feminist theory are not likely to be spoken of out loud. Why are the delights to be had in being *theoretical* very guilty, almost forbidden ones in a feminist setting? Why does theory offend the more rather than the less militant Women's Studies students? Why do the words 'rigorous,' 'disciplined,' 'abstract,' 'analytical,' and, above all, 'rational,' have the same jarring sound in the feminist lexicon that 'metaphysical,' 'imaginative,' and 'normative' have in the positivist one, or that 'subjective,' 'personal,' and 'psychological' have for orthodox Marxism?

It must be said immediately that there are good reasons for anyone to suspect the theoretical enterprise as it is often carried out. Theory is prone to a number of faults which can show up wherever it does — on the page, in the lecture hall, in the kind of conversation endemic to university corridors and coffee shops. Theory can be unnecessarily abstruse, self-indulgently obscure, overly abstract so as to avoid the trouble of stating things as clearly and as sharply as possible. It can be a snobbish exercize in intellectual posturing. In its disregard for literary grace and its impatience with the concrete, it frequently spills out in a prose conjuring up nothing but categories — or, if it conjures up life, does so in such a way that it is made into something hideously boring and grey. At least in the present era, theory driven by a critical impetus easily succumbs to the lure of fadism. It is as though the thrill of subverting the established order of thought becomes habit-forming, so that the critique of an entrenched tradition generates out of itself one briefly fashionable counter-position after another. Those few students whose attraction to feminism is highly theoretical tend to gravitate precisely to the rarefied heights where the pursuit of the latest thinker and thought is most frenetic and fast-paced. Here, there is great intellectual excitement, but also a continual erosion of any sure ground on which one might stand to make sense of the world. This erosion is especially regrettable where students are concerned, because it generally is not chosen by them, but rather happens to them as they follow in the wake of their mentors' speculative twists and turns.

If avant-garde theory can take all its adherents further and further from a fixity and solidity of thought, theory *per se* can take them far from the world to be thought about. Its proclivity for losing connection with the world and feeding off its own concepts and principles is a final fault of which one can legitimately accuse it.

Even when theory is articulate and responsible rather than turgid, fickle or narcissistic, however, anyone who encounters it for the first time is bound to find it difficult. Its idiom is not the idiom of ordinary language; its words, or at least what it does with them, are asymmetrical with the words people use to describe the concrete details of their physical surroundings, their social attachments, their longings and plans. It imposes a cool distance between itself and the direct experience of life. This imposition can be, for the uninitiated, so exasperating that it is wise to consider the reasons for it explicitly in any course in which theory will play a part. Why is it that theory does *not* follow the contours of immediate experience? Why does one begin to do theory, however tacitly or informally, the minute one steps back from immediate experience to reflect on its causes, meaning and implications? Why is the notion of immediate experience itself off the mark, once that experience is informed by prior efforts of self-reflection? Without plumbing the depths of these questions here, I want to suggest two central ways in which reflection is inescapably distinct from the experience it reflects upon (even though the insights it generates may inform future experience). These are the ways in which it secures its status as the analysis, rather than the verbal copy, of the world.

The first way is best illustrated by the kind of theory which presumes that the truth of a social whole is entirely a function of the self-interpretations of its members. Here, if anywhere, theory seems to be a copy of lived experience: its account of the latter is exhausted in an account of what participants intended to do, thought they were doing and believed they had done. In fact, however, even the strictest interpretive theory has already enjoyed a long moment of detachment from the world, during which it reflected on where its truth might be found. This moment is unavoidable because the location of the truth of the world is not, like the key to a map, stamped somewhere on its surface. It must be discovered through thought rather than through observation. Even when theory returns to the world and offers, in its explanation, a repetition of its members' beliefs and intentions, it is a repetition only in a highly qualified sense. Theory must rely on its own distinctive activity to identify the significant and the trivial meanings in any given social context and to ferret out those meanings that are inchoate, diffuse or multilayered.

The second, more striking way in which theory is not a replica of lived experience is illustrated by the kind of theory which claims that social participants may not have a grasp of certain levels of, or constraints on, their thought and action. To the extent that they do not, the truth of their world will not lie with their ideas about it. Hence, theory must distance itself from the world to determine where the key to it can be found, and then it must sustain a distance to fathom aspects of the world hidden from the eyes of its own authors and actors. The refusal to paint the portrait of the world as it appears to its members does not require that theory be blind to the partial integrity of the meanings a culture creates for itself, or to the sense and coherence in people's accounts of what they are doing. It also does not require that it make a sharp distinction between itself and ordinary efforts of self-reflection. Theoretical knowledge of the social world is more systematic and comprehensive than the personal knowledge one acquires by reflecting on the causes, meaning and implications of one's own situation. But becoming theoretical and becoming self-conscious belong to precisely the same genre of mental activity.

The forbidding aura of theory is dispelled when one learns to become conversant in its terms as well as in everyday terms. The ability to do so is given to everyone. Thus, for everyone there is the same promise: that what originally may appear to be a bewildering idiom can become enticing, stimulating and, finally, a part of one's own internal capacities. Nevertheless, theory's initial inaccessibility, as well as the various voluntary sins it is tempted to commit, mean that students will have one understandable and several good reasons for being hostile to it. They often, consequently, must be cajoled into doing the laborious work required to make sense of even relatively lucid theoretical texts. At the same time, they always must be assured that much of what intimidates them about theory has to do with its own pretensions and pomposities — has to do, that is, with its being poor theory and not with their being poor students.

The task of actively winning students over to theoretical discourse is magnified enormously when that discourse is bound up with feminist concerns. There are, I think, three closely related peculiarities of contemporary feminism that have encouraged a staunch anti-theoreticism on the part of many students, members of women's communities and radical representatives of the feminist intelligentsia.

These peculiarities make both teaching and *doing* feminist theory so exceptionally delicate that it becomes imperative to confront them directly.

The first peculiarity is that the very urgency, intimacy and immediacy of sex/gender relations which make teaching Women's Studies so delightful, also present themselves as barriers to abstract thought. That the practical urgency of power relations makes theoretical study a mere indulgence is a familiar claim in every radical social movement. Unfortunately, it is only after an analytically naive movement makes serious political errors that the costs of its naivety become plain; and it is only after its members have undergone theoretical training and come out the other side that they are in a position to know whether it was an indulgence or not.

The belief that theory violates the integrity of close and emotionally intense relations, meanwhile, is a common one — and not only among women. It is a belief with a certain force to it, as a veil of solitude and tranquility descends, however lightly or briefly, upon any person who reflects on any thing. Many women also argue that the theoretical attitude is a license to evade the felt horrors and joys of concrete experience. Often enough, the impulse to analyze has had its secret source in the impulse to deny, and those who have seized the historical moment to speak bitterness of men and love for women are apt to find something disingenuous in the demand that they step back from their active engagements to probe, qualify, investigate and explain. Militant feminists, furthermore, attack intellectual practice *per se* as one acute instance of the general domination of reason over the modern age — a domination also manifested in the festishization of science, the tyranny of bureaucratic institutions, and the rationalization of everyday affairs. The idea of the authoritarianism and impersonality of reason seems persuasive, if only because it is widely current among feminist, ecological and 'New Age' counter-cultural groups. It is also given legitimacy by critical theorists from Adorno to Marcuse to Foucault — but they, after all, must be taken with a grain of salt, as they owe their perspicuity and intellectual sophistication to the very 'history of reason' they condemn.

Despite this protective support for immediacy and intimacy, any easy presumption that theory offends against them is open to serious question. It is telling, for a start, that the very desire to defend immediacy against theory has much to do with ideological habits inherited from the dominant culture by the assorted counter-cultural groups on the American scene. These habits include a belief in the privileged status of the individual self; a penchant for explaining the self in terms of its personal experiences, wants and goals, instead of in terms of larger social forces; and a distaste for acknowledging collectivist practices — whether pernicious or beneficent — of any but the small-scale, face-to-face sort. It can be argued that such conventions of thought are hopelessly antiquated as a description of social reality, or that they are eminently defensible as a set of social ideals, or that they have become the ingredients of an important social critique, given the assault by bureaucratization and technological specialization on spontaneity and autonomy. But however convincing or unconvincing any of these arguments may be, the dominant culture is still the unchallenged source of two primary features of the counter-culture: its preoccupation with the self's immediate experiences and its predilection for 'personal solutions' to the injuries and tragedies of the world.

These preoccupations and predilections are particularly troublesome when they surface in a feminist context. They are grossly inadequate to the task of illuminating or transforming relations between the two largest collectivities in social life. The memberships of feminine and masculine genders are not determined by individual preference, their respective characteristics are not authored by individuals in any self-conscious way, and their mutual interactions are dictated to a great extent by systemic forces individuals often do not fully grasp and sometimes do not know are there. Thus, women who restrict their insights to the immediacy of personally felt life are fated to be unwitting collaborators with the dominant order in imposing debilitating rules of vision, and narrow possibilities for action, on themselves.

The dominant culture, then, stands as a warning against an unreflective glorification of immediate life. Ironically enough, orthodox Marxism stands as a parallel warning against the assumption of an incompatibility between theory and intimacy. Orthodox Marxism insists on the crucial importance of theory in unraveling the truth of history and society. At the same time, it is quite happy to agree that theory is inappropriate with respect to sex and gender. Its most stolid proponents always have assumed that one properly *feels* sexual desire, family ties, the vagaries of friendship and the entire morass of male-female connections. However, to unlock the key to the world, one must learn to *think* the wage-labor/capital relation and all the nefarious dealings and dimensions of the state. What is implicit in the principle that intimacy lies beyond the theoretical pale is, in this context, un-pleasantly clear: that sex/gender relations have no explanatory power for society as a whole; that nothing about them is problematic or complex enough to merit rigorous intellectual attention on their own behalf; that they invite, to the extent that they fulfill no function for productive relations, instinctual responses rather than critical reflect-tions. These intimations reveal that the refusal to theorize about intimacy may signify for it not respect, but disdain.

That theory can illuminate the social causes and consequences of lived experience and intimate relations would surely count in its favor, were it not for a second peculiarity of contemporary feminism. This is the tendency of many of its adherents to identify reason with men. Radical feminists, especially, are prone to describe rational thought — above all, when it is abstract or systematic — as thought 'in a male mode.' It fol-lows from this description that women who think abstractly and systematically have transgressed gender boundaries. Such boundaries are, for all feminists, highly politicized ones. Thus it is that both stu-dents and faculty who do feminist theory find themselves under suspi-cion of having committed what must be one of the oddest and most paradoxical of political sins: they are suspected of having 'male minds,' of having been infected by 'male values,' of being 'anatomically female, spiritually male.' In short, the charge is that they have 'become men.'

   Of course, the notion that reason is alien to true 'women-centered' experience has held a prominent place in men's own reading of the social world. To substantiate their reading, men have pointed to the fact that it is they who have dominated in the production of public knowledge. But while this is evidence of an impressive knack for domination of their part, it is hardly proof of their innate proclivity for intellectual prowess. Historically, there has never been more than an accidental relation between the capacity for wielding power and the capacity for thoughtfulness, insight and the disciplined exercize of mind. Historically, too, there has never been more than an oppor-tunistic relation — a crucial one, to be sure, in shaping the course of human affairs — between the wielding of power and the institutionaliz-ation of academic training for the group to whom power belongs.

   Why, if there is patently so little truth in it, are feminists attracted to the idea that reason is characteristically male? The answer, I think, lies in the twin concepts of reason and emotion which women have inherited from the dominant culture. Modern culture conceives of reason as objective, calculating, instrumental, willfully deaf to emotional sympathies and antipathies. It conceives of emotion as the feeling which attaches itself senselessly to values no argument could possibly support. That many feminists defer to the conventional meaning of 'reason' and 'emotion' but reverse the conventional assessment of them is understandable enough. On the one hand, established conceptual practice has a great deal of power over the way all of us make sense of our inner experience. On the other, a reason divorced from desire, anger and everything that is generally moving about the human world is bound to be derided by women, who have spent much of their time attending to emotional life.

Against both the dominant culture and its feminist critics, however, it must be argued that reason and emotion are not antagonistic opposites. Because emotions are felt does not mean that there is no reason in them. Every emotion entails a pang or welling of the heart. The capacity for such feelings is, along with the capacity for self-reflection, what makes the difference between a person and a thing. But each emotion just as centrally refers to at least partially shared and rationally contestable ideas about which actions of others warrant one's disgust or admiration; which actions count as instances of treachery or sacrifice; and what significance is attached to actions trespassing on conventional expectations. It is the intricacy of such ideas that requires an intricate language of the emotions, a language that can make distinctions between disgust and disappointment, admiration and affection, and so on. If emotional experience has such an intimate connection to thought, there is no more subtle kind of conversation than that which analyzes a particular social context, set of characters and events, in order to determine what passions were felt in a given situation and what passions were warranted or at least reasonable to feel under the circumstances. These are the kinds of conversations women are used to conducting among themselves with great seriousness and pleasure in their everyday lives. In turn, there is no more thoughtful kind of political struggle than that waged over what kinds of circumstances and actions ought to warrant what kinds of emotions, over what feelings ought to be felt when certain kinds of things are done. The feminist movement has waged just such a struggle with the larger society to redefine the circumstances that count as causes for loyalty or indignation, the actions that count as instances of violence or love.

In sum, emotion lies no closer than the deduction of conclusion from premises to some raw thoughtless state. The inchoate moment in emotional experience does not make that experience brute, and it is the richness, not the absence, of a discourse of feeling that signals the complexity of a culture's rational life. As for what is called 'rational argument' — it is always made for particular purposes and with particular interests in mind. Just as the intensity of an emotion does not indicate that it is irrational, the coolness with which an argument is made, while it might show self-control on the speaker's part, does not mean that the argument is innocent of special passions. It is not at all that such passions belie the rationality of the argument. It is, rather, that the test of that rationality is only in part a matter of the argument's coherence; it is just as much a matter of whether the passions behind it are warranted under the circumstances or not. Men may make use of a detached style of argument in their sexual and domestic conflicts with women. Their claims to rationality on that basis, however, can be credited as little as their claims that women are irrational for expressing emotions like resentment or distrust. In truth, the opposite of being 'emotional' is not being 'rational' at all, but rather being 'controlled,' 'closed,' 'tight,' 'repressed,' or 'mechanical.'

If reason and emotion are, in fact, internally related, the task for feminists can be neither to defend emotion against reason nor to reunite the two. Instead, it must be to discover why and how conventional conceptions of reason and emotion distort what people actually do when they think and when they feel. It also may be to discover how people attempt to deform their experiences of thinking and feeling to fit given assumptions about what such experiences should be like. These are perfect questions to take up in the feminist theory class. But whether or not one does so, the fact that they are *appropriate* questions means that women need not prohibit themselves from praising reason for emotion's sake.

In itself, theoretical inquiry is not animated by the desire to violate intimacy, to escape the realities of lived life, or to assume an instrumentalist stance. To be sure, one *can* engage in the inquiry with any of these purposes in mind. However, they are accidental to a mode of thought which, in its pure form, is elicited only by the perplexing and complicated nature of the human world. The theoretical passion is a passion to unravel the complexities of that world, to make clear — if only fleetingly — what is opaque or, at least, to make clear *what* it is that is opaque.

To refuse to acknowledge that one can have the desire to think theoretically about sex and gender is to erase them from the surface of human life. It is to imply that, unlike life, they are not nuanced and intricate enough to ignite a passion like *this*. It is also to forfeit the chance to unravel the hidden strands of exploitation and abuse weaving their way through the ties between women and men. Theory is at its most ebullient when it can uncover, disclose, demystify and undermine that which is buried, masked, distorted or asserted as truth. There is no more fertile ground for buried truths and open pretenses than the systematic subordination of one social group by another. This is why theory is one of the strongest allies subordinate populations can have, and why their rejection of it is always a catastrophic political error. They thereby disarm themselves in front of all the secret manifestations of power the dominant order creates on its own behalf.

The power of knowledge is ordinarily the greatest argument to be made in theory's favor. It is the third peculiarity of contemporary feminism — its ideological prejudice against power — that turns this argument into a point to be hinted at or suppressed. In part, such a prejudice flows out of feminism's strong stand against social oppression. In part, however, it stems from the tendency of its most radical members to portray men as the active agents and women as the passive victims of history, culture and society. This portrait in itself is an extremely crude one, and it encourages the equally crude portrait of power *per se* as male. Thus, the teacher who commends theory's gift of the power of knowledge to her students will first have to rescue power from its place of contempt. To do so, she will have to address a host of difficult questions to do with intentionality, agency and responsibility in sex/gender relations. These are in any case, it seems to me, the most pressing questions facing feminist theory today.

Note

1   Special thanks to Karen Strueing and Suzanna Walters — two students who share with me, each in her own way, a love of theory, a feminist politics, and an iconoclastic attitude towards feminist platitudes. These kindred spirits have kept me the best of intellectual company, and I owe them a great deal for that. Karen's insights about power have influenced my own all too brief discussion of it. I also am indebted to the work of Alasdair Mac-Intyre in my analysis of reason and emotion. Finally, I explore the whole question of reason and emotion in greater depth in another essay, 'Wordless Emotions,' forthcoming in *Politics and Society*.

15

The spectacle of gender: cinema and psyche

Catherine Portuges

The psychoanalytically oriented feminist teacher of film begins, as it were, with three strikes against her: she must overcome her students' desire — a desire she herself knows and shares — *not* to analyze films, those cherished icons of dream and fantasy; she must introduce into such analysis the discourse of psychoanalytic theory to audiences often predisposed to mistrust it; and she must weave into the substance of this inquiry the troubling and persistent questions of gender.

One might well ask why — apart from sheer masochism — anyone would wish to attempt such seemingly doomed pedagogical practice. That question carves out the proper space of inquiry of this essay, for feminist pedagogy — like psychoanalytic feminist criticism — calls attention to the speaking subject as part of the text to be analyzed. Why, indeed, would someone trained in modern French literature subject herself to the daily vicissitudes of this double jeopardy? For any one of these activities places a disproportionate burden of stress upon the practitioner who will more than likely be engaged in situating herself in opposition to traditional academic norms.

It will be immediately apparent that the interdependence of these elements — teaching film as cultural product from the double perspectives of psychoanalysis and feminism, with its concomitant necessity for balancing theory and practice — creates a pedagogical situation of exacting demands. One must bear in mind the multiplicity of potential emotional identifications with any film text, in order fully to respect the varieties of students' responses. In addition, one must work toward developing teaching strategies that seek to interrogate conventional notions of authority and privilege. Still more elusive is to teach a double construct: on the one hand, that film production is embedded in culture, in a social and historical context; on the other, that there are theoretical and critical interpretations which, by virtue of their formalist tendencies, militate against socio-historical claims. And, finally, one must persuade students, some of whom will be mightily seduced by theories seemingly distinct from a basis in practice, that the acts of reading, writing, directing and interpreting are, in fact, profoundly subjective.

I believe that such pedagogical obstacles, which I would be the last to underestimate, are offset by one powerful asset: the deepening conviction that this interdisciplinary method opens up useful directions for students with different talents, highly varied expectations, but often somnolent intellectual drives. I believe that films are works of art capable of affecting people deeply, perhaps even changing them, and that psychoanalytic criticism of a non-doctrinaire kind contains liberating potential for feminist scholarship and pedagogy. The demands on the teacher, however, are great: as reader, spectator, critic and 'professor,' she, like the psychoanalyst, must use her own responses to elaborate the meanings of film texts in constructing a methodology that permits students to remain aware simultaneously of the interactions among film-maker, audience, theorist, character, narrative and cultural context. Yet the demands on the students are perhaps greater still, for they must willingly undergo a period of anxiety and confusion in immersing themselves in the language and particular codes of cinema while they submit to the lure of the screen and, at the same time, remain alert to its most treacherously seductive, latent messages. They must embrace the sense of inadequacy — in some cases, the phobia — of reading and talking about theory, without losing sight of the images before them. (The images themselves can be problematic, spanning, like psychoanalysis itself, nearly 100 years of development, from silent one-reelers to the most technologically sophisticated special effects.) Students and teacher alike must take the risk of exposing themselves to powerful emotional material while managing to maintain firm enough ego boundaries to work intellectually through it. And, finally, both teacher and students together must learn to trust their own interpretations, transcending the realm of pure affect ('I loved/hated the film . . .') in demonstrating the range of operations of the medium — steeped as it is in the language of illusion, distortion and manipulation — upon the viewer.

The reader may already have discerned pedagogical and curricular analogies to the demands of other disciplines, other perspectives. With the possibilities for making such connections in mind, a more general discussion of the contexts of film-viewing might at this point prove worth while before proceeding to an enumeration of specific examples of course content and class settings. When I say 'psychoanalytic' here, I refer first of all to Freud, though I mean to include a great many theorists beyond Freudians. My film students are required to read *The Interpretation of Dreams* at a minimum, and from there, depending on the level of the class, other psychoanalytic readings are incorporated in the study of film scripts and criticism. Even in the most introductory versions of my courses, I find it necessary to speculate, using Freudian and more recent concepts, on the conditions of film-viewing, on cross-cultural implications of such approaches, concepts which underlie some of the most radical feminist critiques of film theory. Most important among these are the habits of viewing with which, unconsciously, most of us grew up. I refer to the darkness of a theater that engenders and sustains, despite the public nature of the medium, a viewer's anonymity, and the play of visual fascination, romance and reverie that characterize so much of our 'Hollywood' experience. Also at a preliminary stage of our investigations, I discuss with students the virulent racist and ethnic bias of most commercial feature films, the attraction of the mirroring screen, its receptivity to narcissistic identification, the tendency of directors to fetishize the human (particularly the female) form, the captivating qualities of images that we have come to associate with pleasure and desire, and the diffuse eroticism that attends so much film-viewing. To this catalogue I add a detail of personal history — the fact of growing up in Hollywood, and hence of being exquisitely aware of its presence as myth and reality — in order to encourage the positioning of the self in terms of regional and class factors in the ongoing discourse of cinema and psyche.

It has been said that every serious film-goer is a fetishist, in that films become eroticized objects of wish-fulfillment, as 'substitutes' for the 'real' world. While some may take issue with this rather orthodox psychoanalytic interpretation of cultural activity, it is nevertheless essential that students be challenged to take some critical distance on these charged issues. I appeal to their critical faculties by contrasting what is being asked of them to what my own generation was expected to do in film study: I was taught to regard the film as object, to assess its image, theme, camera positions and lighting with reference to a director's stylistic and thematic preoccupations. Typical of this approach was the individualist notion that the director was the principal author of what is so obviously a collective endeavor, particularly the French 'auteur' theory that assumed each director left 'his' distinct mark upon each film, irrespective of historical or other mediating circumstances. My film students, by comparison, are encouraged to monitor their responses, to observe the part of the self that wishes to vanish in the hypnotic dreamlike effects of the cinematic apparatus. Always a matter of considerable resistance, this struggle is enacted through note-taking during screenings and writing in the film journals straight afterwards in order to capture the immediacy of the somewhat altered state of consciousness. Obviously, this is asking a great deal: it requires assuming the critical posture of the distanced viewer temporarily unable to 'enjoy' the act of seeing in those old, familiar and treasured ways associated with childhood innocence and rapture. It means giving up a gratifying pastime that has remained largely unquestioned throughout one's life — today's media-literacy notwithstanding. It may even mean accepting a Freudian notion that assumes that pleasure in looking ('scopophilia') is associated with voyeurism and, perhaps, exhibitionism, not to mention fetishism. And who would want to agree to that?

In other words, in all three layers of inquiry resistance must be named, interpreted and worked with: resistance to theorizing about movies, to reading psychoanalytically, and to subjecting adored enter-tainment forms to the scrutiny of considerations of gender, race and class. There is also the larger undergraduate resistance to theorizing about anything, and, within the history of American feminism, a tendency toward skepticism (if not downright hostility) toward the speculative, non-pragmatic theories of continental origin, understood by some as particularly phallic and elitist.

Just as in Women's Studies rescuing women lost to history — their primary documents, their ignored or suppressed position in the world, their silenced artistic voices — has exposed the limitations of an exclu-sively patriarchal vision, so too in film studies researchers and film-makers have been engaged in reclaiming women artists long consigned to oblivion, and reenvisioning the history of movies through new awareness. When I began teaching film regularly, ten years ago, *all* the works shown in class were by male directors. My primary organizing principle at that time was to select a 'representative' group of films as texts, whether the course had as its focus documentary film, films of the 1950s, or the avant-garde. My definitions of excellence remained relatively consonant with those of the avant-garde critical canon of the time (a contradictory notion, of course, since by its own definitions there was no canon for the avant-garde, nor should there be), and with the French tradition in which I was educated — although as a professor of comparative literature I had relative freedom of selection, and was in fact encouraged to work with materials representing several national cultural traditions. Having constructed my syllabus on the basis of stylistic, film-historical and thematic concerns, I grew quickly aware of the overwhelmingly negative portrayals of women in films by nearly every director, regardless of cultural tradition, even by those touted as 'women's directors' or, especially, 'fond of women.' This was the period in which Women's Studies courses entitled 'Images of Women in . . .' were the norm, comprising the first wave of academic offerings. It had not yet occurred to me, nor to most film theorists and critics, that merely describing the roles of women in film did not bring adequate attention to the vexed questions of representation and gender. It was, however, an indispensable step, one which allowed several years of experimentation with classic and contemporary European works as well as the (for me) new terrain of American Hollywood product. An American educated by French professors, wholly devoted to contemporary European narrative cinema, I in time 'discovered' American films of the 1940s and 1950s and began to learn and to teach about the interplay between ideology, women and cinematic representation. To my delight and dismay, students were enthralled: at last, no more subtitles for every film! Classroom hours could also profitably be spent reading the films of their own heritage, using materials on which *they* had expertise as tools of academic investigation. How devastating, then, for them simultaneously to discover that those revered movies were not only laden with unrealistic and unfavorable portraits of female characters, but also contained and embodied innumerable instances of misogyny, in plot and theme, or masked within costumes, lighting, editing and tone.

Nevertheless, the immediacy and familiarity of these films spoke directly to students and engaged them in ways that their European counterparts could not. It grew possible to integrate students' personal knowledge of the films of Bette Davis, Joan Crawford and Humphrey Bogart (knowledge acquired primarily through late-night television and their parents' recollections, the latter of which initiated some stunning intergenerational dialogue concerning sex roles and assumptions about work, sexuality and the family) with contemporary feminist theory. Of particular moment were the theoretical debates proliferating at the same time in psychoanalytic and fictional literature on the developmental complexities of mother-daughter relationships. *Mildred Pierce* (1945) served as catalyst to open up this powerful subject in new ways. To be sure, classroom screenings and discussions of Bergman's *Autumn Sonata* and Fellini's *Juliet of the Spirits* had hardly left audiences unmoved concerning the inner workings of family dynamics, and especially mother-daughter attachments. Nevertheless, the American example, substantiated by other references from the same period (Bette Davis in *Now Voyager* as the oppressed daughter falling love with her analyst) elicited an intensity and richness of response paralleled by few others. That this should be so, very likely says something one might prefer not to hear about cultural chauvinism and the arrogance with which Americans regard other cultures, other languages; yet the film teacher must remain finely attuned to nuance of response in students in order more effectively to employ it in the service of feminist aims. After all, if pleasure is one of the deepest motivating impulses of film-going, making sense of its workings lies at the heart of the critical enterprise. Why not press it into service by teaching 'genre' films — those considered 'women's films' in the 1940s because their world was predicated on the domestic sphere — which may contain real possibilities for subversion to feminist ends through their sometimes unconscious inscription of woman in dialogue and *mise-en-scène*?

For years I had harangued students about the importance of knowing why the spectator is drawn to particular sequences, images, shots or dialogue. Were there differences, I wondered, in the sources of pleasure for female and male viewers? It had been a secret intention and gradually a more public effort on my part to discern reasons for these differences in audience response to male and female screen portrayals, to the array of masculine and feminine gestures, faces, postures and voices represented in films from all historical periods and many different cultures, economic conditions and artistic concerns. Students had been badgered, often with negligible results, to explain, define and analyze their reactions, however subtle, to the portrayals of women, children and men in movies. Although the 'state of the art' in film scholarship had evolved within feminist contexts to call for more positive images of women and more films made by women, little attention had been given to the question of the specificity of spectator-pleasure with respect to gender.

Laura Mulvey's influential article, 'Narrative Form and Visual Pleasure,' (*Screen*, 1973) was perhaps the first to address this gap and to point the way for further research. Appropriating psychoanalytic theory as a 'political weapon,' Mulvey discusses the absence of attention to the specificity of woman's desire and the tendency of patriarchal culture to inscribe the feminine in a symbolic order which maintains the 'look' as male privilege. In this view, the repressed desire of the spectator (assumed to be male) is projected upon the performer (female as object), satisfying a primordial wish for pleasure in looking. If woman is image and man bearer of the look, what are the implications for female spectatorship? By asking such questions, Mulvey confirmed my own inchoate and unempirical interrogations within the space of the classroom.

While gender is not the only category of importance in critical analysis of film, any theory that fails to account for its specificity could not yield the answers then suddenly called for, simply because the wrong questions will continue to be asked. I had been asking probing and provocative questions, to be sure: whose fantasy are we being asked to see as 'reality'? Whose 'imaginary' is translated into these seductive plots and surfaces? Who controls the narrative and for whose benefit? What happens to the female character who tries to transcend prescribed social or psychological boundaries? Even, for that matter, who gets married, who dies, who commits suicide, who has friends, who goes mad? Fascinating as was the evidence, accumulated overwhelmingly — and not surprisingly — on the side of bourgeois values and patriarchal ideology, such questions did not go far enough. Mildred Pierce and her contemporaries did, however, enable me to argue that the place of the mother in filmic discourse, as in psychoanalytic theory, had been repressed or marginalized, just as the voice of the woman as subject of her own narrative was virtually absent. It was no longer acceptable to remain at the comfortable surface. While students were still amused to see Hitchcock's *Spellbound* with Ingrid Bergman as the psychoanalyst treating (and falling in love with) the amnesiac Gregory Peck, and to laugh knowingly when her Hungarian analyst tells her that women make the best analysts until they fall in love (at which time they make the best patients), I felt that a far deeper and more risky pedagogical plunge had to be taken.

Teaching large (75-100) mixed-gender film classes in a state university and without the sophisticated film-projection equipment that permits repeated screenings and close compositional textual analysis had shaped my teaching style and, to some extent, the content of my classes. The time had clearly come to shift focus, to shed the protective mantle of neutrality afforded by the posture of passionate observer, and to enter more fully into what had become my subject — becoming myself the subject at the same time. It was as if several threads converged and offered themselves up for reweaving: theoretical developments had brought feminist psychoanalytic criticism to a moment of questioning combined with creating, not unlike the convergence of theorists, critics and film-makers at the start of the French New Wave in the late 1950s.

Coincident with advances in the field was my impatience with the male bias inherent in deconstructionist theories of representation and my desire to test the newer, feminist, psychoanalytically inspired theories in a more intimate classroom setting with advanced undergraduates drawn from Women's Studies, comparative literature and French. As my own work grew steadily to concentrate upon mother-daughter issues in contemporary art forms, it appeared natural to extend this inquiry to film-makers, as well as to their 'intertextual' dialogue. From the classic paradigm of male director/female star — with all its paternalistic suggestions of representer/represented, bearer and object of the gaze; its history of artist as father/creator and model as mistress/muse — the time had come to shift to the newest experiments of women directors, primarily independent avant-garde directors who had incorporated the radical questioning and subversive techniques of the French New Wave while insisting upon creating their own forms and finding their own subjects.

It did not take long to notice that three shifts were occurring at the same time: as content underwent transformation, so did pedagogy, with student response in some instances leading the way. It is never a simple matter to assign causality in matters of pedagogy. How often do we as teachers plan, anticipate and, with the best intentions and for the best of reasons, attempt to structure inquiry toward certain goals, only to end up mystified or annoyed by the unexpected turns taken by discussion or, for that matter, by a whole semester's work? And sometimes even our best efforts cannot match the results achieved quite by accident due to spontaneous, and irretrievable, happenstance. This is especially common in film teaching where one is dependent upon the vagaries of the perpetual 'present tense' inherent in the medium. Unlike other texts, the film image is a fleeting, ephemeral one, eluding our grasp while fostering the illusion that it presents itself for our individual benefit alone. It cannot be reread or cited by the ordinary spectator, and remains beyond reach while concealing the traces of its operations precisely in order to overcome audience resistance to it. It is not unusual, for instance, to uncover during discussion the most spectacular variations in students' account of what *actually* occurs in a given scene (and here I am referring to the most fundamental narrative level). Consequently, when introducing more demanding material, works that challenge and subvert the workings of cinema itself, films that are hermetic, non-narrative and/or emotionally distressing, I have tended to distance myself more than usual from my own affect, to assume a fairly neutral stance in order to allow students the full range of their responses — to contain them, so to speak.

In the more intimate setting of a small seminar room, screening films with twenty people instead of in an auditorium with 100, such distancing effects are far less possible and perhaps even undesirable. More is demanded of the pedagogical 'self'; or, rather, the formal lecture must give way to an interactive dialogue interspersed with longer discursive moments. While it may be premature to articulate the successes and failures of a course developed in the protected atmosphere of a Mellon Foundation faculty development grant, administered by Wellesley College's Center for Research on Women, and taught only once, this past semester, perhaps others can benefit from my reflections and take heart from my long-delayed risk. What works in one setting often cannot in another; yet I think it is fair to say at this point that what was lost in the 'performance' dimension of the large hall was more than compensated for by the gains of immediacy, subjectivity and informality in the smaller setting.

With Simone de Beauvoir as mentor and muse — and her still unsurpassed text *The Second Sex* as point of departure — my students and I embarked upon a journey into largely uncharted waters. The new course was to be entitled 'French Women Since *The Second Sex*,' to commemorate de Beauvoir as well as to assess her impact on the 'successor' generation of feminists. We would, as I imagined it, explore artistic forms of expression by contemporary French-speaking women writers and film-makers concerned with questions of representation and the female self, the new *écriture féminine*, and its relation to psychoanalytic theory. The first of these intersections to emerge, quite unconsciously as a text that had itself been repressed, was the theme of the artists' (and their characters') dialogue with a mother-figure. This discovery was not without interest to me in my research on the feminist classroom and my hypothesis of its underlying mother-daughter analogies; for, to a degree, each text, each film we studied called attention to a powerful maternal presence in the artist's psyche — subsequently decipherable as either nurturing or limiting and, in some sense, a version of the 'Good and Bad Mother' conceptualization frequently used in object-relations theory. Not only were the readings heavily marked by the writer's concerns with sexuality and maternity, but the films I had chosen also drew a major portion of their focus from those very issues, despite the fact that they had not originally been expected to serve the sole or primary purpose of extending such a mother-daughter inquiry.

While at one level I had still been operating in the professorial mode consonant with my graduate training and subsequent interdisciplinary pedagogy, and therefore anticipating an authoritative positioning with regard to the students by virtue of my more 'advanced' understanding of the complex phenomena we were to investigate, at another, more unconscious, level the material soon began to acquire a life of its own. My students perceived this double operation sooner than I, and by virtue of their own individual claims upon it, the mother-daughter issue became the organizing principle of the course.

In short order, films I had sought to utilize as demonstrations of 'classic' or 'illusionist' narrative modes, as against the more contemporary experiments of the avant-garde women directors, unwittingly suggested themselves as studies in pre-oedipal intertextuality. *The Earrings of Madame de* ... (1953), directed by Max Ophuls, renowned as a quintessential French 'woman's director' (the gallic equivalent of George Cukor), came suddenly to foreshadow most of the works that were to follow: in addition to its tragic romantic elements (a great and impossible love), from its opening frames the film announced itself as a dialogue between a nineteenth-century coquette and her dead mother. Madame de Lafayette's *Princess of Cleves*, which had been intended as an early instance of a woman writing about manners and morals in the court of Louis XIV, revealed itself more profoundly as an imaginative record of a protective, as well as destructive, bond beween mother and daughter.

The foregoing are examples of traditional texts turned to 'feminist' purposes by dint of their inclusion in a particular course, or by the order in which they appear in that course; their use describes a strategy that may be common enough in some disciplines but one that has not, unfortunately, been widely enough appropriated in film studies. As this material in our course made its own affective as well as cerebral demands upon us, I recognized a paradoxical dynamic making itself felt in my teaching practice. In the more traditional pedagogy to which I have referred, the lecturer situates herself or himself *vis-à-vis* the film text in a distanced, 'neutral' fashion to allow for maximum freedom of students' interpretations of a medium whose shadowy seductions have been noted above. Interpretations are customarily encouraged from all perspectives, in the traditional 'humanistic' style I had been perpetuating: the subjective is legitimized when offered ultimately in conjunction with theoretical substantiation. Although in such a mode the professor's opinions are not absent, their status is unarguably mediated. However, in the feminist pedagogy which was unfolding within and before me, the teacher became unconsciously implicated in her own discourse, drawn in by the power of the material and the now undeniable claims of the gendered spectacle played out on the screen. In other words, although I had not relinquished the shaping authority inherent in the role of the person who decides what will be read and screened, I could not have predicted — and, for that matter, would not have wished to — the cumulative impact of the effects of such material upon me as teacher. Contrary to whatever expectations I may have acknowledged, I had begun, however hesitantly, to speak with my own voice. In abandoning the perhaps illusory neutrality of the traditional pedagogical situation, instead of losing what may in fact have been a tenuous 'grip,' I came to acquire a new confidence and authority alongside my students.

It has been noted that a central issue of feminist education within the mother-daughter paradigm is the daughter's gradual awakening to the need to separate from the mother, a realization that engenders inevitable stages of anger, abandonment and anxiety over the fear of destroying the object that is at once loved and dreaded. As a teacher I, too, am a daughter of the paternal figures — professors and film directors — from whom I, too, had to separate, in a process that is still taking place. By leaving behind the filmic fathers to whom I had been so attached, my students and I were able to learn from their successors, the newer generations of women film-makers who were creating their own cinematic language, their own styles of representation. Instead of submitting to the seduction and betrayal of the great pantheon of directors — Renoir, Bergman, Fellini, Resnais, Godard, Truffaut — we encountered the works of Duras, Akerman,

Varda, Poirier and Dulac as they interrogated dominant cinema in their own challenging styles. Perhaps not surprisingly, the majority of these women directors chose to focus upon friendships among women, changes in relationships among mothers and daughters, explorations of the psyche and documentary treatments of work, rape and aging. The presence in the class of two invited film-makers, Agnès Varda and Anne-Claire Poirier, naturally intensified the exchanges among us, as we learned not to equate 'daughter/student' and 'mother/teacher,' for we all, of course, contain elements of both, and represent parts of each to ourselves and to each other.

If spectators surrender a portion of self-definition in their encounter with screen images, feminist pedagogy similarly requires a loosening of the bonds of differentiation between self and other, a shedding of the protective armor of neutrality in order to embrace new opportunities offered by the legitimation of the female subject as text. And just so, in asserting themselves as empowered speaking subjects extending the women's voices on screen and in writing, students mirror the separation-individuation stage in differentiating from the blissful state of pre-oedipal fusion with the teacher — a stage essential in the creation of a whole self. The classroom staging of this scenario of differentiation is heightened when the cinematic dimension is added, for it provides inexhaustible riches for those engaged in seeking to reclaim the hidden truths of representation, here figured in the spectacle of gender.

16

Mastery, identity and the politics of work: a feminist teacher in the graduate classroom

Nancy K. Miller

Let me begin by identifying the political realities that have generated the chain of abstractions structuring the title of my paper. For the context of my local situation has everything to do with my general sense of what is possible or desirable in the feminist pedagogic enterprise and may help to explain the slightly depressive tone of my reflection. I am speaking, then, as a feminist teacher engaged for one-fifth of her time in the education of (primarily) women within the walls and wisdom of an elite institution originally organized by men for the education of men; a teacher, moreover, performing in a classroom in which she herself was a graduate student in the more euphoric moments of the late 1960s and early 1970s.

In 1980, the study of French literature at Columbia is still a pursuit undertaken primarily by women in a department run by men theoretically committed to theorizing the theory of literature. What has changed — at Columbia and elsewhere, of course — is neither the privileged discourse, nor the familiar ecology of power, but the sheer numbers of the unempowered: there are fewer graduate students, with less money to sustain them, and fewer jobs to dream of. These demographic and economic specificities mean, for starters, that the paranoia always inherent in hierarchical organizations is now aggravated by an equally real and altogether appropriate anxiety about survival. What, in such a situation, is an appropriate feminist pedagogy?

What is it, I ask myself, I think I am doing by encouraging these women to continue (or begin) working for a degree that will theoretically entitle them to bear the title of professor? Am I not encouraging them to 'imitate' me — under conditions less favorable to their success? Perhaps this peculiar form of female narcissism — a term more apt, I think, than the cooler and sociological notion of 'role modeling' to describe the psychic miming at the heart of this doubling — is not only irresponsible but wrong. Perhaps a talented young woman should *not* be encouraged to embrace the conditions of a profession agonizing under the threat of continued attrition in the humanities, not to mention the wages of what has been called affirmative inaction. Would she not be better-off doing something else altogether? Or at least, if she is determined to run the risk, should she run it *as* a feminist? I believe this is called double jeopardy.

I have no interesting answers to that well-known dilemma. I have simply taken in my person the willfully naive but no less self-conscious leap of faith that points to the belief that it is possible to bring about difference despite repetition, that it is indeed possible to bring about change because without that wager we guarantee that no change will occur at all. This is part of what I mean by the politics of work; and why, no less obviously, we are all here at this forum.

In the classroom as a feminist teacher, therefore, I maintain — if only by my presence there — that one can survive the vicissitudes of a feminist identity inside the private patriarchal bailiwick I have described. There is, however, one crucial precondition: that this critical identity be perceived as strong within the terms of institutional practice. This may sound a resolutely conservative politics to be proposing under the name of feminist pedagogy, but I believe that I owe my own survival (thus far)[2] as a 'woman who works on women' (as I have come to be known) on the fifth floor of Philosophy Hall (there is a copy of Rodin's *Thinker* in front of the building) to the fact that I was also originally perceived as a structuralist. Today, for graduate students in French post-structuralist times and fiefdoms, other perceptions obtain. But whatever the methodological engagement, a female and feminist mastery of phallocentric mysteries is, I think, an essential strategy for survival. This does not, of course, mean believing that the truth inhabits those systems; rather, it is to recognize that their limits cannot be located without an understanding of their claims to the truth.

I hope it is clear, then, that I understand feminist mastery as a subversive move and not as a gesture of docile complicity and ideological collusion.[3] What I seek to do in the classroom, therefore, is to expose at all times the blind spots in the dominant codes (and modes) of meta-critical discourse as they are pressed into the service of a feminist analysis. This exposure is meant to detheatricalize the scenarios of mastery and to raise the curtains on the stage of its production. In that process, ideally, the classroom becomes not a showcase for exhibitionistic intimidation, but a scene of work.

I shall give one concrete example of this practice. I offered an interdisciplinary course last spring called 'Studies in French Eighteenth-century Fiction and Painting: Ideologies of Representation.' The title was deliberately ponderous and vague, designed to deliver a preemptive strike on the Committee on Instruction. What I wanted to do was to look at − literally and figuratively − the inscriptions of the sexual and social relations between the sexes in eighteenth-century texts. I pretty much knew what I would find − the territory, after all, was not entirely unknown to me − but two pedagogic anxieties immediately emerged: how to present the material (a practical problem); and in what language or meta-language to articulate the findings (a theoretical or methodological problem). The second anxiety was particularly acute since despite the political blandness of the course title, I was teaching from a feminist perspective students − some of whom were men − who did not all necessarily conceive of themselves as feminists in their work or in their lives. I wanted even more acutely to perform a remapping of the territory that would prevent feminist analysis from appearing − to the skeptical − to be a thematics. I wanted, I confess, to seduce.

Paradoxically, though I have no training in art history and machine anxiety to boot, showing slides and 'reading' paintings proved to be the most persuasive tool I had ever used in teaching. Sitting in the darkened room, watching the obsessions of the century − the visual fantasies of the Enlightenment's erotic imagination − it was impossible not to see what lay behind the fictions of desire in the age of reason. The results of this unveiling were compelling in two ways: in the first instance, it brought woman's body − in various stages of undress − physically into the classroom; in the second (a consequence of the first), it identified all of us in the room as gendered and sexual beings − whether we wanted to be identified in that way or not. It was a kind of enactment of the inescapable relations between bodies and theories, the intersections of the personal and the political.

I do not mean to suggest, I should hasten to add, that looking at slides has any inherently feminist value to it, or that an interdisciplinary offering necessarily leads to feminist epiphanies. What I am claiming is that this particular teaching situation − in which I was forced to let go of my own fragile claims to mastery by virtue of taking on the visual — allowed me to bring out into the open the stakes of theorization itself. In the absence of adequate models for articulating the relations between visual and verbal texts, the politics of the image and the erotics of reading, we had to forge our own, building from the strategies available to us, and devising new ones at the scene of their failure. Because, as I have been saying, I think it is crucial for women and feminist scholarship to have a less mystified relation to mastery and theory, I feel that the experiment was both demonstrative and exhilarating.

That is not, however, the whole story. By relinquishing the standard peacock model of graduate teaching designed to dazzle the hens, in favor of a more ambiguous and less predictable pedagogy, I ran the risk of losing my own identity as the teacher — the one who is supposed to know — and the guaranteed seduction that strutting (one's stuff) traditionally effects. That risk is neatly defined in the following aphorism of Nietzsche's I came across in a book called *On Seduction* by a French philosopher: 'We don't believe that the truth still remains the truth once its veil has been removed.' Though there were students who did seem to believe that, in the end, an empowering discourse would have to come from within — not naively, of course, but from patient negotiations with competing claims to authority — I have the distinct impression that there were students who have preferred for me to remain veiled, for identity to remain seamless, for mastery to remain mystifying. I do not know whether their resistance to my unveiling was due to a resistance to a more collaborative pedagogy, or to an inadequacy inherent in the project itself. Perhaps what I took to be their nostalgia for the peacock is merely a projection of my own ambivalence. The desire for his master's voice is not to be underestimated.

In any event, this, I think, is the question of feminist pedagogy in the graduate classroom: how to create a critical identity which understands the discourses of mastery without succumbing to their seductions. For seduced, we are simply the old slaves, or worse, the new masters. In closing, it is not clear to me what metaphorical bird to oppose to the peacock — just us chickens? Nor what erotic model to oppose to the old power politics of seduction and betrayal. It is clear, however, that through the recognition of same to same, despite the mark of difference always inscribed by hierarchy, new identities do emerge — and that is, after all, one of the tasks and joys of any pedagogy.

Notes

1 Originally given as a talk at the Modern Language Association (1980) and published in *Feminist Pedagogy: Positions and Points of View*, Women's Research Center Working Papers Series (Madison, Wisconsin), no. 3, 1981. Reprinted with permission.

2 Recent events (related to tenure and promotion at Columbia, and my personal survival there — but that I cannot elaborate upon here) have made me wonder whether it is wise to regard any strategy for (female and feminist) survival in *institutional* terms as anything more than a self-sustaining fiction (fantasy). However, if a feminist teacher, whatever the denouement of her own specific plot may be, can bring *other* women along within the *provisional* terms of her tenure, all is not in vain.

3 Moreover, I should also make clear here that I do not regard the *production* of theory as masculine in origin. On the contrary. In France today, women intellectuals and writers are producing texts of crucial importance for feminist scholarship: Hélène Cixous, Luce Irigaray, Julia Kristeva — to name just three of the better-known figures theorizing the 'feminine.'

PART SIX

Authority and affect

17

Authority in the feminist classroom: a contradiction in terms?

Susan Stanford Friedman

I choose to address the issue of feminist pedagogy in a personal narrative not only because the cornerstone of that pedagogy has been the validation of experience, but also because my own evolution as a teacher in a university setting over the last twelve years illuminates a pedagogical problem we all must face. Women's Studies classrooms all over the country have brought a new level of energy, motivation and purpose to higher education. As feminist teachers, we have applauded and taken great pride in the revitalization, womanization and humanization we have achieved in the feminist classroom. But beneath the surface and occasionally flaring up into classroom crises there are pressures, dissatisfactions, and conflicts that both teachers and students feel. These problems (often difficult for feminist teachers to admit because we frequently hold impossible standards for ourselves) revolve around such issues as teachers' grading and evaluation, student evaluations; student hostility and fear of feminist material and perspectives; complex student expectations of a Women's Studies teacher; student need for validation, nurturance, and personal relationship with a woman who is both potentially a role model and mother-figure; faculty need to encourage rigorous, excellent work; all the contradictions inherent in a feminist classroom operating within a patriarchal institution. My own experiences shed some light on these issues and can, hopefully, contribute *one* of the many concerns we must address in the theoretical and practical formulations of feminist pedagogy.

I began teaching in the late 1960s during the heyday of the radical challenge to conventional pedagogy. Herbert Kohl and Jerry Farber were my guideposts to becoming the successful teacher who could stimulate students into critical thinking and independent formulations of what they wanted to study and why. Like any new teacher, I had the feelings of inner panic and the pre-class nightmares. Kohl's *36 Children* was invaluable as a warning against projecting that fear into the role of the rigid figure, whose authority in the classroom emerges from the power granted the role of 'teacher.'[2] Farber expanded the attack on professional authority in 'Student as Nigger,' an essay I handed out to all of my classes at the beginning of a semester.[3] Farber argued that teachers in general, and college professors especially, are a timid lot who compensate for their relative powerlessness in a capitalist society by exercizing a tyranny over the minds of their students. Education, he believed, trains students into a 'slave' mentality that inhibits rebellion and independent thought. A profound influence on me as a fledgling teacher, he convinced me that I must break the authority and tyranny of the teacher to establish a classroom where students feel free to challenge all ideas, my own most especially.

As a teacher in a university setting, then, I de-emphasized my authority to establish the course, structure its progression and evaluate the students' work. Attempting to dissolve assumptions of hierarchy in both mine and my students' heads, I thought of myself as a 'resource person' who would 'facilitate' students' development of critical thought. True, I knew a bit more than my students about literature. True, I had to grade them. But we were all equals in a democratic classroom and I would contribute those 'extras' where it was relevant.

My understanding of feminist pedagogy was an outgrowth of the fusion in my professional life of feminism and radical pedagogy. The premises of feminist pedagogy make a familiar list that, in my case, certainly owed a great deal to the feminist movement *and* to writers like Farber: non-hierarchical classroom; validation and integration of the personal; commitment to changing students' attitudes toward women, most particularly women's images of themselves and their potential; recognition that no education is value-free and that our field operates out of a feminist paradigm (as opposed to the patriarchal paradigm of most classrooms). Radical feminist analysis of masculine power structures and modes of thought reinforced the attack on hierarchy in all its forms. As feminist women in the universities, many of us attempted to circumvent the mystique of professional expertise and specialization by emphasizing student 'expertise' based on the authority of their own experience and by de-emphasizing the leadership role the classroom structure demanded of us. We believed we were bringing the organizational structures of radical feminism into our pedagogy.

My students in my small classes, first at Brooklyn College and then at the University of Wisconsin, resisted my attempts at feminist democratization all the way. They enjoyed my supportive reinforcement of all ideas in the classroom; they blossomed under the compassionate tutorials that took place in my office. But student evaluations revealed that they hungered for more of the brief syntheses and 'mini-lectures' I reluctantly scattered throughout the class-period. Evaluations were consistently very high but, always, the anonymous forms asked for more direction, structure and lecture from me. For years, I put these comments down to the socialization of American students to a 'slave' mentality, as Farber put it, so that they devalued students' ideas and gave me the false authority of the expert. We fought a silent battle, the students and I — they demanding ever more of me; I demanding ever more of them. In a feminist context, of course, I felt I was fighting their tendency to devalue women and teaching them self-assertion, self-confidence. For my women students, I was attempting to develop the independence and self-esteem which are the cornerstones of authentic womanhood.

And I was. But I had an epiphany in the shower one morning — where else do epiphanies strike one? It was several months after a series of events and conversations had begun to trouble my ideas about my own teaching and feminist pedagogy. To simplify, I will list these apparently unrelated things. First, for several years my large state university had thrown me into lecture situations where I had to expound and perform for two hours a week in front of 180-200 students. To my surprise, I enjoyed it, especially in my introductory Women's Studies course. Second, a colleague reported to me the discussion of a session on 'The Politics of Nurturance: Psychoanalytic Models for Understanding the Feminist Classroom' at the Simone de Beauvoir Feminist Theory Conference (September 1979). Women's Studies teachers discussed their students' subtle desires to find in their teachers a nurturing mother-figure. Is this expectation compatible with a university teacher's desire to foster rigorous, intellectual work? some asked. Third, the sociologist Norma Wikler came to campus to report the results of her studies on students' differential attitudes and expectations of their male and female teachers.[4] In general, she found students accepting high standards, discipline and toughness from their male teachers and deeply resenting any such behavior from their women teachers, especially in Women's Studies classrooms. Fourth, I watched a bright colleague of mine teach a small and enthusiastic group of advanced Women's Studies students. Discussion went very well, up to a point, on a number of tough theoretical issues about female imagery in women's art. Although I knew my colleague knew perfectly well how to synthesize the disparate issues the students brought up, I watched her suppress her own capacity to conceptualize what the students had discussed. Fifth, a student taking both my Women's Studies class and my husband's political science class told me a dream she had. In her dream, she came to me and begged me to intercede for her by getting Ed to change his take-home exam just distributed. It was much too tough. And, finally, a wonderful colleague of mine was trashed by her students in a Women's Studies class. They were filling out class evaluations on the day she returned their term papers, most of which ignored her careful instructions for use of primary sources. Many grades (Bs and Cs) had reflected the students' unwillingness to do the necessary library work.

All of these coalesced (in the shower) into a single, stunningly simple insight. As feminist teachers, we have paradoxically ignored the lens of gender as it operates in classroom dynamics and pedagogy. Both our students and ourselves have been socialized to believe (frequently at a non-conscious level) that any kind of authority is incompatible with the feminine. That, fundamentally, is what patriarchy does in its definition of woman: deny women the *authority* of their experiences, perspectives, emotions and minds. The denial of intellect is particularly crucial for the scholar and educator who happens to be female. Like her sister the artist, the woman-teacher is caught in a double bind: to be 'woman,' she has no authority to think; to think, she has made herself 'masculine' at the cost of her womanhood. A man stepping into the role of professor has a certain authority granted to him by his students that operates immediatcly. Women, on the other hand, must earn that authority and respect, which is in any event often granted with great resentment, even hostility. Some women become '100 per centers' to achieve authority, often taking pride in being tougher and less personal than many male colleagues. And as Wikler argued, students may pressure any woman-teacher to fulfill the role of the all-forgiving, nurturing mother whose approval is unconditional. Thus, the clashes at grading time. Thus, the hostile challenge to her authority to know that many women have faced.

As for the woman-teacher, she has been subject to socialization to femininity from birth. If she has internalized the patriarchal norm, the last message she needs to hear is Farber's condemnation and analysis:[5]

> teachers ARE short on balls ... the classroom offers an artificial and protected environment in which they can exercise their will to power. Your neighbors may drive a better car ... your wife may dominate you; the State legislature may shit on you; but in the classroom by God, students do what you say — or else. The grade is a hell of a weapon. It may not rest on your hip, potent and rigid like a cop's gun, but in the long run it's more powerful.

The radical pedagogy that so influenced me and a generation of feminist teachers emerged as a critique of *male* authority as it manifested itself in the classroom. What I and other women have needed is a theory of feminist pedagogy consistent with our needs as women operating at the fringes of patriarchal space. As we attempt to move on to academic turf culturally defined as male, we need a theory that first recognizes the androcentric denial of *all* authority to women and, second, points out a way for us to speak with an authentic voice not based on tyranny. I am, of course, not suggesting that feminist pedagogues adopt the power of their male colleagues — that is, in any case, an impossibility for most women. I am arguing instead for the inadequacy of masculine authority (based as it is on oppression) and the feminine (based at it is on the absence of *any* authority). We must move beyond both pedagogical models to develop a classroom based on the 'authority' radical feminism has granted to women in the process of subverting and transforming patriarchal culture.

Writers like Woolf, Rich, Daly and Rowbotham have affirmed woman's right for a fully human *authority* to think, feel, work, play and relate to others as woman. Feminist pedagogy now needs to base the classroom more completely on the accomplishments of the movement. In our eagerness to be non-hierarchical and supportive instead of tyrannical and ruthlessly critical, we have sometimes participated in the patriarchal denial of the mind to women. In our radical and necessary assertion that the feminist teacher must validate the personal and the emotional, we have sometimes ignored the equally necessary validation of the intellect. In our sensitivity to the psychology of oppression in our students' lives, we have often denied ourselves the authority we seek to nurture in our students.

I would suggest that we *add* the following to the list of principles of feminist pedagogy that I outlined before. First, a recognition that we as educators and our students have been socialized in a culture that has negated or trivialized woman's intellect and authority. Second, a celebration of women's intellectual potential — a capacity of the mind that we aim to nourish and to integrate with emotion and relation. Such additions to 'the list' require that our concept of the 'non-hierarchical' classroom must change. As much as we can while working within institutions based fundamentally on hierarchy, we must re-affirm our commitment to dissolving the kind of authority that leads to students' passivity and lack of independent thought (this includes, in my opinion, resisting the temptation to impose a feminist orthodoxy that students do not feel free to critique). At the same time, we must incorporate in feminist pedagogy in the classroom a recognition of the teacher's knowledge and experience within the parameters of the course she is offering.

The feminist teacher can be more than a 'facilitator,' if she will only grant herself the authority to be so. Ideally, she has a rich storehouse of knowledge — intellectual as well as emotional, scholarly as well as personal. Ideally, she has the experience and ability to structure the semester's work, synthesize disparate materials, and challenge the students to precise and rigorous thought. These intellectual capacities can be, I believe, infused with the nuances of nurturance so that the feminist teacher's challenge to her students does not reproduce patriarchal pedagogy. At least, this is a possible ideal — however difficult it is to make real in a world where liberation is a process of becoming.

Notes

1 Originally given as a talk at the Modern Language Association (1980) and published in *Feminist Pedagogy: Positions and Points of View*, Women's Research Center Working Papers Series (Madison, Wisconsin), no. 3, 1981. Reprinted with permission.
2 Herbert Kohl, *36 Children*, New York: Signet, 1967.
3 Jerry Farber, 'The Student as Nigger,' in his *The Student as Nigger*, New York: Pocket, 1969.
4 Norma Wikler, 'Sexism in the Classroom,' paper presented at the American Sociological Association Meetings, New York, September 1976.
5 Farber, 'The Student as Nigger,' p.95.

18

Anger and authority in the introductory Women's Studies classroom

Margo Culley

Teaching about gender and race can create classrooms that are charged arenas. Students enter these classrooms imbued with the values of the dominant culture: they believe that success in conventional terms is largely a matter of *will* and that those who do not *have it all* have experienced a failure of will. Closer and closer ties between corporate America and higher education, as well as the 'upscaling' of the student body, make it even harder to hear the voices from the margin within the academy. Bringing those voices to the center of the classroom means disorganizing ideology and disorienting individuals. Sometimes, as suddenly as the fragments in a kaleidoscope rearrange to totally change the picture, our work alters the ground of being for our students (and perhaps even for ourselves). When this happens, classrooms can become explosive, but potentially transformative arenas of dialogue.

The better we can describe and understand the energy loosed in these contexts, the more adequate our pedagogical theory and processes will be to our tasks. In all the important material written about teaching in the 1960s and 1970s — liberal, progressive, even radical; from Carl Rogers to Paulo Freire, Kozol to Katz — one crucial dimension is missing. None of the discussion of teacher, student, facilitator or learner is gender- or race-specific. And if we are to understand more fully the energy and power of the feminist classroom, we must begin with a focus on this missing information — the gender and race of those participating in the process.

This essay focuses on teaching at the introductory level, and on two central issues of such work: anger and authority in the classroom.

Young white women today, unlike their counterparts of a decade ago, come to the classroom convinced that the revolution has been won. They seek guidance toward that not–too–distant day when success in the workplace will be reinforced by the man at their side committed to co-parenting and his share of the housework. Young black women, while less naive about the promises held out to them by the dominant culture, do hold myths in defiance of facts and are ambivalent about thinking about themselves as black *women*, particularly in a group dominated by white women.

New students of this so-called 'post-feminist' generation come to an introductory Women's Studies course asking: 'Can a young woman from Smithville find happiness as the first (or first black) woman president of Data Corporation?' My task as a white woman now old enough to be their mother, and as an 'elite' member of the dominant culture, is complex. Beginning with what the students *think* they want to know, we move toward what at some level they *do* know — but have largely denied, because if they had not denied it, they could not be asking their question. The process allows them a glimpse, a taste, or a full-face confrontation with the truth that the dominant culture is steeped in the hatred of women. The journey makes students, and at times the teacher, uncomfortable, anxious, despairing and angry. It is a perilous trip undertaken only with my conviction (which I hope they come to share) that we all will emerge stronger, freer, better in control of — because more understanding of — the forces shaping us as women, black and white, in America.

In calling myself a feminist teacher, I take my charge from a statement made by Lucy Stone in 1855: 'In education, in marriage, in religion, in everything, disappointment is the lot of woman. It shall be the business of my life to deepen this disappointment in every woman's heart until she bows down to it no longer.'[2] Lucy Stone would have approved the public service television spot which appeared for a brief time on the air a few years ago. It pictured a girl baby, while across the screen flashed 'born handicapped' with a voice-over telling of the evils of discrimination based on sex. My work in the classroom begins with this realization: the teacher who is a woman and her female students are born into a misogynist culture and are 'born handicapped.' By the time these girl babies, students and teacher alike, find themselves together in the classroom, the damage they have suffered includes some level of self-hatred based on the female body they inhabit, some limits on their capacities and imaginations as the result of sex-role socialization, and some level of blindness to, and denial of, these truths. The most complex and intriguing aspects of what goes on in the feminist classroom derive from the fact that the instructor who is female shares the stigma of her female students. Indeed, only in the classroom where instructor and student share the same stigma — whether it be femaleness or blackness or both — is the potential present for the most radical transformation: the transformation to wholeness, to strength and to freedom.

My students, myself. The feminist teacher can be a potent agent of change who, through combinations of course content and process, has the power to replace self-hatred with self-love, incapacity with capacity, unfreedom with freedom, blindness with knowledge. In accepting my authority (not 'me' as an individual, but as an emblem) to be the agent of that transformation, the students are simultaneously accepting their own rightful claim to those goals. The words 'power' and 'authority' are chosen deliberately here as a challenge to the commonly held notion that a feminist classroom is one where power and authority have somehow disappeared. The radical feminist teacher (this has nothing to do with 'radical feminism,' it has to do with getting to the roots — the roots being the hatred of women) *has* power and must claim her authority if her students are to claim their own. The power she has resides precisely and paradoxically in the source of her stigma: her gender or her race, or both.

No amount of knowledge, insight and sensitivity on the part of a male instructor can alter the deep structures of privilege mirrored in the male as teacher, female as student model. Just as no amount of knowledge, insight and sensitivity on the part of a white instructor can alter these fundamentals if the student is black. One would not want to deny that many positive things can happen when a male is the instructor of female students. And the white teacher can indeed create an authentically anti-racist classroom. But these teachers cannot be the agents of the deepest transformations in a culture where women have been schooled to look to male authority and to search for male approval at the basis of self-worth. Just so, white instructors cannot be the agents of the deepest transformations for their black students in a culture where dominant values are white. These statements, representing the logical extension of my argument, provide the framework for discussion of the more specific issues: anger and authority in the feminist classroom.

Anger is the energy mediating the transformation from damage to wholeness. But to experience anger as a white *woman* is a risk-filled event because it looses, momentarily at least, one's biological, psychological, social, economic and sexual moorings in the dominant culture. To feel anger as a black *woman* may also mean standing outside, for that time, the culture which is a source of identity and strength. While these risks may seem parallel, the consequences will be profoundly different for white and black women so long as one culture is under siege from another.

If done with an awareness of these risks, letting anger out of its Pandora's box and into the classroom can be an important and manageable act. It will be manageable to the extent we understand what is happening when we legitimate one of the many forms of affect the educational system has schooled out of the academy. Manifestations of anger in the classroom setting may include denial and other defensive reactions, as well as the fixing of anger on inappropriate objects, including other students and the instructor herself. The goal of the feminist teacher in daring to lift the lid off what is well buried is not merely cathartic, as some would suggest. The goal is to permit the acknowledgment and claiming of anger as one's own, and to direct its legitimate energy toward personal and social change.

To illustrate, let me consider the large introductory course, 'Issues for Women of the 1980s,' which continues to enroll up to 250 students. I need only mention to this group, for example, the readily available, publicly published statistics on education, employment categories, and income levels and we have begun. These facts are always met with a startling array of reactions: 'Who published those statistics?' (US Department of Labor.) 'When was that?' (Any time before yesterday is pre-history.) 'Those figures must be based on women who work part time.' Or, 'A lot of women choose not to work, you know — are they in there?' Then, soon after, 'You can't get anywhere hating men, you can't blame them.' And quietly to themselves or to each other, 'I heard she's divorced, she's probably a lesbian or something.'

As painful as these efforts to distance, discount and deny may be to hear (and they can be costly semester after semester), they must be allowed or the group will travel no farther. Only a full expression of these defensive responses will allow them to be examined, then to begin to fade, and to be transformed to anger acknowledged. Orchestrating this process always involves trying to sense how far to go, becoming alternately 'Good Mother' and 'Bad Mother,' protecting the students and jolting them, wanting them to hear but not to shut down and tune out completely. Do I respond, for example, by asking them why the culture allows overt and often violent hatred of women, but does not permit, indeed has no word for, anger at men?

Anger felt by students in the classroom often fixes itself upon inappropriate objects, particularly upon other students. One method of dealing with self-hate engendered by a misogynist and racist culture can be to direct negative feelings toward other women, other people of color, and the classroom offers opportunity for this behavior. Students tend to categorize each other and may turn on each other — the 'women's libber' on the one always mentioning 'my boyfriend'; the one who comes to class in jeans and a sweat shirt on the one with heavy make-up and a different skirt every day; the lower-class woman on the one she perceives as privileged. Male students, often uneasy and uncomfortable, can sometimes strike out in extreme responses — as did the one who wrote in his journal, 'These women are like sharks — one taste of blood and they come back and back.' Or the one who was harassing a female member of the class with anonymous phone calls. These last two 'clinical' examples aside,[3] the feminist teacher can turn such free-floating anger into a lesson on the displacement of negative feelings. By directly naming and analyzing these dynamics, she can demonstrate that *every* woman in our culture is the object of the suspicion or disdain of some other woman. The classroom itself can become, at these most difficult moments, a laboratory of what we have set out 'dispassionately' to study.

When anger fixes itself upon the instructor as instigator or mediator of stressful learning, it is here that anger becomes tangled with the issue of authority. If the teacher is female, or black, or both, she comes to the classroom with her authority in question. If she initiates a process challenging the world view and the view of self of her students, she will surely — if she is doing her job — become the object of some students' unexamined anger. And if the feminist teacher embraces any of the following axioms of feminist education, she will also place herself outside available forms of patriarchal authority conferred by her position. These axioms include:

feminist education is interdisciplinary;
feminist education legitimates life-experience as an appropriate subject of analysis;
feminist education concerns itself with process as well as product;

feminist education is multicultural and explores interlocking systems of oppression based on sex, race and class.

Accepting any one of these principles, and surely accepting them in combination, means the feminist instructor cannot be buttressed by 'illusions' of authority, whether it be the authority of tradition, of the academic disciplines, of the dominant culture (if she is white), or of the institutional structures within which she operates.

A painful anecdote will demonstrate what I mean when I say that, as a woman, I come to the classroom with my authority in question. Last fall on the first day of the semester, I walked in to my course 'Man and Woman in Literature.' The group was mixed, men and women (all white but one). The course is a standard introduction to literature class offered by my department, but the section had been misadvertised as taught by a male colleague with whom I had team-taught on other occasions. So, to set the record straight, I began: 'I am Professor Margo Culley, and this is the Women's Studies section of "Man and Woman in Literature."' I was about to say, 'The course carries humanities credit and credit toward the Women's Studies major,' when a young man in the front row stood up, walked in front of me, made gestures and noises as if to vomit, walked to the door, and waved to the students saying, 'See you later, girls.' He then exited to nervous laughter from the class.

The example is extreme, and it only happened once — though I recognized the scene as the stuff one's worst pre-semester dreams are made of. The incident seemed to me a clear demonstration of how this young man's gender gave him permission to act out his misogyny, gave him power over me, the stigmatized. I will not pursue here the origins of that stigma — but I do find the work of Dorothy Dinnerstein on this question illuminating.[4] Her argument that mother-power is frightening, dangerous and overwhelming — as well as (indeed, *because* it is) nurturant, life-giving and sustaining — convinces me. By extension, we can argue that in the face of any female in authority we are all conflicted.

But we do not need to be students of Dorothy Dinnerstein to understand that authority for the teacher who is female is a vexed issue. Some academics who are female (in an effort to deny that they are born without legitimate claims to authority) cling to exaggerated forms of arbitrary power invested in their positions in an effort to 'clean up their act.' They become the sexless terrors who inhabit our myths about teaching spinsters. Others renounce all claims to power and authority, and it has been fashionable among feminist educators to do just this. Most of us muddle about, caught between the contradictory realities of power we shouldn't want — and can't have even if we should want it.

It is here we face the challenging and crucial paradox. Legitimating anger in the classroom is likely to intensify the challenge to the authority of the feminist teacher at one stage of the student's passage from denial and resistance, to anger, to affirmation and change. Yet I would also argue that it is only in *accepting* her authority — by this I mean the authority of her intellect, imagination, passion — that the students can accept the authority of their own like capacities. The authority the feminist teacher seeks is authority with, not authority over, and part of that picture is the authority of our anger.

I say 'our anger' because I must acknowledge that some of the anger I recognize in the students is also my own. Though I had readily accepted that teacher and student alike bring their own 'texts' to the classroom, when it came to facing *my* anger as a factor shaping a course, I had long participated in the denial and resistance I had been ascribing to my students. This response was true for a number of reasons. First, any glimpse of my anger as a factor in classroom dynamics led to the characteristic 'female' reaction — an entire decade of work became thereby suspect. My anger with its roots in the obscure and peculiar psychodynamics of this one individual was invalidated in its likely pathology. An even stronger force than instinctive self-doubt in obscuring my anger was the fact that their anger is one of the most potent weapons used today *against* feminists. *Time*, *Newsweek*, and the *New York Times Magazine* regularly warn us that young women see our generation of activists as bitter and angry women. So, in welcoming new college students to their first feminist classroom, I was busy becoming the 'who me? angry?' feminist, while I was simultaneously engineering the course to make them experience the anger I did not acknowledge.

A black colleague who teaches a course in slavery and the Jewish holocaust helped me out of this bind.[5] After giving a talk about his course, he was asked how he deals with the emotional impact on students of such difficult material. He began his response by saying he felt it his responsibility to allow students to know (intellectually and emotionally) these truths, rather than to protect them from awful realities. As I listened to him speak with conviction about the importance to him and his students of studying this history, I wondered why I had been so apologetic about my anger and reluctant to examine its sources.

The real danger of anger in the feminist classroom, I came to see, is if we cause our students to assume the burden of emotions we will not acknowledge as also our own. When we cease to be apologetic about anger, and rather claim its legitimacy, we thereby neutralize it as a weapon to be used against feminists. Yes, we are angry, and the feminist classroom is one arena where the historic, social, economic, cultural and psychological sources of that anger can be studied.

Anger is one important source of the energy for personal and social change in facilitating the transition from passivity to action. Part of my responsibility as a feminist teacher is to share that energy with my students, not protect them from it. As Toni Morrison-narrator says in *The Bluest Eye*: 'Anger is better. There's a sense of being in anger, an awareness of worth. It is a lovely surging.'[6]

Anger is a challenging and necessary part of life in the feminist classroom. Only when our anger has been felt and acknowledged, not denied, when it has been demonstrated to be grounded in a personal and collective sense of self-worth and not their opposite, can we hope that our students will join us in the remaining work to be done: a semester, and then a life-time, of affirmation and work for social change.

Notes

1　This paper is revised from a talk given at the conference Black Studies/Women's Studies: An Overdue Partnership, held at the University of Massachusetts-Amherst, 22 and 23 April 1983.

2　In a speech to the National Women's Rights Convention, held in Cincinnati, Ohio, on 17 and 18 October 1855, as recorded in Elizabeth Cady Stanton, Susan B. Anthony and Matilda Joslyn Gage (eds) *The History of Woman Suffrage*, vol. 1, Rochester, New York: Charles Mann, 1887, p.165.

3　The examples used in this paper to the contrary, most male students who find their way into Women's Studies courses are thoughtful and aware individuals. On occasion, their 'politics' has even been in advance of their female peers.

4　Dorothy Dinnerstein, *The Mermaid and the Minotaur: Sexual Arrangements and Human Malaise*, New York: Harper & Row, 1976.

5　Julius Lester in a talk given at the University of Massachusetts-Amherst in the spring of 1983. I am paraphrasing his comments as I remember them.

6   Toni Morrison, *The Bluest Eye*, New York: Holt Rinehart & Winston, 1970, p.43.

PART SEVEN

Communication across differences

19

How racial differences helped us discover our common ground

Mary Helen Washington

In September, 1980, I was hired by the University of Massachusetts at Boston as an associate professor of American literature, a specialist in Afro-American literature. That I was black was definitely a consideration in my hiring — there is, of course, only one way to reverse years of discrimination and that is to make one's blackness (instead of one's whiteness) an asset. But one's blackness, in such cases, can also become part of a pattern in which illusions of all kinds flourish wildly. One of the secretaries in the English department explained my coming to U. Mass. in terms that sound like a biblical event.

'Not only did we get black faculty, but we got Mary Helen Washington with a national reputation! And word was passed about the virtual miracle of your coming to our campus. How fortunate we were to have a person of your repute and talent here, how the waters of Boston Harbor parted for your arrival . . . I imagined someone taller. I think . . . someone about thirteen feet tall . . . a superpowered black.'

Luckily, I am on the short side, so this last illusion was easily dispelled. But I myself persisted in another illusory act — I tried not to be noticed, which is fairly difficult in a department of 100 whites and three blacks. The truth of that first semester at U. Mass. is that, in spite of all the hyperbole surrounding my recruitment, I spent the 1980 school year in a fog of fear and unknowing, suffering all the classic symptoms of displacement. I couldn't tell the buildings apart, I didn't know who was an ally and who was to be avoided.

I was team-teaching with a brilliant colleague, Linda Dittmar (a Jewish woman raised in an Israeli kibbutz), who, I thought, had read

221

all the books ahead of time and had the most meticulously kept office I had ever seen — everything in place (filed away in folders with identifying labels), plants blooming profusely but neatly, and even tea brewing cosily on cloth imported from Persia. Next to this orderliness, my office and my life seemed wildly disorganized and incompetent. My normally relaxed, confident and lighthearted manner never asserted itself. I found myself for the entire semester trying not to look bad in front of this woman with the brilliant mind and the perfect office. It was an additional burden, I suppose, that she was white, but the real burden was not her color but the illusion of her perfection.

Illusions prevailed during the entire year, in fact, racial illusions inadvertently became part of the very structure of the 'Images of Women' course I team-taught with Linda. We divided the course into several sections: middle-class women, working-class women, emergent women — each section comparing black women's lives to white women's.

The class was immediately polarized. Since the white teacher taught the white writers and the black teacher taught the black ones, it was easy to assume that whites were supposed to identify with white characters and blacks with blacks. Black students especially were supposed to participate actively in the discussion as soon as we began to talk about black lives — which were, it was assumed, like theirs.

Instead, tension grew, stiffened, hardened. The black students seemed immobilized. The threat of voicing an 'incorrect' racial attitude made the white students silent and edgy. Both Linda and I expected me to buoy the black students as though I had some special talent for keeping blacks afloat (this at a time when I was bobbing around on the water trying to keep myself from sinking). I counted the days when we would be released from this pernicious design that reflected the same illusion about race that was being carried on in my own life.

The class finally exploded when we came to a discussion of Alice Walker's 'Advancing Luna and Ida B. Wells,' which is about the friendship between a black woman and a white woman and the destruction of that friendship when the white woman is raped by a black man (see *Ms*, July 1977). The black woman in 'Luna' is angered by the automatic sympathy that is reserved for the white woman raped by a black man and for the very power she can exert over the black community by crying rape. The black narrator thinks: 'Who knows what the black woman thinks of rape? Who has asked her? Who cares? Who has even properly acknowledged that she and not the white woman in this story is the most likely victim of rape?'

The discussion of this story was so traumatic for me and Linda that we both wrote about this class for a panel at the 1981 National Women's Studies Association conference. Linda described the situation this way:

> The story plugged right into what was going on in class, regardless of the graceful integration of our syllabus. Our white students were upset by the black woman's withdrawal from her white friend. Many saw it as betrayal. What the black students felt, I am yet to find out. I myself looked at my new friend, Mary Helen, with a new anxiety: are we really midnight birds, or are we, above all, a black and a white?

Any real communication among us in that classroom was obscured from the very beginning. The most fundamental illusion, of course, is that there can be any real equality in an institution where racism and sexism accompanied the bricks and mortar of the buildings. And Linda and I didn't help matters by our Ice Cream and Cake duet (vanilla ice cream and chocolate cake). Why did we expect the black students to share their feelings in a class where no one kidded around with them before class, or went to lunch with them after class, or had their telephone numbers to share notes and gossip? Why did both Linda and I think that the white majority dominated the class when actually a few outspoken and confident students dominated the class? Why did students from predominantly Irish Catholic backgrounds, raised on novenas and confession, the nine First Fridays, and the threat of sins against the sixth commandment think they had more in common with a woman raised in an Israeli kibbutz than with me, a woman who survived sixteen years of Catholic school upbringing, who can still recite the Act of Contrition and the Memorare by heart?

What does 'white' mean in this country? It doesn't define a person's ancestry, or culture, or language, or ethnicity. It simply defines their relationship to power and prestige. In contrast to 'Images of Women,' in my English composition class — where students shared their intimate lives in papers based on personal experiences — some very unexpected alliances emerged. One was between a 23-year-old Irish ex-Marine from South Boston and a 40-year-old West Indian woman. By the end of the year, these individuals 'knew' each other in a way that was not possible in the literature class, where we were all defined irrevocably by skin color. It seems to be that this refusal to be known was at the heart of the racial divisions in my classes at the University of Massachusetts.

I, too, had my ways of refusing to be known. I was anxious about my move from Detroit, where blacks are more numerous, where a black professor is not an affirmative action statistic, where the mayor sounds as though he could be a brother or a friend. One of my students described perfectly an experience I had been having since my first days at U. Mass.:

> You know, I get up some mornings feeling good, whistling a little tune as I get dressed for school, look at the sun and the blue sky as I wait for the bus, thinking nice thoughts, and looking forward to my classes. I may even be feeling especially good because I have something I look nice in or because I'm meeting someone for lunch. Then I get off the bus and walk into U. Mass. and as soon as I step into the building I remember that I'm black, I don't even think about the color of my skin until I set foot on this campus.

That is exactly how I felt for most of my first year at U. Mass., and I know that while it reflects what I saw as the fundamental racism in the institution, it also reflects the defensive posture that an 'outsider' will often maintain in order to protect herself.

I had become friendly with one of the secretaries in the English department, a white working-class woman from the suburb of Burlington. I talked with her about my feelings of alienation and being alone at U. Mass., and she responded in a letter:

> You've told me you feel completely alienated here: sad, lonely, as though you don't belong, too many white faces. Well, welcome to our department. I know that feeling too well . . . the feeling that you are completely different. I remember when I started working here, there was a long time when I thought for sure that I had been dropped on an alien planet. Here I was, a new face sitting smack-dab in the middle of the main office, feeling really glad to be in the English department of UMB, the place where I got my degree. (I'm the first member of my family ever to go to college and so a degree has a special importance for me, for us.) And I'm smiling, being cheerful and open as all get-out, and no one, not anyone, said hello to me, or even gave a hint of noticing my

existence. I was here a couple of months before anyone ever really said anything to me, and then it was usually to ask me to do something for them . . .

Here, it is so rare to find someone who is brilliant and yet accessible — who actually makes sense in a down-to-earth way in her writing and her speaking. Someone who has no need for that alienating academic jargon. Who will just sit and shoot the shit like a normal person. Who shops at Filene's. Who cares passionately about literature, not about sounding smart. On and on and on.

Flash: to some people, my being black was not the unique characteristic of my life. For this secretary, I was a single woman in the world, a model of possibility for other working women.

I must have been fairly unapproachable in that first semester. One secretary, whom I saw every day in the department, doesn't even remember my coming to U. Mass., until the second semester. A student stopped me in the halls in March and said: 'I can tell by the look on your face that you're feeling more at home. Last semester I was afraid to talk to you.' My relationship with students had by then begun to thaw. I went to see two student art exhibits; students whom I originally guessed to be twenty years old turned out to be thirty-five; a lesbian raising four children (three teenage sons) taught me a lot about my own prejudices; I learned to tell the buildings apart.

The most important fact about my second semester at U. Mass., is that I taught 'Black Women Writers,' a class composed roughly of twenty white women, four black women (three of whom eventually dropped the class), two black men, and one white man. It was the most satisfying yet emotionally draining class I have ever taught; many of the students felt it changed them deeply. Still, in many ways the class failed and I failed — again because of illusions. In spite of my euphoria over the exciting discussions and my feeling that everyone was as involved as I was, not one of the four black women felt at home in the class, none felt truly respected, and only one stayed long enough to experience any change. I had never faced a problem like this when I was teaching at the University of Detroit, where the students in my Black Studies classes were predominantly black, where they seemed to feel that I, being the teacher, was theirs, the literature was theirs, the discussions belonged to them, and the other students were brothers and sisters who shared the same culture and therefore 'understood.'

In spite of our often heated and hostile discussions and occasional accusations of homophobia, racism, and sexism, 'Black Women Writers' had a different feel from the gelid reserve of the 'Images of Women.'

This course traced the literary history of black women writers from the late nineteenth century to the 1980s. I told the class that since there was no comprehensive literary history of black women, they were, in fact, to write it — to try to determine the shape of black women's literature for the past 100 years. They were as excited as I was about pursuing this pioneering activity. As they stepped westward bearing this burden, it seemed — to borrow an image from a Denise Levertov poem — to lighten as they moved because there was nourishment aplenty to be had.

The journey took us, ironically, to one of the same roadblocks that we had encountered in the first semester's class (the one that Linda and I team-taught). It took three class days to finish the discussion of 'Advancing Luna and Ida B. Wells' — a discussion that aroused so much anger, fear, sadness, outrage, and divisiveness that I thought the class would remain forever fixed at that point. As one student put it: 'We wanted heroines, we wanted women with answers. We didn't want to have to decide this case.'

The following is an account of how, in discussion, we partially resolved the story for ourselves.

One student pointed out that the black narrator was not a particularly admirable character, that she was smug and arrogant, and assumed too much, that her response of her friend's rape was cold and aloof, that she thought her civil rights activities were a fun way to spend the summer, that she was a pretentious Sarah Lawrence girl who was overimpressed with herself. Another student pointed out that Luna, the white woman, was no prize either, that her rule of dating only black men was racist, that she would never and could never escape the life of privilege that she was heir to and which would always be there like a safety-net allowing her to experience these political and cultural escapades.

One inescapable fact emerges from this story: there are no easy answers. Racism and sexism intersect in a way that forces everyone engaged in the story to deal with its implications. A white woman is raped by a black man in the South, where the crime could very well cause him to be lynched if the woman reports it. She decides not to tell. The class agonized over this story because they truly felt it was a moral question that could not be easily answered, but more than that, they wondered what they would do in a similar situation. What choice would they (as white women) make about reporting this rape, and as black women, what choice would they make about friendship with this white woman?

What I want to stress, however, is that the class did not divide strictly along racial lines. The white women did not necessarily identify with Luna, though many identified with the narrator. One lesbian student and a student who worked at a battered women's shelter felt the sense of male domination in the story the most strongly; and I came to feel that the story is really about the failure of friendship. The black woman's inability to respond to Luna, her friend and comrade, tells us that she has refused to be known and has refused to 'know' Luna. Luna does not know her, nor do we. And the rapist's blackness is irrelevant; he is not a disgrace to *his* people — if that means black people — he is a rapist who should have been punished but was not. Not much different from the thousands of other rapists who, for whatever reasons, go unpunished.

The ultimate illusion of race as well as my own failure to be known was brought home to me on the last day of 'Black Women Writers.' We were having champagne to toast the wonderful experience of that class, and the one black woman who finished the class made a statement which she intended as a compliment to me.

Let me put her statement in context: I was constantly referred to as one of the two new *black* faculty in the English department. My life's work has been writing about *black* women in literature. I had just spent nine months trying to decide if I could exist in a city and at a school where there was so little *black* presence.

Nevertheless, on that last day the student said, 'I could tell the first day you came in here and started talking that you weren't black.' And she went on to say that she had since changed her mind and decided I *was* black. What she really meant was that I had succumbed to the temptation most teachers have to deal with: I taught to the quick and the eager and the most confident and outspoken students. The pace and the tone of that class were set by these students — in this particular class, they were mostly white. (In my composition classes, black students were as outspoken and articulate as any students I've had anywhere.) I had not made the special effort to know those four black women students, and they had decided not to know me, either. In their words: 'She's not a sister.'

I will never again divide a course outline and curriculum along racial lines (as I did in 'Images of Women') so that the controlling purpose is to compare the responses of white women and black women, because I see how much the class imitates the syllabus. I do not want to see black women in opposition to white women as though that division is primary, universal, absolute, immutable, or even relevant. It makes students think that integration is like having so many crayons of each color in your crayon box.

In 'Black Women Writers,' we were free of these artificial distinctions and therefore freer to ask different questions and to seek different goals. There were days when the word 'black' was never used. We talked about linquistic authority, the role of community, verbal ingenuity and wit of the writers, male flattery and sexist manipulation of women, the need for independence. We talked about the literary history of black women and the difference between Toni Morrison's *The Bluest Eye* (1970) and Gwendolyn Brooks's *Maud Martha* (1953).

As I come to the end of my thoughts about these classes, I am reminded of a man who said to me that he usually ended up having sex with a woman before he wanted to because when he got nervous, he couldn't think of anything else to do. And I told him that since he didn't do that to men, he must have trouble seeing women as anything other than female. To some extent, that is the problem with the way we set up courses dealing with black women — they get identified as primarily black: their color is their identity, their substance, their uniqueness. Then, because we've made that one fact most critical, we see them only as women whose skin color defines their existence, missing their distinctiveness and diversity.

The illusion of race, the way the racial adjectives 'black' and 'white' obscure meaning, was made even more vivid to me when reading Margaret Atwood's review of my anthology, *Midnight Birds*, in the *Harvard Educational Review*. As a Canadian, Atwood had a perspective on this anthology that startled me into seeing my own racial illusions. She questions, as I had not, why it was necessary to review this book in a special issue devoted to Third World writing, since the writers included in the anthology were more representative of America than the Third World. She writes:

The writers themselves have no doubt about their identity as Americans, nor should they. Their prose is American, their settings are American: even their shared assumption that things can be improved almost by sheer faith, is at its core profoundly American. These women are not writing about genital mutilation, polygamy, or purdah, which luckily are not problems they had to deal with directly. These women are writing — these women can write, which distinguishes them from most women in Third World countries, who have not been taught to write at all, in the most basic sense of the word. These authors are as American as jazz and lynching. By what strange squint — the same one, presumably, that sees white male American writers as the norm and everyone else as the exception — might they be designated by the editors, of this journal as in the 'Third World' category?

There must be a way to teach the work of black women writers other than by racial classification. These are writers whose words deal with evil and moral responsibility, who are attempting to solve the urgent dilemmas of the twentieth century, whose feminism is a deeply felt part of that struggle, who use their inward lives to probe the central social issues of our time. It is ironic that I should come to this old American city of Boston and feel alienated. (There's a reason, isn't there, that none of my ancestors had to be naturalized?) By the same irony, these writers who are *the* American tradition in literature, 'as American as jazz and lynching,' are treated as offshoots, divergent branches of the main tradition. This literature cannot be dismissed by such token language as 'the literature of the oppressed.' These are American lives, these are American sons and daughters, this is the literature of America. In this year at U. Mass., which has been devoted to the shattering of illusions, I have come to understand my presence there and the presence of these writers in the curriculum as a very late admission of our mutual estate.

Note

1   Originally published in *Ms Magazine*, September 1981, pp.60-2, and 76. Reprinted with permission of the author.

20

Toward a pedagogy of Everywoman's Studies

Johnnella E. Butler

Over the past four or five years, I have noticed a significant change in the relationship of black American students to Black Studies. When I began teaching in 1969, Black students expressed a basic uneasiness with the liberal arts curriculum, were eager to take courses in Black Studies, eagerly sought an understanding of past history and recent national events, and were striving to articulate just what Afro-American life and culture is. Of course, one might argue that this is not surprising, for they had experienced the civil rights and Black Power movements, or at least were closer to them in time than present-day students. Nonetheless, it seems that black American students today have little sense of the past, little respect for, or knowledge and understanding of, Afro-American life and culture, are hard-pressed to identify traditions, and all too many have to be convinced of the validity and usefulness of knowing anything about their heritage. They are ambivalent about majoring in Black Studies and about taking courses, although significant numbers do both.

White American students, on the other hand, seem to reflect attitudes not too dissimilar from those of their peers in 1969; however, in my experience, greater numbers are taking courses in Black Studies. A curiosity spurred on by an uneasiness with the content of the existing liberal arts curriculum urges many to seek alternatives in Black Studies courses. Nonetheless, most approach these courses with skepticism and defensiveness about the largely incorrect perceptions, information and distorted images that they bring to the classroom.

In 1969, the academic uneasiness and curiosity of students, both black and white, were reinforced by the civil rights and Black Power movements. Today, the women's movement reinforces the perceived need to challenge the curriculum. Something is missing, however, as the joining of Black Studies and Women's Studies in Black Women's Studies demonstrates. Black women are suspicious of white women's and the women's movement's definitions of them and their roles. Thus, they are wary of dialogues with white women. White women, who are struggling to share a dialogue with black women, often stop short of this goal, afraid of revealing a latent, unconscious bigotry. Thus, frequently, they insist on establishing the definitions and parameters for discussion. Furthermore, mainstream forces seem to be so strong that they successfully prevent Afro-American families, schools, and churches from correctly conveying their traditions and history. Worse, mainstream ideology in general encourages them to deny their traditions and history altogether. Incorrect information and negative images are so ingrained in white American families that even a well-intentioned inquiry into the Afro-American experience may be distorted by lies and, at best, a subtle prejudice. All these attitudes find their way into the classroom and the scholarship, and various classroom situations have prodded me into thinking precisely about a corrective pedagogy. This paper is part of my effort to ascertain the 'lay of the land' for that pedagogy.

During a session of 'The Literature of the Black Woman,' we discussed various interpretations of the Afro-American spiritual, examined styles of singing the spirituals, listened to numerous recordings, and discussed the relationship of the spirituals to the literature. After class, a student — a usually well-informed black student — asked me as she reviewed her notes, 'Now, Ms Butler, what's the name of that spiritual you sang? "Slip Away"?' My mind raced through all the possible reasons she could call what I thought was one of the most well-known spirituals 'Steal Away' 'Slip Away.' She said she had never heard of it before. I thought, 'Well, spirituals aren't sung as frequently as they used to be.' But then, I thought of the black student who asked me last year what gospel music had to do with Afro-American culture. 'What had "Slipped Away"?' I wondered. 'There might be an omen in her question. Maybe her song was bemoaning cultural genocide.'

And then there was the group of white American students who saw nothing amiss in Virginia Woolf's *A Room of One's Own* being taken literally as 'basic feminist dogma,' even though she clearly addressed a specific, small population, restricted by class and culture, and exhibited a benign neglect of the 'negresses' that she wouldn't presume to make over in her image.[1]

I have grappled for years with describing a Black Studies pedagogy, and I am working to illuminate the connections between Black Studies and Women's Studies, both in terms of subject-content and pedagogy.[2] Experience teaching about black women seems to allow me to identify more precisely what 'forces' are at work causing a black student to think there is a spiritual 'Slip Away,' and also to cause a classroom to be polarized, black vs. white, because white students insist on reducing all experience to the same — theirs.

Much of my experience derives from teaching literature classes on either black women's literature or black feminist thought, attended predominantly by women at two private women's colleges; however, a four-year experience at a large, co-educational, public university broadens and reinforces my interpretations. Though both experiences warrant full treatment, my purpose here is to draw on them in order to identify the classroom dynamics that emanate from the subject-matter itself, the interaction of teacher and student, and the mandate of the liberal arts.

The situations in which Black Women's Studies are part of the college curriculum are numerous, ranging from specific courses focusing on black women in various disciplines, to segments of courses, to interdisciplinary courses on black women, to courses on black women in the diaspora, to comparative courses on black women, other women of color and white women. While these courses may differ considerably from one another, teaching about black women is always rooted in the specific black culture of which the women studied are a part, includes examining attitudes toward and perceptions of black men, involves an understanding of racism on national and international levels, and always implies the historical, political, economic, and cultural connection between black women in Africa and black women in the diaspora. Challenging pedagogical issues arise from this subject-content which attacks long-held assumptions and perceptions, ingrained, incorrect information and scholarship, and the 'common wisdom' of everyday attitudes and values.

It should be understood that in each teaching situation, my intention is to employ pedagogy consistent with what might be considered 'an Americanization' of Paulo Freire's methods.[3] Using his insights to illuminate our own situation, I begin with the assumption that:

1 The colonization of minds is characteristic of American education and is maintained by the presence of cultural imposition
and the resultant bias and distortion of subject-matter. Racism,
didacticism, and academic dogmatism support this cultural
imposition.

Combating this colonization of minds as a 'Freirian' teacher of Black
Studies involves the following approaches and methods:

2 The cultural context of the Afro-American reality serves as the
foundation of academic analyses and discussions. In studying
other parts of the African or black diaspora, the specific cultural
situation (French African, Nigerian Ibo, Haitian, etc.) serves as
the foundation.
3 Learning involves an integration of 'all experience into an intricate view of life that includes hopes and fears, loves and hates,
beliefs and expectations, and attitudes toward other people and
toward 'self.'[4]
4 Through student-teacher-subject-content dialogue, and through
employing *both* an either/or *and* both/and approach to problems
posed by the subject-content, generative thinking can occur and
learning and ideas will flourish.

Of course, before 'generative thinking,' or any other kind, can
occur, students must enroll in these courses. The fact is that it is
sometimes difficult to enroll sizeable numbers of students in courses
in Black Women's Studies, and other Afro-American Studies or Women's
Studies courses, primarily because of the strength of negative perceptions of those fields. Many academic advisors and other professors
actively discourage students from taking courses that do not reflect
accepted 'mainstream' scholarship. They imply that such courses are
'victim' studies, are — in the case of Afro-American Studies — for
black students only, that whites may be discriminated against. They
frequently counsel students, as a colleague of mine did, to 'take a real
history course and not one in Afro-American Studies.' This occurred
even in a case when the course was taught by an historian specializing
in United States history and was cross-listed with the history department, counting toward its major. Parents frequently view these fields
as 'militant,' as somehow retarding academic growth. On two occasions,
students told me about their Afro-American parents who admonished

their daughters, 'I didn't send you to college to take a course from a black professor!' Asian-American students have reported to me similar comments of parents about Asian-American professors. The tragic irony is that, while most of the opposition to these disciplines comes from members of the dominant culture, much too much comes from parents, even faculty, of the cultural background these courses address. Such factors, external to the classroom situation, increase pressure on the teacher before any course has even begun. The Afro-American teacher must be credible and personable. Whether she/he likes it or not, she/he must pass tests of credibility and sincerity administered by black and white students alike. Third World USA students of backgrounds other than Afro-American — frequently in attendance in these courses in small numbers, perhaps one or two — administer credibility and sincerity tests. For the Afro-American professor, sometimes the experience is not unlike the classic experience of having to excel before being recognized by others or even their own. Sometimes, as was my experience at a large public university, the Afro-American teacher must convince her/his students (later this applied to other Third World USA students, feminist students, and students in general, struggling to be politically aware) that credibility could come in the form of a black, middle-class professor without an afro and a dashiki. No matter the form of the test, the teacher who passes is the one who consistently demonstrates not only complete knowledge of the subject-matter but also an understanding of, or at least sympathy with, the students' affective responses to having their academic, aesthetic, and social norms challenged.

The Afro-American teacher must also accept that teaching this pariah subject-content is a slow building process. Students of all racial backgrounds come with an acute ignorance about American history and culture. They therefore possess a false sense of self, based on ignorance of ethnicity and the intricate role it can play in not only dividing whites from people of color, but also in dividing whites from each other — indeed, people of color from one another.

The white American teacher, even if of an ethnic background other than WASP, is perceived as white and, as history shows us, usually shares the imperatives of the mainstream. If not, and if she/he opts to teach a course with significant content about black women, then she/he experiences struggles at various levels that are similar to those experienced by the black teacher, if she/he is attempting to accept, as a way of being, the marginality resulting from standing outside of the mainstream scholarship, examining and correcting it. The key, as for the Afro-American teacher, is in how well she/he demonstrates an honest pursuit of the truth in the classroom.

Black students generally are well versed in the dominant culture, because they have lived and are schooled in it from birth. However, because this schooling diminishes in importance or even negates the Afro-American part of their dual cultural existence, many of the strengths gained from knowing and growing through Afro-American cultural values and heritage are lost. The majority see women's issues as 'a white thing,' and, at best, they are confused about the roles of race, gender, and culture in the USA. Frequently, they attempt to deny the importance of racial, gender and cultural difference; they may view such differences negatively, deciding that diversity can only keep them from 'making it.' Many struggle, with little or no assistance from home, it seems, to make sense out of the denial-laden reality of the USA. In doing so, they run the gamut from carefully studying the Afro-American experience through Black Studies, to accepting as their experience mainstream studies and mainstream, white Women's Studies, to rejecting all academic paths and struggling with a superficial sense of identity, sometimes adopting a 'cause' as an identity.

White students often come to these classes viewing themselves as oppressed women. Their first tendency is to equate all forms of oppression and fail to admit their skin/class privilege. Racism and ethnocentrism cause them to refuse to see blacks as distinctly different from whites, encourage them to oversimplify gender issues, and support them in their tendency to define reality for all people. Racial guilt can become a problem, can block fruitful dialogue with the material, and engender hostility among students.

It is important, therefore, to take the time to emphasize and develop the fact that studying black women introduces a specific cultural experience which, while it is American, is distinctly Afro-American. In discussions of black women's literature, for example, the aesthetics, standards and values of Afro-American cultural experience become the central reality. This often raises considerable problems. Black students may be impatient and feel that 'explaining' to white students aspects of Afro-American life is synonymous to Afro-Americans being *patronized*. Generalizations about black culture, necessary to begin the education of white students, may leave individual black students feeling that differences between them are being *ignored*, that they are neglected as individual class members. Black students often sit quietly during such discussions, refusing to be 'categorized' as 'speaking for all black people.' Or, as a black student in 'Philosophy and Women' said after a heated discussion about racism on campus, 'What should *I* say? It's their problem.' Even more problematic for black students may be the feeling that their cultural experience is being *appropriated*, taken possession of and being distorted, like corn-rows becoming 'Bo braids.' White students who have become personally aware of class differences and discrimination, who have experienced ethnic bias, etc., become angry when racism and the black students' experiences seem to take on greater importance in the classroom than the issues that make them uneasy or angry with the women's movement. That the course is about black women does not matter. As white students begin to see serious flaws in feminist thought through the window of studying black women's experience, they scapegoat 'angry, black women' to cloud their anger and frustration.

Consider, for example, a discussion about lynching and rape. The teacher often must begin explaining what lynching is: the horrendous details of its history, its ritualistic aspects, why it involved castration. Focusing on issues of racism and separating them from considerations of sexism raises fears for both black and white students. Black students fear stereotyping in such discussions, while white students fear 'saying the wrong thing.' Black and white students usually display an ambivalence toward the black male as they try to sort through the stereotypes, the facts, their own feelings. The professor must be aware of hidden dialogues among students about, for example, the blonde in the classroom who has a black boyfriend, or the black student who was raped by a white male, and she/he must be able to defuse, either inside or outside the classroom, any negativity that may cause emotional self-protection destructive to constructive dialogue. The fear of being regarded by peers or by the professor as racist, sexist, or 'politically incorrect' can polarize a classroom. If the professor participates unconsciously in this fear and emotional self-protection, the classroom experience will degenerate to hopeless polarization, and even overt hostility. She/he must constantly stand outside the classroom experience and anticipate such dynamics. When necessary, these issues should become the focus of discussion through what I call 'pressure-valve release' discussions. Such 'pressure-valve release' discussions work best when the teacher directly acknowledges and calls attention to the tension in the classroom. In whatever way she/he feels comfortable, she/he may initiate the discussion or allow it to come about through student comments in class.

The hostility, fear and hesitancy that inevitably arise in the first few weeks of a Black Woman's Studies class can be converted to fertile ground for profound academic experiences in the humanities and social sciences. I say 'profound' because the students' 'familiar' is challenged, expanded or reinforced by a subject matter that vibrates with the humanness of life in its form and content. In dealing with Afro-American culture, ethnicity and cultural identity become a central issue for all students. In a literature class, for example, discussing characters and themes relating to women's lives, students begin to grapple with their own identities, and continue a process that perhaps did not begin with a course and that certainly will not end with it. Afro-American women may begin to think seriously about themselves for the first time as part of a distinct American cultural group. To black students for whom the term 'black' has meant primarily skin color, the concept of an Afro-American literary aesthetic (or other cultural content of the term 'black') can be intriguing, even awesome. They delight in seeing themselves in print, reading the familiar language-patterns and idioms. Often texts contain images, themes, plots, characters that are most familiar (whether the familiar has been affirmed, denied, or never thought about), but have never been approached in academic or artistic terms. Students begin to perceive the diversity of Afro-American culture, its Southern, Northern, rural and urban expressions. Some, for the first time, encounter West Indians and Afro-Americans of West Indian heritage. Many of the silences are filled, the taken-for-granteds explored, and self-perceptions begin to change.

For white students, class and ethnicity become the focal points in the wrestling with identity. They resist acknowledging that the USA is a society based on class, but will admit to ethnic differences and tensions among whites. They begin to question not only their academic instruction, but also their parents' teaching and behavior. As they struggle to recast what they have been taught previously in the light of what they are encountering in Black Women's Studies, the responses run the gamut from superficial identification with Afro-Americans to serious self-examination — exploring their own identity and class. Some move toward a radical restructuring of their self-perceptions and identities. Once the appropriation and distortion of ethnicity and cultural diversity is uncovered, and true ethnic and cultural complexity of the USA is understood, paralyzing guilt felt by some may be more easily dispelled and replaced with accepting a responsibility for change.

All students' perceptions of themselves as women are altered as they begin to perceive, if not fully understand, that gender, class, culture and race are necessarily intricately related. Black women students, often for the first time, speak of their women's issues, comfortably seeing gender issues simultaneously as part of and separate from race, class and cultural issues. They begin to seek ways of balancing their necessary struggle with racism, classism and ethnocentrism with gender issues which racism, classism and ethnocentrism reinforce.

White students' often narrow definitions of feminism are assaulted by the recognition of the roles of gender, class, culture and race. Those who define it as anti-men, in white middle-class terms, or who see themselves as post-feminists, often feel overwhelmed by all that must be rethought through, rewritten, redefined. Some, black and white, try to acknowledge that their previous attitudes and definitions are limited — but rigidly maintain them. Classroom time should be devoted to addressing this often unvoiced struggle of students, through, for example, examining works like *The Salt Eaters* or 'Advancing Luna and Ida B. Wells,'[5] and through white and black women guest speakers who have thought through their processes of becoming involved in the civil rights movement and the women's movement.

All this ultimately sounds so optimistic. But the harsh reality is that scholarship on black women is sorely lacking. A teacher can mediate differences in the classroom to a point; however, the history, the sorting-out of race relations and perceptions, political and personal attitudes toward culture, class, race and gender, has not been sufficiently done in either Black Studies or Women's Studies. Knowledge about black women's literary tradition is becoming available. But little is known of their, or other women of color's, feminism. A pedagogy developed without the benefit of the development of the history and understanding of Afro-American and other Third World USA women's organizations, issues and involvement with the white women's movement and experience, will simply continue to point out the gaps and distortions, and leave us with aware students with little substance on which to continue the scholarship and develop a strong, inclusive women's movement.

A pedagogy for Black Women's Studies must be based on the truth — the truth about Afro-American life and culture in the USA, the truth about the historical, political, and social relationships between white and black women, the truth about the ignorance that racial and cultural groups hold about one another in the USA, the truth about the emotional challenge the subject-content brings to black and white women, to Black Studies and to Women's Studies. Such truth heals and leads the way to the human, spiritual renewal we so desperately seek today. If the truth is not sought in actions, words and scholarship, the omen, 'Slip Away,' may have its day, and the part that Women's Studies and Black Studies can play in correcting distortions and bettering society will instead lead to a greater perversion of human potential than we now experience.

Notes

1   Virginia Woolf, *A Room of One's Own*, New York: Harcourt Bruce Jovanovich, 1957, p.52.
2   FIPSE grant, 'Black Studies/Women's Studies: An Overdue Partnership,' held by Smith College, Department of Afro-American Studies, and the University of Massachusetts at Amherst, Women's Studies Program, 1981-3; co-directed with Margo Culley.
3   Johnnella E. Butler, *Black Studies: Pedagogy and Revolution*, Washington, DC: University Press of America, 1981.
4   See Frank Smith, *Comprehension and Learning*, New York: Holt, Rinehart & Winston, 1975, pp.1-2. (Cited in Butler, and employed in her description of pedagogy for Black Studies.)
5   Toni Cade Bambara, *The Salt Eaters*, New York: Random House, 1980: and Alice Walker, 'Advancing Luna and Ida B. Wells,' in M.H. Washington (ed.), *Midnight Birds*, New York: Anchor, 1980, pp.63-81.

21

Combating the marginalization of black women in the classroom

Elizabeth V. Spelman

Both Black Studies and Women's Studies are responses to ways in which the groups they name have been ignored or marginalized in education in the USA. These groups (among others) have been kept at the margins of inquiry, their lives not deemed worthy of serious, sustained investigation. As investigators, they have not been expected to have anything useful to say.

Black Studies and Women's Studies have put to the front and center the lives of those otherwise relegated to the periphery. The very dialogue that we are now engaged in, however, is witness to the fact that marginalization is still very much with us — wherever Women's Studies courses are really White Women's Studies, and wherever Black Studies courses are really Black Men's Studies.[2]

I would like to identify a few of the many factors which have to be taken into account in order to begin to describe that marginalization and to understand what we as teachers, along with our students, might do about it. In a sense, such marginalization is as simple and as complex as racism and sexism themselves are simple, in that these phenomena (along with class bias and heterosexism) are clearly and unambiguously present; complex, in that the process of marginalization has had a long and sturdy history in education, and that educational settings have been likely places for grafting on racism and sexism. Traditionally conceived educational settings, that is, are rife with the kind of hierarchical orderings that authoritarians, bigots, and cultural imperialists need to ensure that inquiry only takes certain directions, that inquirers are only allowed to ask certain questions.

The particular recent experience I speak from is a Women's Studies course that I offered in a predominantly white women's college in the northeastern USA. One-fourth to one-third of the students were women of color, mostly black, and the rest white; I, the professor, am white. The course was conceived of as an attempt to address and discuss in a sustained fashion different perspectives women of different racial and ethnic communities might have with respect to the meaning in their lives of family, learning to be 'women,' work, sexuality, violence, community, and political alliance. Though I speak from that experience in that single setting, I am assuming that the dynamics of marginalization that I observed in that classroom are more or less the same for any classroom in which any group's relevant experiences and perspectives are ignored or kept peripheral.

There are at least two ways in which old pedagogical rules and classroom etiquette can be attacked in order to try to avoid marginalization. One is to use material that has some chance of speaking to (which is different from merely catering to) the lives of all members of the class — maybe not everyone all of the time, but everyone some of the time. The other is to encourage students to voice their opinions on the material at hand — to think out loud with one another, challenge one another, help one another figure out their own considered views. The heart of the educational exchange is not in the delivery of pearls of wisdom from the professor on high, but in the lively exchange among students. (Classroom settings, old-style or new-style, offer all the usual occasions for self-deception plus more. Most of us who teach need to be much clearer than we are about what role or roles we actually do play, or ought to play, in the classroom. All I am trying to do here is point to an attempted shift in classroom attention which I suspect is familiar to many teaching Black Studies or Women's Studies.)

However, it is easily documented that shaping the content of a Women's Studies course so that it will not be essentially a White Women's Studies course and making complicated arrangements for the exchange of different perspectives on the topics at hand do not prevent the marginalization of women of color. Here is a rather short breakdown of some of the forms that marginalization take.

White women and women of color (for different reasons) seem to find it less difficult to refer to the tests written by and about white women. Relatedly, white women's experiences end up being treated as paradigms, with the experiences of black women and other women of color as variations on or divergences from the paradigms.

Women belonging to racial minorities in the USA have a strong sense of being seen and heard *en bloc*, whether or not on any given occasion they wish to be; white women tend to ignore class differences and other differences among women of color.

White women tend to feel that they dare not challenge the opinions of black women and other women of color — with the result that while in another setting black women, for example, would be marginalized by the assumption that they must be wrong, here they are marginalized by the apparent assumption that they must be right.

White women tend to show more concern for black women and other women of color as victims of racism than as members of lively communities with rich cultural identities and traditions.

In addition, black women and other women of color are marginalized by the deafening silence which punctuates the moment at which real conflict might occur, real ground-breaking work might begin. Among the reasons why such silence is troubling is that ultimately it leaves the position of the dominant group in the classroom — in this case, the white women — unexamined and unchallenged. Such silence serves the political status quo as much as silence intentionally and explicitly enforced would, for it usually marks the moment just before white women's privileged status is to be noted, examined, challenged.

Of course, the silence is not unambiguous. It, no less than the issues under conscious exploration, has a variety of meanings, tied to, though not entirely determined by, the different racial and ethnic identities of the women in the class. What are the possible meanings of this silence?

The silence of a few women is a reflection of their lack of concern about what happens in the course. What they want from college is a big boost in the direction of a lucrative career, and they would prefer to have their days in college be as free of pain and self-reflection as possible. This desire cuts across race, class, and ethnic boundaries.

Some may be silent as a form of resistance. It may be that black women's silence is a way of saying that they will not be taken in by spurious claims about the necessity for 'open' discussion, about how everyone's opinions are welcome, and so forth. White women may be merely exercising white privilege, by refusing to engage in activities which might make that privilege more visible — the silence is as if to announce: 'I don't have to say anything that might make me, and others, aware of my own ignorance about the lives of women of color, or of my own racism.'

Fear is, of course, a great silencer — fear of saying 'the wrong thing,' of saying something hurtful or oppressive, of saying something that is not well thought out. It does not help matters that fear has always found many places to lodge in educational settings. Among the particular fears important to single out is the fear of having or showing emotions. (Again, it does not help that there is a sense in which education has been conceived of as expunging the emotions, freeing us from their 'insidious influence' on our capacity to reason.) For example, women of color and white women may be fearful of each other's anger, though for quite different reasons. Whatever else may be going on, the history of racism in the USA makes us see that a black woman's anger at a white woman presents a challenge to white skin privilege; that a white woman's anger at a black woman might well be an expression of the privilege which says, 'Don't dare to challenge me.' These are not the only facts about our anger at each other but they are important facts.

The silence also reflects our lack of knowledge about ourselves and each other. We are in the process of trying to uncover and/or write about our own histories and identities, and sometimes our silence may be a reminder of the work that is yet to be done. But here again, there is hardly perfect symmetry across race lines, for, as has often been pointed out, people of color have had to learn about the ways of white people in order to survive in the USA while whites' ignorance of blacks and other minorities is yet another expression of white supremacy.

There is a lack of trust engendered by the history of racism; by the competitiveness historically intended to be characteristic of the classroom; by the limited amount of time the participants spend together, by the well-known habit among students and faculty of acting one way in class and another elsewhere.

For the most part, educational institutions do not know how to reward students for learning about themselves, or about others unless the others are (1) male, (2) white, and (3) dead. It is easier to speak up when the avenues of reward are clearly charted.

In short, the opportunities for silence in the kind of classroom I am talking about are vast. But that silence cannot be ignored or underestimated if we are serious about preventing marginalization in Women's Studies courses (or similarly in Black Studies courses), for such silence ultimately serves the racial or sexual status quo, despite the fact that at any given moment in such courses silence may be an important way of withdrawing consent to oppressive classroom assumptions and proceedings. We who are hoping for a dialogue between Black Studies and Women's Studies might find it useful, as the dialogue begins, here and in our classrooms, to raise these questions, among others, about the conditions under which such discussion takes place:

1 We are aware of the powers we do not have. Do we know what powers we do have and want to have? Do we know what powers our students have, and what powers we hope they might come to have? Are we *clear* about the powers, *wanted and unwanted*, that we as teachers have?

2 What are the explicit and implicit rules we expect to be followed by those engaging in the dialogue? What do we think the participants have consented to?

3 What are our expectations for the result of such dialogue? To what extent do we have contradictory expectations about the classroom? For example, do we encourage students to read and talk about material that is meant to be agitating, and then expect them to keep their agitation out of the classroom?

4 Are our expectations about what can happen in educational institutions realistic? For example, do we overestimate the extent to which the classroom can be a place where relations of dominance and subordination are challenged? On the other hand, to what extent are we all too ready to use the limitations of the classroom as an excuse for not trying to challenge such relationships?

All of these thoughts are, of course, exceedingly sketchy. But I hope they can provide some points of departure for our own dialogue, as well as for examining what goes on in our courses.

Notes

1 Originally published in *Women's Studies Quarterly*, vol. 10, no. 2, summer 1982, pp.15-16. Copyright ©by The Feminist Press, 1982. Reprinted with permission.

2 I have found it very useful to listen to a work-in-progress project on marginalization by Susan Geiger, Jacquelyn Zita, Naomi Scheman, Susan Heinemann and Susan Bernick, at the University of Minnesota.

22

Teaching the feminist minority

Barbara Hillyer Davis

In Women's Studies conferences during the past few years, I have heard many descriptions of pedagogical approaches to specific student groups — working women, displaced homemakers, business majors, and so on. I admire and learn from these presentations and at the same time I am uneasy. For some reason my classes are never like those described. The longer I teach them, the less homogeneous they seem. I am working out my role as a Women's Studies teacher in a university in which — as in most others, I suspect — no class consists of *just* working-class women, *just* reentry women, *just* Native American women. It is time to discuss the work of the feminist teacher in a *mixed* classroom, where any constituent group may be a minority — and the smallest consistent minority group is feminist students.

When the field of Women's Studies began its phenomenal growth about ten years ago, teachers and students alike were beginners in a process of self-education. Most of us had been socialized as 'traditional women'; we learned together what that meant. By the time Women's Studies classes were offered in our region — the Bible Belt — there were valuable resources, printed and experiential, to facilitate this reeducational process. Our first classes were demanded by women who had learned feminism from books and xeroxed essays and who had experienced its practical necessities in the state legislature, in marriage, in consciousness-raising groups. These women, self-educated feminists like their teachers, filled our first classes.

My own first 'Women in Literature' course was very conservative in its content: it focused mainly on Victorian literature and included such male authors as George Meredith, Thomas Hardy, and D. H. Lawrence. My students and I, however, were very well informed about the legal and sociological situation of women in our own time. We brought our personal and political experience into a conventional university classroom and examined the relationship between the two worlds. Together we reread traditional literature in the light of our experience and in the light of contemporary feminist theory. Our expectations of the university classroom itself were traditional; we had no idea that conventional class discussions would soon be inadequate in terms of feminist process. What was radical in our approach was our collective questioning of course *content*.

That was in 1972. By now the situation has almost reversed itself. Gradually the course has changed, literally one volume at a time, so that it now includes 'non-traditional' forms, and only women authors — for example, Zora Neale Hurston, Harriette Arnow and Sarah Wright. A much smaller percentage of the students are feminists, and their awareness of the legal and sociological situation of women in our society is less specific and exact. Less well informed about sexual politics, the majority now are reading non-traditional literature from a more traditional perspective than the earlier students, who had lobbied for the ERA before they petitioned for Women's Studies.

Both traditional and feminist students are with us still, but their proportions are reversed. This is a sign of our success. Women's Studies enrollments are much larger: women from a much wider range of backgrounds now see the study of women as appropriate to university classrooms. The class, therefore, is not for an initiated group only, but for all women and some men. In these circumstances the norms of the university are much more influential. The challenge to me as the teacher is no longer to explore with feminist colleagues the relationship between the legal-sociological condition of women and the literature I learned in graduate school, but to educate students who know relatively little about either.

The 'traditional' woman assumes as she enters my class that she will spend her life in conventional subordination to men (boyfriend, husband, professor, boss) and, because she has not examined the implications of this assumption, she believes this to be a desirable outcome, freely chosen. 'Feminists' share an impatience with the traditional perspective and a belief, ironically similar to that of the traditional students, that women who accept traditional subordination have freely chosen to do so. I am in fact less a peer of these students than I was of the earlier ones; I know more about women's literature and about feminist theory than they do, and I embody the contradictions fostered by the institution in which we work.

The university has taught us well how learning should be done. Because I do 'know more' than most of my students, I am easily persuaded that I should impart knowledge for their reception. The institutional pressure to do so is reinforced by the students' well-socialized behavior. If I will tell them 'what I want,' they will deliver it. They are exasperated with my efforts to depart from the role of dispenser of wisdom.

On the other hand, what I know about feminist process makes me feel an obligation to renounce the professorial role, to serve instead as a role model for sisterhood, disclaiming any stance of superiority and presenting myself as one who learns instead of teaching. Struggling to maintain myself between these conflicting pressures, I work out a role as teacher which leans toward a peer relationship but includes enough of the professor to reassure those students who feel comfortable in a more traditional classroom.

In their midst sits a feminist minority — women who have rejected the condescension of the professoriat and who have themselves read some feminist theory. What they want from me is a model of sisterhood, and from the other students, emotional and intellectual support.

Every year, then, I am teaching, at the same time in the same classroom, 'kindergarten' and 'graduate school,' though it is sometimes very difficult to tell which is which. Some students who consider themselves 'advanced' in Women's Studies are separatist/elitist; some who have never before given feminism any thought have a sort of instinct for sisterhood.

Teachers of Women's Studies have standard devices for bringing these buried contradictions to group or individual consciousness: class journals, small group discussions, readings of feminist essays. The problem is using these tools on two (or ten) levels at once — starting where the individual student is 'here and now' when collectively they are in many places. Initially designed to encourage the development of consciousness among traditional women, these devices still seem to work more effectively with that group. We use them in institutions which assume that students-as-beginners and the teacher-as-expert are the norm. Students or teachers who do not share these expectations will seem out of place, even to themselves.

It is commonplace among us that studying women is a painful

experience for women, and that Women's Studies classrooms should provide an environment in which women can support one another through this pain. But there is also joy in the process, as we discover mutual support and rejoice in the recovery of women's past and women's culture. My recent experience is that this pleasure comes more frequently to 'traditional' than to 'feminist' students. The process is not, initially at least, so helpful to the small minority whose 'consciousness has already been raised.' They come to the Women's Studies classroom with higher expectations, gained especially from feminist literature and also from some limited work in women's groups. They expect, for example, that as they meet the emotional and intellectual needs of other women, their own needs will be met — that their growth into more complex feminist modes will also be supported by the group. But the majority do not know how to support people whose pain is over factions in the women's movement instead of housework.

A traditional student, asked to examine the sexual politics in literature or history, very quickly sees its relationship to her own life. She will grow and change and learn faster in small group discussions with other women who are already clear about their feminism. As traditional students learn from feminists how to analyze their lives as women, they also develop some respect — perhaps even admiration — for the feminists' non-traditional choices. But the feminist students, however 'advanced' their intellectual and emotional grasp of feminist issues, often lack empathy with or respect for the hard choices and important conflicts of traditional women.

It is as important for feminists to learn to listen as to be heard - to understand the complexity of traditional women's lives as to present the alternatives of their own. Otherwise, no one is 'advanced'; we are all still in first grade. The challenge to us *as teachers* is to keep these two groups together long enough to facilitate their forming relationships and beginning to listen to each other.

The challenge is complicated by the ambiguities in the feminist teacher's dual roles as sister—peer and professor. We may have a commitment to the sister—peer role that makes the conservative majority's obedient cooperation with the professorial role problematic. Our experimental solutions confusingly encompass both roles. We may use professorial power to 'require' disclosure, to control group formation, to 'facilitate' communication.

This is not all bad. People have to write journals for a while before they understand their importance; they have to stay in a group to develop its effectiveness. To provide structure may be the best way to encourage growth. Having acknowledged this, we wish that we could do better for the feminist students. Precisely because their reasons for making additional demands are feminist ones, we want to meet them.

One of the easiest ways to alleviate the distress of feminists in a conservative classroom is to permit students to segregate themselves into 'beginning' and 'advanced' subgroups. If we permit or encourage such segregation, we may in the guise of 'freedom' be encouraging a decision to avoid a more difficult but potentially more rewarding choice. If, on the other hand, we insist that the groups remain 'mixed,' we must beware of oppressing the feminist minority. We don't want feminist students to go away, nor should we expect them to become adjunct teachers whose own needs for growth and support are not met.

The most typical ways of helping the desired female bonding to take place are variations on traditional women's roles. We may choose to play superwoman, wife, or mother. Superwoman is a feminization of the professorial role: by adding responsibilities for interpersonal relationships to our work as discussion leaders, evaluators, role models, and paper graders, we 'humanize' the classroom. Feminist students encourage the teacher's superwoman role because they, too, have been taught by the educational system that learning is transmitted from teacher to student. Anticipating a different quality of learning from the Women's Studies classroom, they expect to be reinforced and supported as feminists, not 'just as women' (I quote a student). Since (because the institution shapes the way we expect education to take place) even feminists are more comfortable with being *told* than with being *shown*: they expect, like the majority, a better experience through conventional forms, and therefore prefer additions to those forms, not substitutes for them. So we play the role of superwoman, killing ourselves with overwork and denying the students' responsibility for their own relationships.

The role of wife is more insidious. 'Let me help you be more comfortable,' we suggest. 'You're OK, dear, and I will work to reassure you.' The role is closely related to that of mother — the role both we and our students probably prefer. I want to meet the student's needs and she wants me to — nurturing, protecting, loving. The catch to these two solutions is that the proper correlative roles are those of husband and child, neither of which seems appropriate to a feminist classroom.

None of these responses to the plight of the feminist student works very well, but all are serious efforts to work *as women* — not in the professorial father role. What we need — and what I believe we are learning to do — is to develop a new role for teachers of these mixed groups, another way of learning, which blends realism about the institutional context with belief in the feminist future.

A more effective, more intellectual, and more feminist role than that of superwoman, wife, or mother is that of simultaneous translator. This role involves hearing and giving back in other words what another person has just said, and at the same time presenting an explanation in another language which will illuminate the issue for a second group without alienating the first. A statement from a still traditional student will, in this model, be fed back to the speaker in a way that tells her she is indeed being heard and understood, while at the same time an explanation in theoretical feminist language is provided for another member of the group. This is a practical illustration of the slogan that decorates many of our office doors: 'Feminism spoken here.'

The translator intends to teach the 'second language' at the same time that interpretation is occurring and the discussion being advanced to its next stage. The translator works in both languages, without making value-judgments about either, but with sensitivity to the nuances of each.

Feminist students have access to a descriptive vocabulary, drawn from their reading of Adrienne Rich or Mary Daly or Susan Brownmiller, which will be new to other students. The concept of translation may enable them to apply this vocabulary to their own behavior in new ways, as that behavior is interpreted to the others.

For example, when some feminist students threaten to drop out because they can't bear listening to women who conventionally affiliate with men, what they are doing is dichotomizing: dividing women into 'good' and 'bad' categories on the basis of life-style, much as anti-feminist groups have done (naming dependent housewives 'good' and 'women's libbers' 'bad'). Recognizing the dichotomy in the context of feminist analysis of masculinist reasoning is useful both for the students who make such announcements and for the listeners who will be surprised and probably threatened by them. Both groups need to consider how and why such reasoning is masculinist and integral to the institution in which their discussion is taking place.

When students complain that 'women are our own worst enemy,' the statement can be explored in terms of what Mary Daly has said about women as the enforcers of mutilation (foot-binding, for example) and also as a further example of dichotomizing. The use of Daly's language, which engages us in her analysis, reassures the feminist student that we do speak feminism while asking her to see the connection between her own vocabulary and that of traditional women.

Although the immediate goal of the teacher who performs such philosophical or linguistic analysis may be to alleviate or confront the students' immediate distress, the eventual goal is a change in the teacher's relationship to both groups. As group members learn the second language, they will begin to use it, becoming translators themselves. And as the teacher shares this role, she becomes more like the sister—peer of her ideology. Although her knowledge may remain greater in quantity, it will have become similar in kind. All will be bilingual.

The translator has to have two vocabularies which are consistent with each other and must be able to slip back and forth in response to non-verbal clues as well as words and other symbols. She connects the philosophical with everyday experience. Students who have already read Mary Daly and Susan Griffin may learn much by developing a sensitivity to the language and perspective of women who have never heard of either. It is seriously feminist, after all, to recognize that some women's values are important and different from men's and that traditional women's language and culture are valuable in their own right.

Students who enter a class with the rigid ideology of the university, believing that good teachers dispense wisdom and good students absorb it, learn only with difficulty how to think critically. Those who condemn past attitudes as less valuable than present ones, or beginners as less deserving of respect than those who have rejected their beginnings, will also learn only with difficulty how to think in other ways. Both groups share a cultural expectation that there are right answers and that they can be learned from good teachers. Since we want students to struggle with questions that do not have 'right' answers, we are ourselves struggling against that deeply acculturated expectation.

Recognizing this may enable us to understand the paradoxes of our own behavior as teachers. My own teaching strategies, for example, have become more radical. This reflects the conservatism of my students and my belief that within a conservative institution only carefully constructed support will permit the transition to other modes. At the simplest level this may require me to *explain* how women's experience is devalued in our economic and social system, or to *state* that a group's frustration may come from the difficulty of attempting a non-hierarchical relationship in a political context that enforces hierarchical norms, so that what we attempt and the ways we fall short become conscious. At a more complex level, what is effected by the process of translation is awareness of the shaping power of language: that understanding of the crucial life-experiences of women involves learning to 'think like' other women.

Literature is often used to develop students' empathy for women whose lifestyles are different from their own. Class members' experiences can be used in the same way, though the teacher may have to interpret as the novelist has done. When some students describe their own inclination to 'mother' their husbands, their dilemmas can be interpreted to others who cannot imagine being so male-dominated by references to Adrienne Rich and Nancy Chodorow, but it can also be presented to both groups as illustrating women's values. The feminist student is thus asked to appreciate the skills involved in balancing the emotional needs of husband and children, while the traditional student comes to understand how the institution of motherhood limits people. This can be accomplished by echoing the language of the traditional students and the language of feminist theory in the same discussion, thus expanding both vocabularies while affirming both.

Citation of feminist theory meets everyone's expectation that wisdom will be dispensed in the classroom. Translation of that theory into the languages of several populations of the class helps to meet the needs of students who want a more personal satisfaction from a Women's Studies course. To the extent that this strategy succeeds, both traditional students and the feminist minority will learn to understand a wider range of women's experience and the consciousness of both will be gently raised.

Note

1   Originally published in *Women's Studies Quarterly*, vol. 9, no. 4, winter 1981, pp.7-9. Copyright ©by The Feminist Press, 1981. Reprinted with permission.

23

Pedagogy of the oppressors?

John Schilb

I get uneasy when people describe their political conversions in language more appropriate to religious ones. While such vocabulary evokes learning as a mystical flash of awareness, hard for mortals to reproduce, I count on shifts of ideology occurring in more ordinary and gradual sorts of ways. Yet I realize how difficult it can be to tell others how you came to know or believe something, let alone help them through a similar process. As a teacher of writing, for example, who never had to take English 101 and rarely had to brood about what it meant to compose an essay, I struggle now to understand students who routinely agonize over paragraphs. As a teacher of Women's Studies who suddenly grew interested in it for reasons I still do not fully comprehend, I struggle now to influence students who routinely oppose my values.

In the first role, I benefit from the articles, books, and conferences on the teaching of writing that have proliferated in recent years. In the second role, though, I often look fruitlessly for texts and seminars enabling me to *converse* with resolute anti-feminists — rather than to argue with them, or demand conformity from them, or utterly capitulate to them. Although I have encountered many feminist teachers in similar plights, and exchanged strategies in those private talks, I think public discourse has not focused enough on how to deal with the kinds of students we face. Instead, we are more likely to hear at a Women's Studies convention about how to collaborate with students basically predisposed to the insights feminism can offer. As Barbara Hillyer Davis has commented, 'It is time to discuss the work of the feminist teacher in a *mixed* classroom, where any constituent group may be a minority

— and the smallest consistent minority group is feminist students.'[1] Attempting here, then, to construct my own version of a feminist pedagogy, I inevitably center on moves I have evolved in trying to prevent schisms between my Women's Studies classes and me.

In reporting such moves, I naturally hope that my concrete analysis will have larger applicability, and I will stress ways it might as I go along. Nevertheless, I do not want to claim that my practices necessarily have universal relevance. As I have already indicated, the realities of individual teaching situations expose even the shrewdest effort to codify feminist pedagogy as a futile gesture of will. Generally speaking, theorizing about any type of instruction sooner or later compels the theorist to drift in one of two directions: toward purity or toward pragmatism. Nowadays I operate more with the sense that even though feminist educators should affirm some common ends, they should also tolerate a considerable diversity of means — if, that is, they sincerely wish to succeed on a wide scale. The careful, deliberate evolution of strategy to fit a particular situation has, of course, distinguished the most productive feminist politics over the last two centuries. The historian, teacher, and activist Sara Evans underscored this fact when she noted how contemporary fears of cooptation and impurity can subvert potential coalitions of women. She went on to call for an organizing mentality which does not try to get everything 'right' at once, but rather lets the complexities of the process itself guide the organizer as it proceeds.[2]

With this injunction in mind, I often call upon the writing teacher in me to advise the Women's Studies teacher, because the first has learned principles of rhetoric that the second could use. I know that to teach Women's Studies effectively at my particular institution, I must contemplate the nature of my audience and the possible repertoire of techniques for reaching it, along with the purposes I want ultimately to achieve. What precisely constitutes my students' backgrounds, their own desires and needs? What persona should I cultivate to gain their trust while not unduly compromising my own temperament? How might I bridge their personal experiences and those of other people I want them to acknowledge? How might I nurture a class discussion so they walk out enlightened and not just alienated? Obviously I back away from the premise that directness and honesty always prove best; at the same time, I recoil from the prospect of becoming a Machiavellian. Answers representing a middle ground, however, can elude me on terribly inconvenient occasions. But over the long run, I have in fact managed to secure enough of them to teach with some confidence a Women's Studies course at my school. I will elaborate them first by profiling in greater detail the students I must address, then by citing specific methods I have used in the classroom, focusing on how I have modified precepts of Paulo Freire and how my gender has played a role in my teaching.

When pressed to summarize with one neat adjective the place where we work, those of us who teach Women's Studies at Denison University often resort to the term 'schizophrenic.' We do not invoke it as a clinically precise diagnosis, except at moments of extreme rage. Instead, it serves us as a metaphor for the contradiction between a basically progressive curriculum and a basically reactionary clientele. On the one hand, Denison has supported a Women's Studies program for an entire decade. Moreover, for the past five years, it has boasted a general education requirement special enough to warrant national publicity: each student must take a course in Women's or Minority Studies. On the other hand, Denison's applicant pool continues to be flooded with the children of the USA's corporate elite, bringing with them myths which reinforce its dominance: the validity of traditional sex roles, the fairness of established business practices, the sinister parasitism of the welfare state. The principal mode of social organization on the campus is the Greek system, which trains young men for the executive brotherhoods of the future and young women for their auxiliaries. Alumni encourage the fraternities' dedication to their own pleasures and their disdain for social responsibility on a local or national level. When, in her recent book, Carol Gilligan contrasts a masculinist ethic that exalts self-autonomy with a historically female ethic that values connectedness to others, she describes the fraternity morality that reigns at Denison and the sorority morality that in effect buttresses it.[3]

Social class, therefore, strikes me as the main factor to consider in an analysis of Denison students' perceptions — even if it becomes necessary to consider as well how class interacts with gender and, for that matter, with other socio-cultural variables like race and sexual preference. Yet I have also found it increasingly useful to apply theories of cognitive development in trying to understand my students, whether such theories explicitly acknowledge political circumstances or not. Because my courses in Women's Studies essentially serve to introduce the subject, they tend to consist of freshmen and sophomores; this situation, in turn, has made me reflect on how particular ages correlate with particular degrees of intellectual maturity. I have grown especially interested in the scale of cognitive development formulated by William Perry, since it has repeatedly illuminated the ways my students appear to learn. Briefly, he charts how college youths move through different mental stages, the three main ones being: (1) dualism, where they deem propositions absolutely right or absolutely wrong and feel authorities should not be questioned; (2) relativism, where they believe that no absolute truths exist and everyone has a right to his or her own opinion; and (3) committed relativism, where they feel a plurality of views remains possible but find some more worth while than others.[4] When students resist new information that clashes with inherited wisdom, they may be defending class privilege, yet they may also be expressing the sort of logic that characterizes most young people at Perry's stage one. This possibility should not drive a teacher to despair. On the contrary, the idea of cognitive development precludes by definition the acceptance of cognitive determinism, and should instead lead instructors to plan ways of helping students progress through more advanced stages. At any rate, the notion has at least helped me better grasp where my own students might be psychologically located right now, supplementing my awareness of the societal matrix where they also stand.

The language I have used in describing them may seem unduly scornful. Indeed, perhaps I have indulged too much in caustic generalizations. Admittedly a number of Denison students have exchanged their native bourgeois spirit for a larger social conscience and others sometimes claim they would like a more heterogeneous student community. But the ingrained prejudices of the vast majority cannot vanish upon request and my uneasiness with their worldview survives. It intensifies when students take my courses in resentful submission to the requirement instead of genuine sympathy for its concerns. Although I avoid wallowing in my rancor as if it constituted a holy mood, I have grown more willing to reveal it to my colleagues, despite the cherished stereotype of the feminist classroom as a scene of perpetual collaborative bliss. Only if feminist educators examine the breaches they might feel between themselves and their students do they stand a chance of overcoming mutual alienation and establishing a climate of generative trust. In my personal case, I usually wind up assuming that I am the party who must change to begin with, implementing strategies which might prove effective. Somehow I need to transform my negative feelings into positive action.

I realize that Women's Studies faculty at other colleges might envy me my problem. After all, it represents the kind of difficulty which comes from a significant amount of success. I encounter it because my school has decided that Women's and Minority Studies ought to figure in the learning of all Denison students, especially those who prefer a white, androcentric world. Needless to say, most colleges make feminists grieve by refusing their courses a stable life even on the margins of the academy. I take small comfort, though, in the knowledge that getting to teach Women's Studies to captive hordes of conservatives is a chance denied many, a landmark in mainstreaming granted few. But since this feature of Denison's curriculum might indeed be a harbinger, portending the greater influence of Women's Studies across the land, I feel a unique pressure to devise and communicate ways of coping with its results.

Naturally, coping must entail demonstrated respect for the students in question, and it should extend to professed interest in their views. If the dynamics of a Women's Studies class become such that Self-Righteous Teacher merely lectures to Sinfully Ignorant Pupils on the defects of their minds, critics of the field will reap new evidence for their old charges of indoctrination. Worse, ritual sermons from on high will probably just affirm the young congregation's fondness for hierarchical systems and modes of thought. I acutely sensed the value of an opposite approach on the first day of a seminar at the National Institute in Women's Studies last summer. The participants had to write about one of their best teaching experiences, and when we compared notes, we found that all of us had recounted an occasion when we ourselves had said very little, our students quite a bit — with genuine intellectual achievement still taking place. Clearly, we now had empirical proof that a student-centered classroom, in some meaning of the term, lay at the heart of our pedagogical dreams.[5]

Yet just as clearly, my burst of awareness left open to investigation exactly how I might go about literalizing my ideal. The conflict between my hope of involving my classes in their education, and my skepticism about the validity of what they might contribute, proved a constant personal theme during the seminar. More precisely, I found myself struggling to apply the works of Paulo Freire, our major texts, to my own teaching situation. How could Freire's pedagogy of the oppressed — the title of his most famous book — develop with people who, by virtue of their social stratum, could reasonably be labeled oppressors?[6]

The seminar was not actually the first time I had read Freire and grappled with the accompanying dilemma. A few years back, when I was intensely thinking about both my incipient feminism and my traditional penchant for lecturing, I had read *Pedagogy of the Oppressed* upon the advice of a friend. Right away I had liked how it connects true reciprocity in the educational process with a truly humanistic praxis in the larger world. Freire protests the 'banking' method of education, whereby the instructor 'deposits' information into allegedly empty heads. Fearing that it threatens to keep the oppressed numbly compliant with the structures oppressing them, he advocates instead a real dialogue between their teachers and them, entailing a critical analysis of the contradictions afflicting their everyday life. They would thus attain a new power to distinguish the ineradicable laws of nature from the transient institutions of culture, along with a new optimism about the prospect of social change. Although I had, indeed, subsequently tried to realize his vision in my classroom procedures, the sheer rigor of shifting it from the political arena of Third World peasants to the comfortable halls of an American private college had proven too formidable. While I had by no means renounced his principles, I had let his account of them slip to the back of my mind, relaxing my determination to enact them. Still, like some dybbuk who continues to haunt on the edges of consciousness, Freire did not altogether depart from my thinking. And the experience of the seminar certainly returned him to the forefront of it — with newly beneficial consequences for my theories as well as my actions, whatever the problems of importing his pedagogy to the milieu I inhabit.

Freire would be the last person to grant all his methods ontological status, necessary for any setting no matter what its particular characteristics. He himself painstakingly elaborated them in response to the specific conditions he faced. Yet, as I have suggested, they can hold a powerful appeal for the feminist who teaches the wealthier people of this country. To make them useful to me, though, I had to ask myself throughout the seminar — and before it as well as after it — if I could in any sense consider my students 'oppressed.' Do they suffer in ways identifiable enough to motivate their engagement in critical inquiry? Can they viscerally feel the worth of conducting the sort of dialogue Freire describes, even if it winds up challenging their society? My answer to both these questions has gradually become a tentative, shaky, hesitant, qualified, but still productive 'Yes.'

The students have undeniably escaped the pain of extreme material want. However, they can be thought of as entrapped in a certain profound fatalism. Unaware of the conceivable relationships between one institution and another, one historical event and another, one human being and another, they themselves experience life as a fragile web of monadic units that cannot afford to depend too much on the prospect of mutual aid. Given their own apprehension of culture as incorrigibly opaque, they follow the specific edicts of their parents and the general doctrine of social Darwinism as the only means of mental and physical survival. The term 'Me Generation,' esteemed as a label for the well-off children of the 1970s wrongly implies that they enjoy a stable conception of self. But they do suffer doubts and inner schisms, exacerbated by their continued blindness to social relations and their continued reliance on ideological clichés. Confronting the supposed onslaught of feminism, therefore, the men resist notions of their own complicity in the structures it attacks, while still vaguely intuiting the justice of at least some of its ideals. The women automatically defend their strategic investment in the patriarchal family and its associated codes, branding feminists as 'selfish' and 'extremist'; at the same time, they cannot help responding on some level to the promise of genuine choice, equality, and exchange of care.

I have not, to be sure, let my classes become mere therapy sessions, focused simply on purging the students of their existential malaise. Rather, I aim to tap their latent despair, bring it to the surface of their minds, and enable them to see how resolving it depends on knowing not only how their own freedom gets limited, but also how the whole world functions, how others feel agony in more tangible forms, how social change on a global scale remains a possibility and a need. In classic feminist style, therefore, I often pivot discussions around the students' personal lives, but I have us quickly situate them in a network of relationships that include oppressed people otherwise absent from the room. By encouraging the students to place their experiential texts in broader social contexts, I hope they will discern the links between their internally disruptive paradoxes and the external forces of division that harm multitudes.

For example, on the first day of a course I taught last semester entitled 'How Women's Studies and Black Studies Connect,' I asked the students to give brief accounts of jobs they once had. As usual, I did not want to waste the occasion simply dispensing the syllabus and intoning the course requirements, as if official business of that sort really served as a meaningful prelude to the topics that would preoccupy us. Testimonies of work experience give the class some immediate knowledge of one another, introduce what always becomes a major subject of a Women's Studies course, and start people thinking about how they generally interact with others in the world beyond the classroom door. On this particular day, the anecdotes proved especially useful because several members of the class described summer jobs in factories, emphasizing how they had to consort for the first time on a daily basis with members of a social stratum they normally did not confront much. Admitting their own discomfort with the monotonous routines they performed, along with their new pity for those still entrenched in them after Labor Day, these students provided grounds for the whole class to examine their anxieties about the spiritual worth of their future employment, the possible value or lack of value of work for all human beings, and the mechanisms which assign dreary tasks to one group while enabling other groups to do them just briefly. The very fact that the various issues hung together as parts of the same discussion suggested the holistic kind of approach needed for each. The class did not suddenly produce a complete Marxist analysis of the stories, nor did I thump down one myself. Rather, we talked only a little this first day about the implications of what we had narrated, with me being content simply to tease out a few. I have come to understand that working *with* students, as opposed to preaching *at* them, means that I have to be satisfied with sequencing insights over the span of an entire semester, letting the students hatch them at their own pace — or at least with only some hastening interventions now and then. I would have shattered the chance of prolonging the dialogue if I had prematurely announced the ideas it had confirmed. When the first period ended, the students were still just budding theorists, but they had begun to generate a responsible awareness in concert with themselves and their teacher.

The awareness began to grow considerably, I think, with an activity they carried out soon afterward. I paired students and had them interview each other outside of class; next, they used their findings to introduce each other during a regular class session. Although they certainly could ask about any autobiographical details that interested them, I had them focus on the topic that would eventually serve as the basis of their first writing assignment. They would be gradually composing it through dialogue instead of privately scribbling it all at once the night before it was due. Such an activity, overall, has two general virtues: it initiates close collaboration early in the semester, and it implies that thinking as well as writing is a process of evolution rather than a quick glimpse of certainties. I chose the subject of these interviews, introductions and papers in a renewed attempt to widen the students' normal framework for analyzing their existence. Specifically, they had to consider what it meant to be black or white or male or female at their high school, choosing a category to which they did *not* belong. They would thereby be *re*viewing their personal backgrounds, yet in an unfamiliar light, one that encompassed people whose orientation they had not shared. In the classroom introductions and in the actual papers, they signified a new awareness of certain sociological data. For instance, the reality of segregation loomed. We talked much about their burgeoning insights, as well as about how they achieved them: namely, by pondering their relationship to people different from themselves, and the negative consequences for both groups of their previous neglect.

Again, the class did not attain right away a highly sophisticated understanding of how discrimination operates. At this point in the course, for one thing, they still tended to believe that racism and sexism basically involve just individual attitudes. They found it hard to stand back and comprehend how institutions like the American high school — in which, after all, they had recently been immersed — perpetuated inequality in a variety of forms. They would move toward a firmer theoretical base as the course ensued, directly confronting the matter of institutional discrimination near the end, when we read Feagin and Feagin's *Discrimination American Style: Institutional Racism and Sexism*.[7] At that stage, we found ourselves automatically referring back to our first talks, incorporating them into our elaborated perspective. So, the nature of the first major class activity became the nature of the course itself: carefully revisionary at the students' own best speed. In one sense, the semester featured a linear movement, a cumulative gathering of ideas; in another sense, it would be more precise to depict the shape of the course as a spiral, looping back to previous events and sweeping them up into refined interpretations. While teaching a course like this one, I try to keep the latter image in mind, for it enables me to maintain patience when the students do not immediately lift their remarks to the theoretical plane where I wish for them to rise.

Engaging in writing assignments and discussions about them throughout a course tallies with Freire's emphasis on the study of language as a means of demystifying the world. Collectively ruminating on terms and definitions can indeed move a class from issues of semantics to truths of politics. Shortly before my formal reacquaintance with Freire, I had hit upon this fact with conspicious effects. I was struggling to discuss with another Women's Studies class a subject that Denison students much prefer to avoid, lesbianism. Previously, I had discovered that no matter how many plain statistics I might accumulate, no matter how many stirring poems by Audre Lorde I might read aloud, students would accord the topic little more than giggles and snorts. With this class, however, I decided to focus on linguistic analysis and their own compositions. We spent three class periods in a row unpacking, so to speak, a statement which I had put up on the blackboard: 'Lesbianism is not natural.' Obviously, we converged upon the various meanings behind the last word. While I wondered at the start if this approach would be too intellectually detached to elucidate the subject of lesbianism more than superficially, it came to provoke valuable responses. The more the students explored the implications of 'natural,' the more they saw the term rooted in cultural biases instead of scientific proof, and the more they realized even heterosexuals could be victimized by its thoughtless currency. They pieced together more glaring evidence of the damage homophobia can wreak when I required them to write an analysis of the upcoming weekend at Denison from a homosexual student's point of view. Not surprisingly, the assignment initially elicited a high degree of tension, which I tried to alleviate with the promise of richer understanding. Unbeknown to me, the weekend centered around fraternity formals, so the students had a veritable gallery of heterosexist behavior to patrol. In our subsequent discussions of their reportage, they exchanged dozens of stories about how the community expresses fears of homosexuality, through loud jokes and whispered accusations. Fraternity men emerged as utterly obsessed with demonstrating their sexual 'propriety.' The most significant perception the students reached through the exercize was that pressure to show 'natural' sexuality afflicted heterosexual students too, albeit in a different fashion. It became obvious in class that the assignment helped them locate their own sexual insecurities in the context of rampant social coercion, whatever their preferences might actually happen to be. By recording the language of others, composing their own written discourse, and speaking about the whole process as a group, privileged students did manage to connect problems of their particular lives to those of the blatantly tormented. My own later reunion with the texts of Freire compelled me often to try recreating such events.

In adapting Freire's pedagogy to my Women's Studies courses, or in transporting any pedagogy to them, I cannot blur one apparent contradiction. The fact that I am a male teacher of Women's Studies inevitably makes a difference, and it becomes only prudent for me to reflect on what the difference might ideally be. Since I have argued elsewhere for the validity of my taking on my job in the first place,[8] I prefer to focus here not on defending it but on noting the basic effects of my gender when I carry it out.

The advantages lie in having a fair amount of persuasiveness at some moments of controversy. When a female colleague and I team-taught a Women's Studies class a few years ago, we regularly found that while the students construed as militant even innocuous remarks of hers, they greeted my explicitly partisan judgments with less hostility. I have continued to sense that although I may indeed provoke abrasive responses with several of my observations, a feminist woman would probably face greater contempt in making them. Similarly, my students feel more comfortable asking me questions about the women's movement than they probably would if they had to ask someone from its overwhelmingly female majority. No doubt they tend to assume, whatever statements I make to the contrary, that I speak more as an enthusiastic spectator of the movement than as a fully engaged participant in it. Moreover, I stand a chance of promulgating feminist insights when I supply personal accounts of coming to them as a man. Speaking, for example, of the sisterly warmth I saw expressed at an institute where I was the only male, I can impart an air of authenticity to a claim that might otherwise elicit suspicion.

Of course, disadvantages underlie the advantages. Much as I appreciate the rhetorical leverage granted my sex even in my Women's Studies classroom, I shudder to think that only a man's voice could legitimize what mine says. I realize the danger of affirming patriarchal authority in the name of my administrative convenience. When, in a course, I stress class discussion instead of lecture, the worth of the student as opposed to the prestige of the instructor, I do so in part because I want to assert that a course does not need male power at the helm. I remind students who utterly depend on my testimony as the basis for assenting to feminism that such reliance betrays its ideals. I further try to offset my authority by having female teaching assistants run several discussions and female guest speakers explain their work.

Lately, I have wondered if my difficulty with controlling my temper in a recalcitrant Women's Studies class stands as another disadvantage of my gender. I know that I regret not having participated in the feminist consciousness-raising groups of the past two decades. Without sentimentalizing them out of ignorance, I suspect they afforded their members valuable training in honestly resolving conflict. Many men who profess new interest in feminism want to spend their time intimately talking with one another, and while I fear they may slight political exigencies which directly threaten women, I understand their desire to capture now for themselves a group experience they once trivialized or disdained. Still, I persistently feel a commitment to the teaching of Women's Studies, at Denison or elsewhere. And with the help of theorists like Paulo Freire, of many women friends, and yes, even of my students on distressing as well as joyful occasions, I persistently seek better ways of enacting that commitment.

Notes

1 Barbara Hillyer Davis, 'Teaching the Feminist Minority,' this volume, p.245.
2 Lecture at Great Lakes Colleges Association, National Summer Institute in Women's Studies, University of Michigan, 29 June 1982.
3 Carol Gilligan, *In a Different Voice: Psychological Theory and Women's Development*, Cambridge, Mass.: Harvard University Press, 1982.
4 See especially William Perry, *Forms of Intellectual and Ethical Development in the College Years*, New York: Holt, Rinehart & Winston, 1970.
5 The participants in the seminar besides myself were Nancy Barnes (leader), Virginia Beauchamp, Sister Carol Berg, Ryn Edwards, Mary Johnson, Bonnie Lamvemeyer, and Joan Scott. I thank them for their various contributions to my thinking.
6 Paulo Freire, *Pedagogy of the Oppressed*, trans. Myra Bergman Ramos, New York: Seabury Press, 1970; see also his *Education for Critical Consciousness*, New York: Continuum, 1973.
7 Joe R. Feagin and Clairece Booher Feagin, *Discrimination American Style: Institutional Racism and Sexism*, Englewood Cliffs, New Jersey: Prentice-Hall, 1978.
8 John Schilb, 'Men's Studies and Women's Studies,' *Change*, April 1982, pp.38-41.

Selected bibliography

The bibliography does not attempt to include material on the feminist transformation of the curriculum. The selections below focus directly or by implication on the dynamics of the feminist classroom.

Aptheker, Bettina, ' "Strong Is What We Make Each Other": Unlearning Racism Within Women's Studies,' *Women's Studies Quarterly*, vol. 9, no. 4, winter 1981, pp.13-16.

Arce, Jenny Valcarel, 'The Broken Wing: Teaching Literacy to Rural Peruvian Women in the City,' *Women's Studies International*, no. 2, 1982, pp.27-33.

Beck, Evelyn Torton, 'Teaching About Jewish Lesbians in Literature: From *Zeitl and Rickel* to *The Tree of Begats*', in Margaret Cruikshank (ed.), *Lesbian Studies: Present and Past*, Old Westbury, New York: The Feminist Press, 1982, pp.81-7.

Bennett, Sheila Kishler, 'Student Perceptions of and Expectations for Male and Female Instructors: Evidence Relating to the Question of Gender Bias in Teaching Evaluation,' *Journal of Educational Psychology*, 74, April 1982, pp.170-9.

Bernard, Michael, *et al.*, 'Sex Role Behavior and Gender in Teacher Student Evaluations,' *Journal of Educational Psychology*, 73, October 1981, pp.681-96.

Berry, Linda and Judith McDaniel, 'Teaching Contemporary Black Women Writers,' *Radical Teacher*, 17, November 1980, pp.7-10.

Bose, Christine, 'Teaching Women and Technology at the University of Washington,' *Women's Studies International Quarterly*, vol. 4, no. 3, 1981, pp.374-7.

Boxer, Marilyn, 'For and About Women: the Theory and Practice of Women's Studies in the United States,' *Signs: Journal of Women in Culture and Society*, vol. 7, no. 3, spring 1982, pp.661-95.

Bulkin, Elly, 'Heterosexism and Women's Studies,' *Radical Teacher*, 17, November 1980, pp.25-31.

Bulkin, Elly, '"A Whole New Poetry Beginning Here": Teaching Lesbian Poetry,' *College English*, vol. 40, no. 8, April 1979, pp.874-88.

Bunch, Charlotte, 'Not By Degrees,' *Quest: A Feminist Quarterly*, vol. 5, no. 1, summer 1979, pp.7-18.

Butler, Johnnella E., *Black Studies: Pedagogy and Revolution, A Study of Afro-American Studies and the Liberal Arts Tradition Through the Discipline of Afro-American Literature*, Lanham, Maryland: University Press of America, 1981.

Cannon, Ellen, and Carey Kaplan, 'An Experiment with Innovative Teaching in a Small Conservative, Liberal Arts College,' *Radical Teacher*, 3, 1976, pp.34-6.

Cantarow, Ellen, 'The Social Uses of Literature: Reclaiming Our Roots,' *Radical Teacher*, 3, 1976, pp.34-8.

Clarricoates, Katherine, 'The Experience of Patriarchal Schooling,' *Interchange on Educational Policy*, vol. 12, nos 2/3, 1981, pp.185-205.

Davis, Barbara Hillyer, 'Finding New Forms: A Study of Autonomy in a Patriarchal University,' *Women's Studies Newsletter*, vol. 7, no. 2, spring 1979, pp.22-4.

Davis, Madeline, 'Learning Through Teaching: A Lesbianism Course in 1972,' in Margaret Cruikshank (ed.), *Lesbian Studies: Present and Past*, Old Westbury, New York: The Feminist Press, 1982, pp.93-6.

Denyer, Joyce, and Helen La Fountaine, 'More Than Just a Course.' *Canadian Newsletter on Women*, vol. 1, no. 2, winter 1978-9, pp.120-1.

Douglas, Carol Anne, 'Can A Radical Feminist Find Happiness Teaching Women's Studies?', *Off Our Backs*, 7, December 1977, pp.11ff.

Duelli-Klein, Renate, 'Women College Students and Feminism,' *Radical Teacher*, 21, n.d., pp.12-13.

Fausto-Sterling, Anne, 'The Myth of Neutrality: Race, Sex and Class in Science,' *Radical Teacher*, 19, n.d., pp.21-5.

Fausto-Sterling, Anne, 'Women's Studies and Science,' *Women's Studies Newsletter*, vol. 8, no. 1, winter 1980, pp.4-7.

Fausto-Sterling, Anne, *Feminist Pedagogy: Positions and Points of View*, Women's Studies Research Center, Working Papers Series, no. 3, Madison, Wisconsin: University of Wisconsin, 1981.

Fausto-Sterling, Anne, 'Course Closeup: The Biology of Gender,' *Women's Studies Quarterly*, vol. 10, no. 2, summer 1982, pp.17-19.

Ferguson, Ann, 'Feminist Teaching: A Practice Developed in Undergraduate Courses,' *Radical Teacher*, 20, n.d., pp.26-9.

Fisher, Berenice, 'What Is Feminist Pedagogy?' *Radical Teacher*, 18, n.d., pp.20-4.

Fontaine, Carolyn, 'Teaching the Psychology of Women: A Lesbian-Feminist Perspective,' in Margaret Cruikshank (ed.), *Lesbian Studies: Present and Past*, Old Westbury, New York: The Feminist Press, 1982, pp.70-80.

Freire, Paulo, *Pedagogy of the Oppressed*, trans. Myra Bergman Ramos, New York: Seabury Press, 1970.

Freire, Paulo, *Education for Critical Consciousness*, New York: Herter & Herter, 1973.

Glenwick, D. S., S. L. Johannson and J. Brady, 'Comparisons of Self-Images of Female and Male Assistant Professors,' *Sex Roles*, 4, August 1978, pp.513-24.

Gonzales, Sylvia, 'Toward a Feminist Pedagogy for Chicana Self-Actualization,' *Frontiers: A Journal of Women Studies*, vol. 5, no. 2, summer 1980, pp.48-51.

Grant, Julia, 'The Dynamics of the Women's Studies Classroom,' *Radical Teacher*, 22, n.d., p.24.

Grumet, Madeleine, 'Pedagogy for Patriarchy: The Feminization of Teaching,' *Interchange on Educational Policy*, vol. 12, nos 2/3, 1981, pp.165-84.

Gurko, Jane, 'Sexual Energy in the Classroom,' in Margaret Cruikshank (ed.), *Lesbian Studies: Present and Past*, Old Westbury, New York: The Feminist Press, 1982, pp.25-31.

Hall, Judith A., Karen G. Braunwald and Barbara J. Mroz, 'Gender, Affect and Influence in a Teaching Situation,' *Journal of Personality and Social Psychology*, 43, August 1982, pp.270-80.

Higgins, Kathy, '"Making It Your Own World": Women's Studies and Freire,' *Women's Studies International Forum*, vol. 5, no. 1, 1982, pp.87-98.

Hoffman, Honey, 'A Class of Our Own,' in Elaine Showalter and Carol Ohmann, *Female Studies IV: Teaching About Women*, Pittsburg: Know, 1971, pp.14-27.

Howe, Florence, 'Identity and Expression: A Writing Course for Women,' *College English*, vol. 32, no. 8, May 1971, pp.863-71.

Howe, Florence, 'Literacy and Literature,' *PMLA*, vol. 89, no. 3, May 1974, pp.433-41.

Howe, Florence, 'New Teaching Strategies for a New Generation of Students,' vol. 11, no. 2, summer 1983, pp.7-11.

Issues of Pedagogy in Women's Studies: A Preliminary Bibliography of Monographic Materials, University of Wisconsin, Madison, 1979.

Jenkins, Lee, and Kris Kramer, 'Small Group Process: Learning From Women,' *Women's Studies International Quarterly*, vol. 1, no. 1, 1978, pp.67-84.

Jorge, Angela, 'Issues of Race and Class in Women's Studies: A Puerto Rican Woman's Thoughts,' *Women's Studies Newsletter*, 8, fall/winter 1980, pp.17-18.

Kaschak, Ellen, 'Another Look at Sex Bias in Students' Evaluations of Professors: Do Winners Get the Recognition That They Have Been Given?' *Psychology of Women Quarterly*, vol. 5, no. 5, Supplement 1981, pp.767-72.

Kaye, Melanie, 'Closeup on Women's Studies Courses: Feminist Theory and Practice,' *Women's Studies Newsletter*, summer 1978, pp.20-3.

King, Ynesta, 'Feminist Pedagogy and Technology: Reflections on the Goddard Feminism and Ecology Summer Program,' *Women's Studies International Quarterly*, vol. 4, no. 3, 1981, pp.370-2.

Kinnard, Cynthia and Jean Robinson, '"It Applies Directly": Introducing Students to Women's Studies,' *Radical Teacher*, 18, n.d., pp.15-19.

Knowles, Mary Tyler, 'All Male Students and Women's Liberation,' in Elaine Showalter and Carol Ohmann (eds), *Female Studies IV: Teaching About Women*, Pittsburg: Know, 1971, pp.35-9.

Krasno, Francine, 'On Teaching a Feminist Writing Workshop,' *Women's Studies Newsletter*, 5, fall 1977, pp.14-17.

Lanser, Susan S., 'Beyond *The Bell Jar*: Women Students in the 1970s,' *Radical Teacher*, 6, December 1977, pp.41-4.

Longino, H. E., 'Scientific Objectivity and Feminist Theorizing,' *Liberal Education*, fall 1981, pp.187-95.

Lowenstein, Sophie Freud, 'The Passion and Challenge of Teaching,' *Harvard Educational Review: Women and Education, Part II*, vol. 50, no. 1, February 1980, pp.1-12.

McCracken, Ellen, 'Teaching *Cosmopolitan*: Theory and Practice,' *Radical Teacher*, 13, March 1979, pp.5-8.

McNaron, Toni, 'Out at the University: Myth and Reality,' *Women's Studies Newsletter*, vol. 8, no. 4, fall/winter 1980, pp.20-1.

McNaron, Toni, 'A Journey into Otherness: Teaching *The Well of Loneliness*', in Margaret Cruikshank (ed.), *Lesbian Studies: Present and Past*, Old Westbury, New York: The Feminist Press, 1982, pp.88-92.

Mackie, Marlene, 'On Congenial Truth: A Perspective on Women's Education,' *Canadian Review of Sociology and Anthropology*, 14, fall 1977, pp.117-28.

Maglin, Nan Bauer, 'Journal of a Women's Course,' *University of Michigan Papers in Women's Studies*, vol. 1, no. 3, October 1974, pp.55-81.

Maglin, Nan Bauer, 'Women's Studies at Manhattan Community College: Teaching Next to the Tango Palace,' *Radical Teacher*, 6, 1977, pp.5-9.

Maglin, Nan Bauer, ' "Full of Memories": Teaching Matrilineage,' *College English*, vol. 40, no. 8, April 1979, pp.889-98.

Manahan, Nancy, 'Homophobia in the Classroom,' in Margaret Cruikshank (ed.), *Lesbian Studies: Present and Past*, Old Westbury, New York: The Feminist Press, 1982, pp.66-9.

Martin, Jenny, J. P. Powell and Chris Wieneke, 'The Experience of a Group of Older Unqualified Women at University,' *Women's Studies International Quarterly*, vol. 4, no. 2, 1981, pp.117-31.

Martin, Wendy, 'Teaching Women's Studies — Some Problems and Discoveries,' in Elaine Showalter and Carol Ohmann (eds), *Female Studies IV: Teaching About Women*, Pittsburgh: Know, 1971, pp.9-13.

Miller, Janet L., 'The Sound of Silence Breaking: Feminist Pedagogy and Curriculum Theory,' *Journal of Curriculum Theorizing*, vol. 4, no. 1, winter 1982, pp.5-11.

Miranda, Wilma R., 'Implications in Dewey for Feminist Theory in Education,' *Educational Horizons*, vol. 58, no. 4, summer 1980, pp.197-202.

Mitrano, Barbara, 'Feminism and Curriculum Theory, Implications for Teacher Education,' *Journal of Curriculum Theorizing*, summer 1981, pp.5-85.

Moraga, Cherrie and Barbara Smith, 'Lesbian Literature: A Third World Feminist Perspective,' in Margaret Cruikshank (ed.), *Lesbian Studies: Present and Past*, Old Westbury, New York: The Feminist Press, 1982, pp.55-65.

Morgan, Ellen, 'On Teaching Women's Studies,' *University of Michigan Papers in Women's Studies*, May 1978, pp.27-34.

Morgan, Ellen, 'The One-Eyed Doe,' *Radical Teacher*, December 1978, pp.2-6.

Nawy, Martha, 'Women's Studies: Education as Healing,' *Women: A Journal of Liberation: Healing*, 7, 1981, pp.56-8.

Nelson, Randle W., 'Reading, Writing and Relationship: Toward Overcoming the Hidden Curriculum of Gender, Ethnicity and Socioeconomic Class,' *Interchange on Educational Policy*, vol. 12, nos 2/3, 1981, pp.229-42.

Neumann, Stephanie G., 'Wife, Mother, Teacher, Scholar, and Sex Object: Role Conflicts of a Female Academic,' *Intellect*, 10, fall 1978, pp.302-6.

Pederson, Lucille M., 'Pedagogical Methods of Teaching "Women in Public Speaking,"' *Communication Education*, 30, July 1981, pp.256-64.

Perun, Pamela, *The Undergraduate Woman, Issues in Educational Equity*, Lexington, Mass.: D.C. Heath, 1982.

Pheterson, Gail, 'The Struggle of an Academic Feminist: Elitism versus Excellence,' *Women's Studies International Forum*, vol. 5, no. 1, 1982, pp.83-5.

Porter, Nancy, 'Liberating Teaching,' *Women's Studies Quarterly*, vol. 10, no. 4, winter 1982, pp.19-24.

Porter, Nancy M., and Margaret T. Eileenchild, *The Effectiveness of Women's Studies Teaching*, Women's Studies Monograph Series, Washington, DC: National Institute of Education, 1980.

Radner, Susan, 'Changing Approaches to Teaching "Women in Literature,"' *Frontiers*, 6, spring/summer 1981, pp.3-5.

Register, Cheri, 'Brief, A-mazing Movements: Dealing with Despair in the Women's Studies Classroom,' *Women's Studies Newsletter*, 7, fall 1979, pp.7-10.

Rich, Adrienne, 'Toward a Woman-Centered University,' *On Lies, Secrets, and Silence: Selected Prose 1966-1978*, New York: W. W. Norton, 1979, pp.125-56.

Rothchild, Joan, 'Teaching and Learning About Women and Technology,' *Women's Studies International Quarterly*, vol. 4, no. 3, 1981, p.369.

Rowley, Rotunno, and William Dobken, 'Strategies for the Teaching of Women's Studies,' *Social Science Record*, 10, September 1973, pp.37-9.

Schlib, John, 'Men's Studies and Women's Studies,' *Change*, April 1982, pp.38-41.

Schneidewind, Nancy, 'Feminist Values: Guidelines for Teaching Methdology in Women's Studies,' *Radical Teacher*, 18, n.d., pp.25-8.

Shanley, M. L., 'Invisible Woman: Thoughts on Teaching Political Philosophy,' *News for Teachers of Political Science*, 24, 1980, pp.2-4.

Shaw, Linda, L., and Diane G. Wicker, 'Teaching about Racism in the Classroom and in the Community,' *Radical Teacher*, 18, n.d., pp.9-14.

Showalter, Elaine, 'Teaching About Women, 1971,' in Elaine Showalter and Carold Ohmann (eds), *Female Studies IV: Teaching About Women*, Pittsburg: Know, 1971, pp.i-xii.

Singer, Katie Herzfeld, 'One Student's View of Women's Studies,' *Women's Studies Quarterly*, 10, summer 1982, pp.26-7.

Spender, Dale, 'Learning to Create Our Own Knowledge,' *Convergence: An International Journal of Adult Education*, vol. 13, nos 1-2, 1980, pp.14-23.

Spender, Dale, 'Education: the Patriarchal Paradigm and the Response to Feminism,' *Men's Studies Modified*, Oxford and New York: Pergamon Press, 1981.

Speizer, Jeanne J., 'Role Models, Mentors, and Sponsors: The Elusive Concepts,' *Signs: Journal of Women in Culture and Society*, 7, summer 1981, pp.692-712.

Stanley, Julia, 'The Lesbian Perspective: Pedagogy and the Structure of Human Knowledge,' paper presented to the National Council of Teachers of English, Chicago, November 1976.

Stitzel, Judith, 'Conversations,' *New Directions in Teaching*, 50, spring 1977, pp.14-16.

Stitzel, Judith, 'Unlearning Not to Speak,' *Frontiers: A Journal of Women Studies*, vol. 4, no. 1, spring 1979, pp.47-9.

Stitzel, Judith, 'Toward the New Year: From A Journal,' *Trellis*, 3, summer 1979, pp.53-6.

Stitzel, Judith, 'A Third Chance,' in Warren Bryan Martin (ed.), *New Perspectives on Teaching and Learning*, San Francisco: Jossey-Rass, 1981, pp.125-8.

Strobel, Margaret, 'Fighting Two Colonialisms: Thoughts of a White Feminist Teaching About Third World Women,' *Radical Teacher*, 6, 1977, pp.20-2.

Strong, Bryan, 'Teaching Women's History Experimentally,' in Elaine Showalter and Carol Ohmann (eds), *Female Studies IV: Teaching About Women*, Pittsburg: Know, 1971, pp.40-7.

Tilly, Louise A., and Mary Edwards, 'Women's Studies in Process: Overviews and Case Studies in Teaching and Research on Women,' *University of Michigan Papers on Women's Studies*, May 1978, pp.9-13.

Tobias, Sheila, 'Teaching Female Studies: Looking Back Over Three Years,' *Liberal Education*, 58, May 1972, pp.258-64.

Toomey, Beverly G., and William D. Eldridge, 'The Interactive Team: A Non-sexist Teaching Approach,' *College Student Journal*, 16, spring 1982, pp.4-8.

Westcott, Marcia, 'Feminist Criticism of the Social Sciences,' *Harvard Educational Review: Women and Education, Part I*, vol. 49, no. 4, November 1979, pp.422-30.

White, Barbara, 'Up from the Podium: Feminist Revolution in the Classroom,' in Elaine Showalter and Carol Ohmann (eds), *Female Studies IV: Teaching About Women*, Pittsburg: Know, 1971, pp.28-34.

Zimmerman, Bonnie, 'Lesbianism 101,' *Radical Teacher*, 17, n.d., pp.20-4.

Notes on contributors

Gloria Bonder is the Director of Centro de Estudios de la Mujer in Buenos Aires, Argentina. A psychologist, she has written articles including 'Women's group therapy: a transitional space for the reconstruction of female identity,' available with other publications from the Center at OLLEROS 2554, P.B. (1426) Buenos Aires, and is an active participant at conferences addressing feminist issues in an international context.

Johnnella E. Butler, Associate Professor Afro-American Studies at Smith College, is chair of her department. She teaches 'Afro-American Literature,' 'Introduction to Afro-American Studies' and 'Theory and Research in Afro-American Studies.' During the past four years, she has been actively involved in curriculum development that allows a dialogue between Black Studies and Women's Studies. As an accomplished soprano, she performs lecture/recitals on the Afro-American spiritual and music by black women composers. She continues to explore ways to use her talent most effectively as a cultural worker.

Robert Bezucha, Professor of History at Amherst College, teaches the social, cultural and political history of modern Europe. His most recent publications include studies of the social history of work, the transformation of popular culture, and the history of French painting in the nineteenth century.

Joan Cocks, a political theorist, has taught a variety of courses in

273

274/Notes on contributors

feminist theory at Mount Holyoke College and the University of Massachusetts, Amherst. She is writing a book entitled *The Oppositional Imagination: Critical Reflections on Radical Feminism*, which explores the philosophical dilemmas generated by radical feminism in its struggle to create itself against the grain of the dominant culture.

Margo Culley teaches Women's Studies within the English department at the University of Massachusetts, Amherst. The editor of the Norton Critical Edition of Kate Chopin's *The Awakening*, she has published a number of articles on American women writers. With Johnnella Butler, she was Co-Director of the Black Studies/Women's Studies Faculty Department Project supported by the Fund for the Improvement of Post-secondary Education. She has taught graduate courses in feminist pedagogy and with Catherine Portuges has offered workshops for faculty on the topic. She is completing a book on the diaries and journals of American women.

Barbara Hillyer Davis, Director of the Women's Studies Program of the University of Oklahoma, has published widely on feminist pedagogy. Her present work concentrates on building connections between academic Women's Studies and the broader feminist community. Her research interests include feminist theory in relation to the experiences of women who care for individuals with disabilities.

Arlyn Diamond, a feminist and a medievalist, has co-edited with Lee Edwards a collection of women's fiction, *American Voices, American Women*, and feminist criticism, *The Authority of Experience*, and is currently working on a feminist study of courtly love. She is a union activist and an expert in dressage.

Lee Edwards, former editor of the *Massachusetts Review*, is the author of *Psyche as Hero: Female Heroism and Fictional Form*, Wesleyan University Press, 1984. She is Professor of English and Women's Studies at the University of Massachusetts, Amherst.

Susan Stanford Friedman, Associate Professor of English and Women's Studies, University of Wisconsin, is the author of *Psyche Reborn: The Emergence of H.D., 1981*, co-author of *A Woman's Guide to Therapy, 1979*, and has published articles on H.D., Adrienne Rich and others. She is currently at work on *Sagas of the Self: A Study of H.D.'s Prose* and *Portrait of an Analysis with Freud: The H.D.—Bryher Letters, 1933-1934.*

Nancy Jo Hoffman teaches at the College of Public and Community Service, University of Massachusetts, Boston, where she is Associate Professor of Humanities. In addition to articles on Women's Studies, education and literature, she is the author of *Spenser's Pastorals, Women's 'True' Profession: Voices from the History of Teaching,* and co-editor, with Florence Howe, of *Women Working: Stories and Poems.* From 1979 to 1981 she worked as a program officer at the Fund for the Improvement of Post-secondary Education.

Helene Keyssar has been a theater director, film and drama critic, and university teacher for almost twenty years. In addition to numerous articles on film, theater and communication, she is the author of *The Curtain and the Veil: Strategies in Black Drama,* Burt Franklin, 1981; *Right in Her Soul: the Life of Anna Louise Strong,* Random House, 1984; *Landscapes of the Feminist Theater,* Macmillan, 1984; and *New Roots for the Nation: The Films of Robert Altman* (in progress). Her most recent venture has been the production of a series of simultaneous videocasts between San Diego and Moscow. She currently chairs the Communications Department at the University of California, San Diego.

Sara Lennox, Associate Professor of German, is Director of the Social Thought and Political Economy Program at the University of Massachusetts, Amherst, where she also works closely with the Women's Studies Program. She is the editor of *Auf der Suche nach den Barter unserer Mutter: Feministische Kultackritik aus Amerika* and the author of essays on contemporary East and West German literature, concentrating particularly on the works of recent German women writers.

Judith McDaniel now considers herself an ex-academic. She lives and writes from an old farmhouse in upstate New York and occasionally teaches in non-traditional situations. Her article, 'We Were Fired: Lesbian Experiences in Academe,' published in *Sinister Wisdom,* 20, spring 1982, tells the rest of the story.

Frances A. Maher, Assistant Professor of Education at Wheaton College, Norton, Massachusetts, has been active in efforts to integrate the new scholarship on women into the undergraduate curriculum. Though her work focuses on women and the education curriculum, she is interested in feminist pedagogy as it applies to all fields. Until 1981 she worked as a high school teacher of Social Studies in Brookline, Massachusetts.

Nancy K. Miller, Associate Professor of Women's Studies and Chair of the Women's Studies Program at Barnard College, Columbia University, is author of *The Heroine's Text: Readings in the French and English Novel, 1722-1782*, Columbia, 1980. She has written widely on issues in feminist literary criticism, and is currently writing a book of essays on female authorship and the novel in France.

Catherine E. Portuges is Director of the Women's Studies Program at the University of Massachusetts, Amherst, where she teaches film in the Department of Comparative Literature. A consultant to colleges and universities on curriculum and program development, she has also been a Mellon Fellow at the Wellesley Center for Research on Women. She has published articles, reviews and interviews on the intersections of psychoanalysis, feminism and cinema and is currently at work on a book on the representations of gender in avant-garde European film.

Janice G. Raymond, Associate Professor of Women's Studies at the University of Massachusetts, Amherst, works in the field of medical ethics. She is the author of *The Transsexual Empire* and is currently writing a book on female friendship, to be published by Beacon Press in 1985.

Adrienne Rich, a lesbian—feminist writer—teacher, has published twelve books of poetry and two of non-fiction prose, the most recent being *On Lies, Secrets and Silence*, W. W. Norton, 1979, and *Sources*, The Heyeck Press, 1983. She has taught at The City College of New York, Columbia University, Bryn Mawr College, Douglass College (Rutgers), Cornell University, and Scripps College, among other places.

Janet Rifkin, Associate Professor of Legal Studies at the University of Massachusetts, Amherst, is the founder and director of the University of Massachusetts Mediation Project. In that capacity, she has mediated a wide range of interpersonal and institutional disputes.

She has developed a training program for community mediators and has consulted with dispute resolution projects throughout the USA.

Michele Russell has been a writer, teacher, artist and community organizer for over two decades. Her personal and political roots are in Chicago, where she was born, and she has recently lived and worked in Grenada, West Indies.

John Schilb has taught English at the State University of New York at Binghamton, Carthage College, Denison University, and at the University of North Carolina at Wilmington. At Denison College he also taught Women's Studies for five years. He has published articles on Women's Studies in the *Women's Studies Quarterly* and *Change: The Magazine of Higher Learning*.

Diedrick Snoek, a professor of psychology, teaches both social and developmental psychology at Smith College. As co-investigator with the Project on Women and Social Change, he is working on the relationship between gender and ideology based on case studies of the lives of contemporary American women.

Elizabeth V. Spelman (Vicky) has been living and working in Western Massachusetts since 1973 and presently is teaching philosophy at Smith College. She is the author of 'Theories of Race and Gender/The Erasure of Black Women,' *Quest*, vol. 5, no. 4; and with Maria Lugones, 'Have We Got a Theory for You! Feminist Theory, Cultural Imperialism, and the Demand for "The Woman's Voice,"' forthcoming in *Hypatia: A Journal of Feminist Philosophy*. Her work explores the ways theory-making as a feminist activity marginalizes women of color. She is writing a book called *Out of Their Minds: Philosophers on Women, Slaves, Emotions and the Body*.

Erlene Stetson is an Associate Professor of English at the University of Indiana. She is the author of *Black Sister: Poetry by Black American Women, 1946-1980* (Bloomington: University of Indiana 1981) and numerous articles on black women writers. She was a founding editor of *Sojourner: A Third World Women Research Newsletter* and has served as co-chair of the Committee on the Status of Women of the Modern Language Association.

Mary Helen Washington, Associate Professor of English at University of Massachusetts, Boston, teaches Afro-American literature. She is the editor of two anthologies, *Midnight Birds: Stories of Contemporary Black Women* and *Black-Eyed Susans: Classic Stories By and About Black Women* and is at work on a literary history of black women writers. She has recently been Visiting Professor at Mills College in Oakland, California.

Index

Abel, Richard, 105, 106
academic disciplines, 51-2
Adams, Maurianne, 139
Adorno, Theodor Wiesengrund, 177
AFDC, 165-6
Afro-American: students, 233-5, 237;
    Studies, 233; teachers, 234; see also
    black
Akerman, Chantal, 193
Amherst College, 82-3
anger: in classroom, 19, 71, 209,
    211-16, 226; in drama classroom,
    117, 122
Anzieu, Didier, 67
Arnow, Harriet, 246
Asian-American students, 234
Atwood, Margaret, 228
Auber, Vilhelm, 106
authority: and anger in classroom,
    209-16; female, 11; in feminist
    classroom, 203-8; male, 89, 92;
    linguistic, 228
autobiographies, student, 41, 137

Bambara, Toni Cade, 239
Barber, Benjamin R., 95
Barnes, Nancy, 264
Barzun, Jacques, 25
Beard, Mary, 88
Beauchamp, Virginia, 264
Beauvoir, Simone de: on father/mother
    split, 11-12; Memoirs of a Dutiful
    Daughter, 16; as professor, 19; The
    Second Sex, 3, 12, 60, 191; works
    used in class, 136, 191

Berg, Sister Carol, 264
Bergman, Ingmar, 188, 193
Bergman, Ingrid, 189
Berkman, Joyce, 85, 93
Berkshire Conference on Women's
    History, 85, 91
Bernick, Susan, 244
Bezucha, Robert, 4
black: feminists, 127-9; professors,
    221, 224; students, 211, 222-3,
    230, 235; teachers, 215; women,
    155-67, 210, 232, 240-4; women
    writers, 225-9; see also Afro-
    American
Black: Power movement, 230-1;
    Studies, 46, 155, 225, 230-2, 240,
    259; Women's Studies, 233, 237-8
Bledstein, Burton, 59, 60
Bonder, Gloria, 4
Boston, Mass., 221, 229
Boxer, Marilyn, 46
Brecht, Bertold, 163
Brooklyn College, 205
Brooks, Gwendolyn, 228
Brownmiller, Susan, 250
Bunch, Charlotte, 40, 131
Butler, Johnnella, 6

California, University of, 108
Cassell, Joan, 68
CEM (Women's Studies Center, Buenos
    Aires), 64, 66
Chinoy, Helen, 123
Chodorow, Nancy, 14, 37, 252
Chopin, Kate, 137

279